The Great Big
BUTTER
COOKBOOK

Because Everything is
Better with Butter

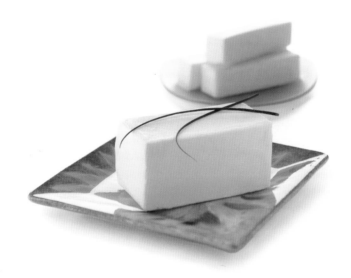

Edited by Diana C. von Glahn
Foreword by James Robson, CEO Wisconsin Milk Marketing Board

Running Press
PHILADELPHIA · LONDON

3 - 08
20 -

Printed in China

9   8   7   6   5   4   3   2   1
Digit on the right indicates the number of this printing

Library of Congress Control Number: 2007920534

ISBN-13: 978-0-7624-3169-4
ISBN-10: 0-7624-3169-5

Cover and interior design by Frances J. Soo Ping Chow
Edited by Diana C. von Glahn
Recipe development: Wisconsin Milk Marketing Board
and Priscilla Warren
Typography: Congress Sans, ITC Berkeley, P22 Corinthia,
and Type Embellishments

This book may be ordered by mail from the publisher.
Please include $2.50 for postage and handling.
But try your bookstore first!

Running Press Book Publishers
2300 Chestnut Street
Philadelphia, Pennsylvania 19103-4371

Visit us on the web!
www.runningpresscooks.com
www.butterisbest.com

Contents

Foreword

Butter holds a unique place in kitchens around the world. From four-star chefs to culinary novices, cooks overwhelmingly choose butter as an ingredient and spread. And it's easy to see why. Its rich, pure, and appealing nuanced flavor is indisputably favored. Its smooth mouth feel and contribution to the texture of silky sauces and flaky pastries are unparalleled. Butter is equally at its best in a tender pie crust or assertive garlic bread. It can comfortably enhance a piece of toast or a succulent lobster. Its versatility is truly remarkable.

One of the oldest dairy products, butter is thought to date to 2000 BC; yet it perfectly fits into the most contemporary trends. Butter is one of our most natural and minimally processed foods, simply relying on cream and sometimes salt. It is fresh and richly satisfying. Interestingly, many shoppers consider butter to be more caloric than margarine, when in fact, butter and margarine are absolutely equal—in both calories and grams of fat. What's more, butter contains no trans fats, an undesirable component found in many spreads, fats, and oils.

Wisconsin Milk Marketing Board is pleased to be able to help bring this book, a celebration of butter, to you. Our recipe collection contains hundreds of recipes that feature butter, and we're happy to share some of the finest with you.

Best wishes to you as you head to your kitchen; you can be assured that butter will help you achieve your best cooking, baking and eating.

James Robson
Chief Executive Office
Wisconsin Milk Marketing Board

Cooking with
BUTTER

SALTED OR UNSALTED?

Salted butter enhances flavor and has a longer shelf life. Use salted butter as table butter and for general cooking.

Unsalted butter contains no preservatives and has a shorter shelf life than salted butter. Use unsalted butter for baked goods such as crusts and sweets.

. . . .

Other Butter Varieties

CLARIFIED BUTTER—Butter that has been melted and made clear by separating and discarding the milk solids and water. It is ideal for cooking or as a base for sauces because it will not burn at high temperatures.

To make one pound of clarified butter, melt 1¼ pounds unsalted butter over medium heat. Stir without allowing it to boil. The butter will form three layers: milk solids on top, clarified butter in the middle, and milk solids on the bottom. As the butter continues to warm, skim off the top layer and discard. Carefully pour off the clear, melted butter into a separate container and discard any remaining milk solids.

CULTURED BUTTER—Made from cultured sour cream with a rich, complex flavor. It is ideal for baking because the lower moisture content produces flakier pastries and fluffier cakes. Cultured butter is most popular in European countries, but is increasingly available in the U.S.

EUROPEAN-STYLE BUTTER—Made from cream that is churned more slowly and for a longer time. It has higher butterfat content than standard butter, producing a more flavorful butter that is beneficial for cooking and baking and can be used at higher temperatures without burning to produce a lighter, flakier pastry.

WHIPPED BUTTER—Butter that has had air or other acceptable gases whipped into it, resulting in a product with greater volume, reduced density and improved spreadability at colder temperatures.

General Rules of Thumb for
Cooking with Butter

Use unsalted butter with seafood and in baking—its delicate flavor brings out the best in these types of dishes.

For maximum flavor, heat butter before using. Heating releases natural flavor compounds, allowing butter to develop its full, rich taste. Drizzle over veggies, pasta, grains, potatoes, fish, poultry, and experiment—butter's delicious on almost everything.

Use butter sticks when preparing recipes to ensure even measurements. Whipped butter contains more moisture and air and is better for toppings and spreads.

Appetizers, Snacks, and Beverages

———— ∞ ————

Spiced Nuts

4 tablespoons butter, melted

½ teaspoon garlic powder

½ teaspoon ground cumin

¼ teaspoon cayenne pepper

1 cup whole almonds

1 cup whole pecans

½ cup Brazil nuts

½ cup whole pecans

Kosher salt

Preheat the oven to 375°F.

In a large microwavable bowl, add the butter, garlic powder, cumin, and cayenne pepper, and melt in the microwave for 30 seconds over high heat. (Alternately, melt on the stovetop in large pan or Dutch oven.) Add the nuts and stir to coat evenly. Pour out onto a foil-lined baking sheet and bake for 15 minutes, until the nuts are browned and fragrant. Salt to taste.

Candied Nuts

Makes ½ pound

½ cup granulated sugar

⅓ cup water

⅛ teaspoon cinnamon

1 tablespoon butter

1 cup blanched almonds

Place the sugar and water in a heavy skillet and heat over low heat to form a light brown caramel.

Add the cinnamon, butter, and almonds, stirring constantly until the almonds are toasted and coated with the syrup, about 12 minutes.

Pour onto a greased cookie sheet, spreading the nuts quickly with forks. Cool before serving.

Amaretto, Mascarpone, and Fontina Purses

Chef Suzanne Pherigo

Makes 16

8 ounces (2 cups)
  fontina cheese, grated

8 ounces (1 cup)
  mascarpone cheese

½ cup chopped almonds

1 tablespoon Amaretto*

1 teaspoon white pepper

½ cup dried tart cherries

25 (14 x 8.5-inch) sheets
  phyllo dough, cut in half
  (7 x 4.25-inches)

4 to 5 tablespoons
  butter, melted

*Substitute with 1 tablespoon of non-alcoholic Amaretto syrup.

In a heavy-bottomed pan set over medium heat, blend the fontina and mascarpone cheeses together until smooth. Add the almonds, Amaretto, white pepper, and cherries. Mix well and chill for at least one hour, up to overnight.

When you're ready to continue, preheat the oven to 375°F.

Cover the phyllo sheets loosely with plastic wrap. Place a half sheet of phyllo on your work surface and brush with melted butter. Top with another half sheet of phyllo, brush with butter, and repeat with one more half sheet. Put a tablespoon of cheese filling in the center. Bring up the edges of the phyllo to form a purse-shaped (pouch) packet. Place the packet on a baking sheet and brush with melted butter. Repeat to form 16 purses, placing them approximately 1-inch apart on the baking sheet. Bake until golden, approximately 10 minutes. Serve hot.

DID YOU KNOW?
It takes 21.8 pounds of whole milk to make a pound of butter.

Feta Cheese Beggars' Pouches

Makes 8

16 sheets phyllo dough cut
   into 32 (5-inch) squares
¼ pound (1 stick)
   butter, melted
3 cups cooked,
   chopped spinach
10 ounces (2 cups)
   feta cheese, crumbled
1 tablespoon chopped garlic
3 eggs
Salt and pepper, to taste
1 cup spicy marinara sauce,
   for serving
Freshly ground black pepper
Fresh basil, cut in long thin
   strips, for garnish
2 ounces (½ cup) aged
   Asiago cheese,
   shredded, for garnish

Preheat the oven to 375°F.

Brush each square of phyllo with melted butter and stack them in eight stacks of four. As you stack them, turn each sheet slightly so the corners do not match up evenly.

Cover the stacks with a slightly moistened towel or plastic food wrap. This will keep the phyllo from drying out.

Combine the spinach, feta cheese, garlic, eggs, and salt and pepper. Place a portion of the spinach-feta mixture on each of the stacks of phyllo. Pull the phyllo up over the mixture and pinch it together to make a pouch. Place the pouch on a baking sheet and brush with melted butter. Repeat to form 8 pouches, placing them approximately 1-inch apart on the baking sheet.

Bake the pouches for 20 to 25 minutes, or until golden brown.

To serve, pour some marinara in a large serving bowl and set the pouches on top. Grind fresh pepper over the top of each pouch and garnish with basil and Asiago cheese. Serve hot.

Bagna Cauda

Makes about 1 cup

6 tablespoons
unsalted butter

¾ cup extra-virgin olive oil

12 anchovy fillets

6 cloves garlic, chopped

Blend all ingredients in a blender and transfer to a heavy saucepan. Cook over low heat until all of the ingredients are melted and blended together.

Ripe Olive and Walnut Brie Torte

Makes 12 to 18 servings

1 (14-ounce) wheel Brie cheese

¼ pound (1 stick) butter,
at room temperature

1 large garlic clove,
finely chopped

⅓ cup finely chopped walnuts

⅓ cup finely chopped
ripe olives

2 tablespoons chopped
fresh basil leaves,
or 2 teaspoons dry basil

Place the Brie in the freezer for about 30 minutes, or until firm. Carefully cut the wheel in half through the center of the wheel (horizontally) and set aside.

In a small bowl, cream the butter and garlic. Mix in the walnuts, olives, and basil; blend thoroughly. Spread this mixture evenly on a cut side of one of the Brie halves. Top with the other half, cut side down. Press together lightly; wrap and chill. Bring to room temperature before serving.

Savory Brie-En-Croute

Makes 32 servings

⅓ cup walnuts, toasted
  and finely chopped

1½ tablespoons, plus
  2 teaspoons butter, melted

½ teaspoon dried
  rosemary, crushed

Dash of cayenne

1 sheet refrigerated
  pie crust pastry,
  at room temperature

1 (8-ounce) round
  Brie cheese

Baguette slices, toasted,
  for serving

Fruit chutney, for serving

Preheat the oven to 400°F.

In a small bowl, mix together the walnuts, 1½ tablespoons of butter, rosemary, and cayenne; set aside.

Unfold the pie crust on a greased baking sheet and spoon the walnut mixture into the center of the dough. Spread into a 5-inch circle. Place the Brie on top of the walnut mixture and fold the dough over the Brie, starting at two opposite sides, bringing to the center and pinching to seal. Fold in the remaining pastry ends to the center, crimping as necessary, and press to seal. Invert the Brie onto a baking sheet and brush the top with the remaining melted butter.

Bake for 20 to 25 minutes, or until the pastry is browned. Cool to room temperature before serving with toasted slices of baguette and fruit chutney.

Baked Brie
with Almonds and Garlic

Makes 40 servings

1 (16-ounce) wheel Brie cheese

¾ cup slivered almonds

1 garlic clove, minced

4 tablespoons butter

French bread, sliced,
   for serving

Fruit, for serving

Preheat the oven to 350°F. Place the Brie on an oven-proof serving plate.

Sauté the almonds and garlic in the butter until just browned. Pour over top of the Brie. Bake at 350°F. for 12 minutes or until warm throughout, or microwave on medium heat for 3 to 5 minutes.

Serve with French bread slices and fruit.

Cheese Puffs

Makes about 4 dozen

½ pound (2 sticks) butter,
   at room temperature

16 ounces (1 pound) Cold Pack
   cheese,* any variety

3 cups all-purpose flour

*Cold Pack cheese is sold in the dairy aisle of the grocery store, in plastic, often transparent, tubs. It is a blend of cheeses that is smooth and spreadable, but no heat is used in the process (as opposed to a cheese "spread.") For more information, visit www.wisdairy.com.

Preheat the oven to 375°F.

Cream together the butter and cheese. Mix in the flour until thoroughly blended. Roll into 1-inch balls using 1 level tablespoon of dough for each ball.

Place on an ungreased baking sheet about ½ inch apart. Bake for 15 to 20 minutes or until golden brown. Serve warm or cool.

TIP: The dough can be made ahead and refrigerated until ready to use.

Asiago Cheese Puffs

Makes about 4 dozen

1 cup water

¼ pound (1 stick) butter

¼ teaspoon salt

1 cup all-purpose flour

4 eggs

7 ounces (1¾ cups) Asiago
    cheese, shredded

Preheat the oven to 375°F.

In a 2-quart saucepan over medium heat, combine the water, butter, and salt; heat to boiling. Reduce the heat to low and add the flour, stirring constantly, until the dough forms a ball and leaves the sides of the pan. Remove from the heat.

With a whisk or mixer, beat in the eggs, one at a time, until the mixture becomes smooth and glossy. Stir in most of the Asiago cheese reserving about ½ cup. Drop the dough by scant tablespoonfuls onto a buttered baking sheet about ½ inch apart. Lightly press a little of the remaining cheese onto each dough ball.

Bake for 30 minutes or until evenly browned.

Remove the puffs from the oven and reduce the oven temperature to 300°F. Prick each puff with a toothpick to release the steam. Return the puffs to the oven for 5 minutes.

Remove the cheese puffs from the baking sheet and let cool on a wire rack.

Spicy Cheese Puffs

Makes about 3 dozen

¼ pound (1 stick) butter,
   at room temperature
8 ounces (2 cups) Cheddar
   cheese, shredded
½ teaspoon
   Worcestershire sauce
Dash of cayenne pepper
1 cup all-purpose flour

Using an electric mixer, cream the butter, then mix in the cheese and seasonings. Gradually incorporate the flour. Shape the resulting dough into a smooth ball, wrap in plastic wrap, and chill thoroughly.

When you're ready to proceed, preheat the oven to 350°F.

Using only about one-quarter of the dough at a time, shape the dough into 1-inch diameter balls, flouring hands to make rolling easier.

Arrange the balls about 2 inches apart on an ungreased baking sheet and bake for 12 to 15 minutes; serve hot.

TIP: The dough may be rolled in advance and kept refrigerated or frozen until needed.

Savory No-Bake Basil Cheesecake

Makes 1 (8- or 9-inch) cheesecake,
serves 12 to 14

1 cup fine Italian breadcrumbs

3 tablespoons butter, melted

1 cup basil leaves, packed

2 garlic cloves, chopped

½ cup light mayonnaise

15 ounces ricotta cheese
   (or mascarpone)

2 ounces (¼ cup) blue cheese

4½ ounces (1½ cups) Parmesan
   cheese, grated

½ cup almonds, finely chopped
   and toasted, optional

Slivered almonds, for garnish

Fresh chives, for garnish

Assorted crackers, for serving

Vegetable slices, for serving

Toast slices, for serving

Combine the breadcrumbs and butter and press into the bottom of a lightly greased 8- or 9-inch springform pan. Chill until the crust sets.

Meanwhile, combine the basil, garlic, and mayonnaise in a blender, and blend until smooth. Set aside.

In mixing bowl, beat together the ricotta, blue, and Parmesan cheeses until blended. Beat in the basil mixture. Spread this cheese mixture over the set crust, pressing and smoothing the top. Chill for at least 8 hours or overnight.

When you're ready to serve, remove the sides of the springform pan and place the cheesecake on a platter. Press the toasted almonds onto the sides of the cheesecake.

To garnish the top of the cheesecake, make a "flower" with slivered almonds and chive stems. Serve with assorted crackers, vegetable slices and toast.

Cheddar and
Horseradish Cheesecake

Makes 1 (8- or 9-inch) cheesecake, serves 12 to 14

Cracker Crust

⅔ cup buttery cracker crumbs

5 tablespoons butter, melted

Filling

16 ounces cream cheese

2 eggs, beaten

1 cup sour cream

12 ounces (3 cups) Cheddar
   cheese, shredded

½ cup prepared horseradish

1 (2¼-ounce) can sliced
   black olives

1 (2-ounce) jar pimentos

Preheat the oven to 350°F. Prepare an 8- or 9-inch springform pan by removing the sides and covering the bottom with foil paper. Replace the sides and wrap the foil paper up the sides of the outside of the pan.

To make the cracker crust, combine the cracker crumbs and butter, stirring well. Firmly press the mixture evenly to the bottom and 1 inch up the sides of the pan.

Bake for 5 minutes. Set aside.

To make the filling, combine the cream cheese, eggs, and sour cream. Add the Cheddar cheese. Drain the horseradish, olives, and pimentos and add to cream cheese mixture. Pour into the prepared crust and spread evenly. Place the springform pan in larger pan and fill the larger pan with hot water so it reaches halfway up the sides of the springform pan.

Bake at 350°F. for approximately 45 minutes or until browned. Refrigerate for at least 2 hours to set before serving.

Camembert Almond Balls

Makes about 3 dozen

1 (8-ounce) wheel
  Camembert cheese
1 cup dry white wine
¼ pound (1 stick) butter,
  at room temperature
1 cup salted almonds,
  finely chopped
Crisp crackers, for serving

Soak the Camembert in the wine for at least 8 hours or overnight, turning occasionally.

Drain and discard the wine. Press the cheese through a coarse sieve or food mill and combine with the butter. Chill until slightly firm.

Shape the chilled cheese mixture into small balls about ¾-inch in diameter, then roll in the chopped almonds. Serve with crackers.

Herbed Smoked Gouda Rice Squares

Makes 12 to 14

1¾ cups water

1 cup uncooked medium-
  or short-grain rice

1 teaspoon salt

1 large egg

1 egg white

6 ounces (1½ cups) smoked
  Gouda cheese, shredded

4 tablespoons butter, melted

½ cup milk

¼ cup finely chopped green
  onions, including green tops

3 tablespoons chopped
  fresh dill

3 tablespoons chopped
  fresh parsley

¼ teaspoon cayenne pepper

Preheat the oven to 350°F.

In medium saucepan, bring the water to a boil. Add the rice and salt. Cook for about 18 minutes, until the rice is tender but not mushy. Remove from the heat and toss with a fork.

In large bowl, lightly beat the egg and egg white. Add the rice, Gouda, butter, and milk. Add the green onions, dill, parsley, and cayenne; stir gently until well mixed. Press the mixture into a lightly greased 9-inch-square baking pan.

Bake for about 35 minutes, or until the rice begins to brown lightly around the edges and become crusty. Cool on a wire rack for 20 minutes. Cut into squares.

Serve warm or at room temperature.

Cheesy Spinach Crescents

Makes about 3 dozen

Pastry

6 ounces cream cheese,
  at room temperature
½ pound (2 sticks) butter,
  at room temperature
2 cups all-purpose flour
¼ teaspoon salt

Filling

1 (10-ounce) package frozen
  chopped spinach, thawed
  and squeezed dry
6 ounces (1½ cups) Pepato
  or Pesto Monterey Jack
  cheese, shredded
2 eggs
¼ teaspoon salt

NOTE: Crescents may be
prepared and frozen up to
4 weeks before baking.
Do not thaw before baking.

To make the pastry, beat together the cream cheese and butter. Add the flour and salt; blend well. Shape into two oval discs. Wrap each disc in plastic wrap and refrigerate until firm, about 40 minutes.

Preheat the oven to 350°F.

To make the filling, in a medium bowl, combine the spinach, cheese, 1 egg and salt; mix well.

On a lightly floured surface, roll out the pastry (one oval at a time) to ⅛-inch thickness. Cut into circles with a 3-inch biscuit cutter or the mouth of a wine glass. Spoon one heaping teaspoon of filling onto the center of each circle. Fold the dough in half over the filling to form a crescent; press the edges together firmly to seal.

Beat the remaining egg until frothy; brush evenly over the crescents.

Place the crescents on an ungreased baking sheet about ½ inch apart. Bake for about 20 minutes or until golden brown. Serve warm or at room temperature.

Scone Sandwiches

Makes about 3 dozen

4 cups biscuit mix

1½ cups milk

2 eggs

4 tablespoons butter, melted

10 ounces (2½ cups)
  sharp Cheddar cheese,
  finely shredded

Choice of deli meat,
  thinly sliced

Preheat the oven to 400°F.

Combine the biscuit mix, milk, eggs, butter, and cheese; mix well until ingredients are moistened. Drop by tablespoonful onto a lightly greased baking sheet. Bake for 12 to 14 minutes or until golden brown.

Remove from the oven and let cool.

To serve, slice the scones in half and fill with your choice of deli meat.

Crispy Bacon and Cheese Triangles

Makes 6 dozen

½ pound (2 sticks) butter

½ cup dark brown sugar,
  packed

2¼ cups all-purpose flour

4 ounces (1 cup) Monterey Jack
  cheese, shredded

4 strips bacon, crisply cooked
  and crumbled

¼ teaspoon salt

¼ teaspoon pepper

¼ teaspoon red pepper flakes

Preheat the oven to 325°F.

Cream together the butter and brown sugar; gradually beat in the flour until the mixture forms a stiff dough. Beat in the cheese, bacon, salt, pepper, and red pepper flakes.

Spread the dough into a 13 x 9-inch baking pan. Bake for 40 minutes, or until browned. Remove from the oven and immediately cut into squares and then again diagonally to make triangles. Let cool before removing from the pan.

Sherried Cheese Toasts

Makes 10

10 slices French bread,
  1-inch thick, toasted

8 ounces (2 cups) mozzarella
  cheese, shredded

4 tablespoons butter,
  at room temperature

1 teaspoon Dijon-style mustard

¼ to ½ teaspoon bottled
  hot pepper sauce

2 tablespoons dry sherry

Preheat the broiler.

Combine the mozzarella cheese, butter, mustard, and hot pepper sauce. Using an electric mixer, beat at low speed until well-mixed. Gradually add the sherry, beating until well-combined. Spread onto toasted bread slices, covering the entire surface of each slice. Place on a baking sheet and broil 4 to 5 inches from the heat for about 2 to 3 minutes or until cheese mixture is bubbly and golden brown.

Chicken Empanadas

Makes 12

Filling

12 ounces ground chicken

3 tablespoons extra-virgin
   olive oil

1 teaspoon ground cumin

2 teaspoons chili powder

½ teaspoon salt

¼ teaspoon pepper

½ cup chicken stock

2 tablespoons
   chopped cilantro

½ teaspoon onion powder

1 (6-ounce) can tomato paste

1 cup shredded
   Cheddar cheese

Pastry

3 cups all-purpose flour

1½ teaspoon baking powder

1 teaspoon granulated sugar

¼ teaspoon salt

4 tablespoons butter,
   chilled and diced

¼ cup ice water

To make the filling, cook the chicken in olive oil in a large skillet set over medium-high heat. Cook until browned, about 5 minutes, being sure to crumble the meat as it cooks. Stir in the cumin, chili powder, salt, and pepper, and cook an additional minute.

Stir in the chicken stock, cilantro, onion powder, and tomato paste and cook until it thickens, about 2 or 3 minutes. Make sure that the tomato paste is incorporated thoroughly. Remove from the heat and stir in the cheese. Pour the mixture into a bowl and set aside to cool to room temperature.

Sift the flour, baking powder, sugar, and salt together into a bowl. Add the butter and beat until it resembles coarse cornmeal. (You may use a food processor, pulsing until about 4 times.) Add the ice water and stir to incorporate until it is a soft dough. (With the food processor running, add the water and pulse until just combined.)

Turn the dough out onto a lightly floured surface and knead briefly with floured hands, about 2 minutes. Divide the dough into 12 portions. Working with one portion at a time, roll out into a circle, adding flour to prevent sticking.

Spoon 2 tablespoons of the meat mixture onto half of the circle, being careful not to overfill. Fold the dough over the filling and press the edges together to seal. Repeat with the remaining dough and filling until you have 12 empanadas. Cover with plastic wrap and refrigerate until firm.

Preheat oven to 375°F.

Divide the empanadas among two baking sheets and bake until the bottoms are golden brown and the tops are brown, about 15 to 20 minutes, checking at 10 minutes.

NOTE: Traditionally, empanadas are fried. You may fry them over medium-high heat in canola or vegetable oil until the dough is golden and blistered, about 7 to 10 minutes.

Pumpernickel Cheese Bowl

Makes 1 (14-inch) bowl, or 3 (4-inch) bowls

19 ounces cream cheese, at room temperature

6 ounces (1½ cups) Cheddar cheese, shredded

5 tablespoons butter, at room temperature

2 tablespoons minced onion

2 teaspoons Dijon mustard

1 (14-inch) round pumpernickel loaf, or 3 (4-inch) round loaves

Additional pumpernickel bread, for serving

Crackers and fresh vegetables, for serving

Combine the cheeses, butter, onion, and mustard until well-blended. Cover and refrigerate overnight.

Preheat the oven to 375°F.

Cut a slice from the top of the pumpernickel loaf and hollow out the center, creating a bowl. Cut the center pieces into cubes, place on a baking sheet and bake for 10 minutes.

Fill the bowl(s) with the cheese dip mixture. Serve with pumpernickel bread cubes, crackers and fresh vegetables.

Cheddar, Chive, and Brie Crackers

Makes 2 dozen

¼ pound plus 4 tablespoons
  (1½ stick) butter

2 ounces (½ cup) Cheddar
  cheese, shredded

2 ounces (⅓ cup) Brie cheese,
  rind removed

1 teaspoon garlic salt

½ teaspoon dried parsley

1 teaspoon fresh chives,
  chopped, or ½ teaspoon
  dried chives

2 cups whole wheat
  all-purpose flour

Preheat the oven to 375°F.

In a large mixing bowl, cream the butter and the cheeses. Mix in the remaining ingredients. Shape the mixture into a log, 1½-inch in diameter. Wrap in plastic wrap and chill for 2 hours or overnight.

Slice thinly (about ⅛-inch thick). Place the slices on a greased baking sheet about ½ inch apart and bake for 7 to 10 minutes.

Dilly Cheese Crackers

Makes 5 dozen

7 ounces (1⅔ cups) sharp
  Cheddar cheese, shredded
¼ pound (1 stick)
  plus 2 tablespoons
  unsalted butter
2 cups all-purpose flour
2 teaspoons dill weed
1 teaspoon paprika
1 teaspoon salt
½ teaspoon baking soda
½ cup heavy cream
1 egg yolk
2 teaspoons water
Poppy seeds

Combine the cheese and butter, mixing at medium speed with an electric mixer until well blended. Combine the flour, dill, paprika, salt, and baking soda and add to the cheese mixture; mix well. Add the cream and blend well.

Divide the dough in half and shape each half into a small disk. Wrap the dough in plastic wrap and chill for 1 hour.

Preheat the oven to 375°F.

On a lightly floured surface, roll each disk of dough to ⅛-inch thickness. Using a 2-inch cookie cutter, cut out the cracker shapes and place them on a greased baking sheet about ½ inch apart. In a small bowl, lightly beat the egg yolk with the water and brush this mixture onto the tops of the crackers. Sprinkle with poppy seeds and bake for 10 to 12 minutes or until lightly browned.

Pepper Jack Crackers

Makes 6 dozen

8 ounces (2 cups) Pepper Jack
cheese, cut in small cubes

½ pound (2 sticks) unsalted
butter, cut into pieces,
at room temperature

2½ cups all-purpose flour

1 teaspoon salt

1 teaspoon cayenne pepper

1 cup chopped pecans

In the bowl of a food processor, combine the cheese and butter. Pulse the mixture, scraping down the sides of the bowl frequently. It will take several pulses until the mixture is smooth. Add the flour, salt, and cayenne pepper, pulsing until combined. Add the pecans and pulse just to mix. Form the dough into two rolls, each about 1½-inch in diameter and 20 inches long. Wrap the rolls in plastic wrap and refrigerate for 1 hour or overnight.

Preheat the oven to 350°F.

Cut the rolls into ¼-inch slices. Place the slices on an ungreased baking sheet about ½ inch apart. Bake for 12 to 15 minutes, just until lightly browned. Cool on racks. Store up to 1 week in airtight tins.

Parmesan Bread Chips

Makes 4 to 6 servings

6 pita breads

¼ pound plus 4 tablespoons
  butter (1½ stick), melted

4½ ounces (1½ cups)
  Parmesan cheese, grated

Garlic powder

Preheat the oven to 350°F.

Split each pita bread along its side, creating 12 circles. Brush each rough side with melted butter and sprinkle with Parmesan cheese, then dust lightly with garlic powder. Cut each bread circle into 16 triangular pieces and place on an ungreased baking sheet. Bake for 13 minutes or until crisp and golden.

Blue Cheese Walnut Wafers

Makes 4 dozen (see photo on page 30)

5 ounces (1 cup) crumbled
  blue cheese, at room
  temperature

4 tablespoons butter,
  at room temperature

1 cup all-purpose flour

1 cup finely chopped walnuts

Cream the blue cheese and butter with an electric mixer until fluffy. Thoroughly mix in the flour and walnuts. Form into a log about 2 inches in diameter. Wrap in plastic wrap and chill for at least 1 hour or overnight.

Preheat the oven to 375°F.

Cut the log into ¼-inch thick slices and place them ½-inch apart on baking sheets. Bake for 12 to 14 minutes, watching them closely so they don't burn, until the bottoms are lightly browned. Cool on a wire rack.

Cheese Wafers

Makes 4 dozen

2 cups all-purpose flour

½ teaspoon salt

¼ teaspoon paprika

¼ pound (1 stick) butter,
   at room temperature

1 pound (4 cups) Cheddar
   cheese, shredded

1½ cups chopped nuts

In a small bowl, sift together the flour, salt, and paprika. Set aside.

In a separate bowl, using an electric mixer, cream the butter and cheese, then add the flour mixture, combining well. Add the nuts.

Shape the dough into rolls about 1¼-inches in diameter, wrap in plastic wrap, and chill for at least 1 hour or overnight.

Preheat the oven to 350°F.

Slice the dough into ¼-inch thick wafers. Place the wafers ½ inch apart on greased baking sheets and bake for 12 to 15 minutes or until lightly browned. Transfer to racks to cool.

DID YOU KNOW?

Butter was reportedly used as early as 2000 BC. The word butter comes from *bou-tyron*, which seems to mean "cowcheese" in Greek.

Cheese Turnovers

1 cup all-purpose flour

¼ pound (1 stick) butter,
   at room temperature

3 ounces cream cheese,
   at room temperature

2 eggs, slightly beaten

2 cups (8 ounces)
   medium-aged Brick cheese*
   or mild Cheddar cheese,
   shredded

2 tablespoons finely
   chopped onion

½ teaspoon ground coriander

⅛ teaspoon salt

1 egg white, slightly beaten

½ cup sesame seeds

*Brick cheese is a semi-soft, cow's milk
cheese originating in Wisconsin. For more
information, visit www.wisdairy.com.

In a medium bowl, mix the flour, butter, and cream cheese until well-blended. Shape the soft dough into a flat ball, wrap it in waxed paper, and refrigerate it for about 2 hours.

Preheat the oven to 375°F.

To make the filling, combine the eggs, cheese, onion, coriander, and salt until thoroughly blended. Set aside.

On a lightly floured surface, roll out the dough to ⅛-inch thickness. Cut out 36 rounds using a 2½-inch round cookie cutter.

Place 1 teaspoon of filling in the center of each round, then fold the dough in half and seal the edges with a fork. Brush the tops of the turnovers with egg white and dip in sesame seeds. Arrange the turnovers on a lightly buttered baking sheet about ½ inch apart, and bake for 20 minutes or until golden brown. Serve warm or cool.

NOTE: Feel free to experiment with this recipe by changing your fillings. Add cooked shredded chicken or ground beef, leave out the cheese, or make some with grilled vegetables.

Stuffed Mushrooms

Makes 24

2 links sweet Italian sausage

3 tablespoons
  chopped shallots

1 tablespoon chopped
  bell pepper

24 button mushrooms,
  cleaned and stems removed
  and reserved

4 tablespoons butter

½ cup herb stuffing mix

2 tablespoons grated
  Parmesan cheese

Preheat the oven to 350°F. and lightly grease a baking sheet.

Remove the sausage from its casing and cook in a skillet set over medium high heat until no longer pink, about 7 to 10 minutes. Add the shallots, bell pepper, and mushroom stems until the vegetables are soft and shallots are opaque, about 10 minutes.

In large saucepan, melt the butter and add the herb stuffing mix. Add the vegetables and sausage mixture to the herb stuffing mixture and mix well to incorporate completely.

Carefully stuff the mushroom caps with the filling and place on the prepared baking sheet. Sprinkle with Parmesan cheese and bake about 10 to 15 minutes, or until the mushrooms are golden on top and they give off their juices.

Cheese and Onion-Stuffed Mushrooms

Makes 20

20 large white or
  Portobello mushrooms

6 tablespoons butter, melted

Salt and pepper, to taste

3 tablespoons minced
  green onions

1 tablespoon all-purpose flour

¾ cup heavy cream

2 ounces (½ cup) Parmesan
  cheese, grated

3 tablespoons minced parsley

2 ounces (½ cup) Swiss
  cheese, shredded

Preheat the oven to 375°F.

Clean the mushrooms, remove the stems, and reserve. Brush the caps with melted butter and arrange, hollow side up, in a 13 x 9-inch baking dish. Season with salt and pepper.

Finely chop the mushroom stems and sauté them with the green onions in the remaining butter for 10 to 12 minutes, or until most of the liquid is evaporated. Stir frequently. Lower the heat and stir in the flour, cooking for 1 minute. Add the cream and simmer until thickened. Stir in the Parmesan and parsley.

Fill the mushroom caps with the mixture. Top each cap with 1 teaspoon of Swiss cheese. Bake for 15 minutes.

TIP: These mushrooms can be made a day in advance. Prepare and stuff the mushrooms; top with cheese. Cover and refrigerate until ready to bake and serve.

Mushroom Pâté

1 medium-sized leek, white
part only, chopped

2 tablespoons minced shallots

2 cloves garlic, minced

½ pound (2 sticks) butter

1½ pounds fresh mushrooms
(button or any combination),
coarsely chopped

2 tablespoons chopped parsley

1 teaspoon dry thyme, crushed

1 teaspoon dry marjoram,
crushed

½ cup extra dry vermouth

2 tablespoons dry sherry

Salt and pepper to taste

Over medium heat, sauté the leek, shallots, and garlic in the butter for about 8 minutes, until the leek is tender. Stir in the mushrooms, parsley, thyme, and marjoram and sauté about 10 minutes or until the mushrooms release their juices. Stir in the vermouth, sherry, and salt and pepper. Cook, stirring constantly, until the liquid is reduced and thickened, about 10 minutes. Remove from the heat and cool.

Pour the mixture into the bowl of a food processor and process until smooth or desired consistency. Transfer to a covered serving bowl and refrigerate for several hours or overnight to set.

Green Olive Pastries

Makes about 3 dozen

8 ounces (2 cups) Cheddar
cheese, finely shredded

¼ pound (1 stick) butter

1 cup all-purpose flour

1 teaspoon paprika

40 pimento stuffed olives

Preheat the oven to 400°F.

Combine the cheese and butter, mixing until well-blended. Add the flour and paprika; mix well.

Shape 1 teaspoon of the cheese mixture around each olive, covering completely. Place on an ungreased baking sheet about ½ inch apart. Bake for 15 minutes.

TIP: To make ahead, prepare as directed, except for baking. Freeze unbaked pastries on baking sheet for 2 hours; place in plastic bag. When ready to serve, bake at 400°F. for 18 minutes.

Butterfly Shrimp with Pancetta

Makes 18

6 ounces pancetta, very finely
  chopped (substitute with
  8 slices of bacon)

6 ounces (1½ cups) smoked
  Baby Swiss cheese, shredded

½ cup breadcrumbs

4 tablespoons unsalted butter,
  at room temperature

1 tablespoon chopped
  fresh chives

Salt and pepper, to taste

18 jumbo (10 to 15 count)
  shrimp, cleaned
  and butterflied

Sour cream, for garnish

Chopped fresh chives,
  for garnish

Sauté the pancetta over medium heat until the fat is translucent; about 15 minutes. Cool. Combine the pancetta, cheese, breadcrumbs, butter, and chives; mix well. Shape into an 8-inch log. Wrap in plastic wrap; chill until firm.

Preheat the oven to 400°F.

Lay the shrimp on a baking sheet. Slice the cheese log into ⅛-inch slices and place 2 slices on each butterflied shrimp. Bake for 5 to 10 minutes or until the shrimp tails curl up.

Serve garnished with sour cream and chives.

Shrimp Mozambique

Makes 4 servings

5 tablespoons butter

¼ cup finely chopped onions

½ cup water

9 garlic cloves, finely chopped

4 tablespoons chopped fresh
  flat leaf parsley

1 teaspoon turmeric

½ teaspoon assafroa*
  or paprika

½ cup red wine

3 teaspoons fresh lemon juice

1½ pounds medium shrimp,
  peeled and deveined

2 teaspoons salt

½ teaspoon white pepper

1 teaspoon crushed
  red pepper

*Assafroa is a Portuguese spice that is very
much like a smoky paprika.

Melt the butter in a large skillet over medium-low heat. Add the onions and sauté until golden, about 5 minutes. Pour in the water, then add the garlic, parsley, turmeric, and assafroa. Cover and simmer for 4 minutes.

Add the wine and lemon juice, raise the heat, and cover, bringing the sauce to a boil. Reduce the heat and simmer an additional 2 minutes. Add the shrimp and cook until shrimp are pink and just cooked, about 5 minutes, depending on size of shrimp. Season with salt, white pepper, and crushed red pepper.

Crispy Chicken Strips
with Sweet and Sour Dipping Sauce

Makes 8

Chicken Strips

1 cup buttermilk

1 teaspoon hot pepper sauce,
   optional

2 pounds chicken breast
   tenders or boneless,
   skinless chicken breasts
   cut into long strips

1½ cups seasoned
   breadcrumbs

3 ounces (¾ cup) Parmesan
   cheese, grated

½ cup yellow cornmeal

1½ teaspoons salt

½ teaspoon freshly ground
   black pepper

¼ pound (1 stick) butter, melted

Sweet and Sour
  Dipping Sauce

1 cup apricot preserves

3 tablespoons seasoned
   rice vinegar or white
   wine vinegar

2 teaspoons dry mustard

Preheat the oven to 400°F.

Combine the buttermilk and hot pepper
sauce in a large bowl. Add the chicken and mix
well. Let stand for 10 minutes.

Combine the breadcrumbs, Parmesan
cheese, cornmeal, salt, and pepper in a shallow
pie plate or dish.

Roll each piece of chicken into the
breadcrumb mixture to coat. Place on nonstick
baking sheets, then drizzle the breaded chicken
with melted butter. Bake for 8 minutes, then
turn the chicken and continue baking for
8 more minutes or until chicken is golden
brown and no longer pink in the center.

Meanwhile, in a small bowl, combine the
preserves, vinegar, and mustard; mix well.
Serve the chicken warm, at room temperature,
or cold with dipping sauce.

Escargots

Makes 4 servings

¼ pound (1 stick) butter,
  at room temperature
1½ tablespoons minced shallot
2 tablespoons finely chopped
  fresh parsley
2 teaspoons minced garlic
Salt and pepper, to taste
1 (7-ounce) can snails, rinsed
Clean snail shells*

*Available at gourmet food stores.

Preheat the oven to 400°F.

In a food processor, purée the butter, shallots, parsley, and garlic until smooth. Season with salt and pepper.

Carefully divide the butter mixture among the snail shells, then stuff each with one snail. Put the snails on a baking sheet and bake for 10 minutes, until the butter oozes from the shells.

Taco Popcorn

Makes 12 cups

4 tablespoons butter
1 tablespoon minced
  fresh cilantro
½ teaspoon taco seasoning
1 ounce (¼ cup) Mexican
  Blend cheese, shredded
12 cups popped popcorn
  (about ¾ cup kernels)

In a small saucepan, melt the butter; stir in the cilantro, taco seasoning, and cheese.

In a 4-quart mixing bowl, drizzle the seasoned butter over hot, freshly popped popcorn. Stir popcorn gently to coat kernels. Serve immediately.

Zesty Parmesan Popcorn

Makes 8 cups

8 cups popped popcorn
 (about ½ cup kernels)

3 tablespoons butter, melted

1 ounce (¼ cup) Parmesan
 cheese, grated

1 teaspoon dried oregano

½ teaspoon salt

Place the popcorn in a large bowl and drizzle with melted butter. Toss lightly, then quickly stir in the cheese, oregano, and salt to taste.

Holiday Butter Corn

Makes about 20 cups

16 cups popped popcorn
 (about 1 cup kernels)

1 cup pecan halves

1 cup blanched whole almonds

1 cup walnut halves

2 cups brown sugar,
 firmly packed

½ pound (2 sticks) butter

½ cup dark corn syrup

½ teaspoon salt

½ teaspoon baking soda

Preheat the oven to 250°F.

Put the popcorn and nuts in a large roasting pan and keep warm in the oven.

Combine the brown sugar, butter, corn syrup, and salt in a large saucepan. Bring to a boil, stirring constantly. Stop stirring and cook to 250°F. on a candy thermometer, about 5 minutes. Stir baking soda into the caramel.

Drizzle the caramel over the popcorn and toss to coat. Bake for 5 to 10 minutes. For crispier corn, bake for 15 to 20 minutes.

Caramel Corn

24 cups unsalted popped
   popcorn (about 1½ cups
   kernels)

2 cups salted peanuts

½ pound (2 sticks) butter

2 cups dark brown sugar,
   packed

½ cup white corn syrup

1 teaspoon baking soda

1 teaspoon salt

1 teaspoon vanilla

Preheat the oven to 250°F. Measure the popcorn and nuts into two 13 x 9 x 2-inch baking pans and bake for 5 minutes.

In a heavy saucepan, melt the butter, then add the brown sugar and corn syrup. Bring to a full boil over medium-high heat, stirring constantly. Boil for 5 minutes. Immediately remove from the heat and add the baking soda and salt, then the vanilla.

Pour the caramel over the popcorn and nuts, stirring to coat evenly. Bake for 50 minutes, stirring every 10 minutes.

Cool on waxed paper.

Snack-Time Oat Bars

Makes 3 dozen

¼ pound plus 4 tablespoons
  (1½ stick) butter

⅓ cup white Karo syrup

1 cup brown sugar

1 teaspoon vanilla

4 cups oats

1 cup flaked coconut

½ cup chopped walnuts

1 cup chocolate chips

½ cup peanut butter

In a large saucepan over low heat, melt and stir the butter, Karo syrup, brown sugar, and vanilla. Stir in the oats, coconut, and walnuts. Continue to cook over low heat, stirring occasionally for 3 minutes.

Using a buttered spatula, press the mixture evenly into a buttered 9-inch square pan. Cool for 15 minutes.

In a small saucepan set over low heat, melt the chocolate chips and peanut butter together. Spread over the oatmeal in the pan. Cool completely and cut into 1½-inch squares.

Party Mix

Makes 8 cups

2 cups crisp corn and
   rice cereal

2 cups oat bran high oat
   fiber cereal

2 cups mini buttery
   round crackers

2 cups mini 100% whole wheat
   wafer crackers

1½ cups pecan halves

1 cup raisins

6 tablespoons butter, melted

1 tablespoon lemon juice

1 tablespoon Worcestershire
   sauce

1 teaspoon garlic salt

½ teaspoon onion salt

Preheat the oven to 250°F.

In a large bowl, combine the cereals, crackers, pecans, and raisins.

In a separate bowl, combine the butter, lemon juice, Worcestershire sauce, garlic salt, and onion salt; mix well. Pour over the contents of the larger bowl, tossing lightly until evenly coated. Spread the mixture onto a jelly roll pan or into a large roasting pan. Bake for 45 minutes, stirring every 15 minutes. Cool before serving.

Microwave Directions: Microwave the butter in a 2-cup container on high for 45 seconds or until melted. Stir in the lemon juice, Worcestershire sauce, garlic salt, and onion salt. Place the remaining ingredients in a 4-quart glass bowl and pour the butter mixture over all, tossing lightly until evenly coated. Microwave on high for 5 to 7 minutes or until evenly toasted, stirring after 3 minutes.

VARIATION: Substitute sweetened dried cranberries for raisins. Substitute 2 to 3 teaspoons hot pepper sauce for lemon juice.

Buttery Mulled Cider

Makes 8 servings

½ cup brown sugar

Juice of 1 orange

Juice of 1 lemon

8 cups apple cider

4 whole clove

2 cinnamon sticks

1 teaspoon whole allspice

¼ pound (1 stick) unsalted butter

In a large saucepan, stir the brown sugar, orange and lemon juice, cider, cloves, cinnamon sticks, allspice, and 4 tablespoons of butter. Simmer covered for 30 minutes, stirring occasionally.

Remove the whole spices. Pour into mugs, top each with ½ tablespoon of butter, and enjoy.

Hot Buttered Rum

Makes 12 servings

½ pound (2 sticks) butter,
   at room temperature

1 cup brown sugar

1 cup granulated sugar

1 teaspoon ground nutmeg

1 teaspoon ground cinnamon

2 cups French vanilla ice
   cream, at room temperature

1½ cups (12 ounces) rum

6 cups boiling water

In a mixing bowl, cream the butter, sugars, and spices until light and fluffy. Beat in the ice cream. Transfer to a container, cover and freeze.

To serve, spoon ⅓ cup frozen ice cream mixture into a mug. Add ⅛ cup (1 ounce) rum and ½ cup boiling water. Stir well and serve.

TIP: Try substituting hot coffee for the water or substitute different flavors of ice cream, like chocolate.

Chocolate Hot Buttered Rum

Makes 6 servings

4 tablespoons butter,
  at room temperature

¼ cup brown sugar, packed

½ teaspoon ground cinnamon

¼ teaspoon ground nutmeg

½ cup dark rum

½ cup granulated sugar

⅓ cup cocoa

4 cups milk

Combine the butter, brown sugar, cinnamon, and nutmeg in a small bowl, mixing until well-blended. Drop six spoonfuls of the butter mixture onto a plastic-wrap-lined plate and chill, then form into balls.

Combine the rum, sugar, and cocoa in a 2-quart saucepan. Heat to boiling over medium heat, stirring constantly. Simmer for 1 minute; then add the milk. Cook until heated through; do not boil. Pour into six mugs; place one butter ball in each cup.

Breakfasts and Breads

Croissants

Makes about 2 dozen

1½ cups warm whole milk
  (105°F. to 110°F.)

¼ cup light brown sugar,
  packed

1 tablespoon plus ¼ teaspoon
  active dry yeast

3¾ to 4½ cups unbleached
  all-purpose flour

1 tablespoon kosher salt

¾ pound (3 sticks) unsalted
  butter, chilled

In the bowl of a standing mixer with the dough hook attachment, add the milk, brown sugar, and yeast; let stand until foamy, about 5 minutes.

Add 3¾ cups of flour and the salt and mix at low speed until the dough is soft and smooth, about 7 minutes.

Transfer the dough to a lightly floured work surface and knead by hand for 2 minutes, adding more flour as necessary, a little at a time, until you have a soft, slightly sticky dough. Form the dough into a 1½-inch-thick rectangle, wrap in plastic wrap, and chill for about 1 hour.

Place the sticks of butter on a work surface next to one another horizontally, with their sides touching. Pound the butter with a rolling pin to soften it slightly and form it into one large block of butter. Scrape the butter into a block and set on a tea towel (avoid towels with lots of fluff), then cover with another towel. Roll and pound the butter on both sides until you have an 8 x 5-inch rectangle. Wrap the butter and place in the refrigerator to chill while you roll out the dough.

On a lightly floured surface, roll out the

dough, dusting with flour as needed. Lift and stretch the dough until it forms a 16 x 10-inch rectangle. With the shortest side of the dough near you, put the butter in the center of the dough so that the long sides of the butter are parallel with the shorts sides of the dough. Fold the dough in thirds, like you are folding a letter, placing the bottom third of the dough over the butter, then the top third down over the dough. Brush off any excess flour with a pastry brush.

Roll out the dough into a 15 x 10-inch rectangle, rolling just to the ends. Brush off any excess flour, then fold the dough in thirds again. Wrap the dough in plastic wrap and chill for 1 hour.

Continue rolling out the dough, folding it in thirds, and chilling it for 1 hour three more times, for a total of four times. (If any butter oozes out while rolling, sprinkle it with flour to prevent sticking.) Wrap the dough tightly in plastic wrap and chill for at least 8 hours.

To shape dough into croissant shapes, cut the dough into approximately 24 (3 x 5) pieces. With a rolling pin, lightly roll each piece into a triangle shape. Starting with the end opposite of the triangle's point, roll the dough into the shape of a croissant and place on baking sheets. Place the baking sheets in a large enough bag to encase them, propping the bag up with something (a glass or skewers work nicely) so the bag won't touch the dough. Let the croissants rise for 2 hours.

Preheat the oven to 425°F.

With a spray bottle filled with water, spray the oven and close the door. Place the baking sheets in the oven and spray the oven again.

Reduce the heat to 400°F. and bake for 10 minutes. Rotate the baking sheets 180 degrees, lower the heat to 375°F., and bake the croissants for an additional 10 minutes, until they are golden brown and flaky.

Popovers

Makes 9 to 12

1 cup all-purpose flour

½ teaspoon salt

1 teaspoon granulated sugar

2 eggs, beaten

1 cup whole milk

1 tablespoon butter, melted

Preheat the oven to 475°F. Grease a muffin pan and put it in the oven. It needs to be piping hot when you pour in the batter.

In a large mixing bowl, sift the flour, salt, and sugar.

In a separate bowl, combine the eggs, milk, and butter. Add this mixture to the flour mixture and beat for 2 minutes, until well incorporated. Pour the batter quickly into the heated greased pans and bake for 12 minutes, then reduce the temperature to 350°F. Bake an additional 12 minutes, or until golden brown and puffed. Pierce the popovers with a skewer and bake an additional 3 minutes until nicely browned. Serve immediately.

Hot Cross Buns

Makes 16

Buns

½ cup granulated sugar

1 teaspoon salt

½ cup whole milk, scalded

2 (¼-ounce) packets
   active dry yeast

¼ cup lukewarm water

3¾ cups all purpose four, sifted

2 eggs, beaten

½ cup butter, melted and
   slightly cooled

½ cup dried currants,
   plumped*

¼ cup finely diced citron

1½ teaspoon cinnamon

1 egg white mixed
   with 1 tablespoon water

*To plump currants: pour hot water over
the currants and let them sit until the
currants re-hydrate

Icing

⅓ cup confectioners' sugar

1 tablespoon whole milk

1 tablespoon light corn syrup

½ teaspoon vanilla

Pinch salt

Add the sugar and salt to the milk and stir thoroughly to incorporate. Set aside to cool.

Proof the yeast in additional lukewarm water for 5 minutes. Add the cooled milk and 1¼ cups of flour, and blend until smooth. Add the eggs and then the butter, stirring to distribute throughout. Stir in the remaining flour and beat for 2 minutes.

Cover the dough and set aside to let rise in a warm place until the dough doubles in size, about 1½ hours.

Add the currants, citron, and cinnamon to the dough and knead until the fruit and cinnamon are distributed. Cover and place in the refrigerator for 2½ hours.

Turn the dough out onto a lightly floured surface and knead for a minute. Cut the dough into 4 equal portions and shape the portions into uniform balls. Cut each ball into fourths. Shape into 16 buns and place onto greased baking sheets. Brush the buns with the egg white mixture, then cover with a damp cloth and let rise in a warm place until they double in size, about 1½ hours.

Preheat the oven to 350°F.

Bake the buns for 18 to 20 minutes.

Meanwhile, combine the icing ingredients together until smooth. When the buns are out of the oven let them cool, then make crosses on top of each bun with the icing.

Buttermilk Waffles

Makes 9 servings

1¾ cups all-purpose flour

2 teaspoons baking powder

½ teaspoon baking soda

¼ teaspoon salt

2 egg yolks, beaten

2 cups buttermilk

¼ pound (1 stick)
   butter, melted

2 egg whites, stiffly beaten

Assorted fresh fruit,
   for serving

Plain or fruit-flavored yogurt,
   sour cream, or whipped
   cream, for serving

In a mixing bowl, combine the flour, baking powder, baking soda, and salt.

In another bowl, combine the egg yolks, buttermilk, and butter. Stir to mix well. Add the yolk mixture to the flour mixture all at once. Stir just until blended. Batter should be slightly lumpy. Carefully fold in the beaten egg whites. Do not over-mix.

Pour the batter onto a preheated, lightly greased waffle maker. Close the lid quickly and do not open the waffle maker during baking. Remove the waffle from grid. Repeat with remaining batter. Serve waffles warm with fresh fruit and yogurt, sour cream, or whipped cream.

Sweet Roll Dough

Mary E. Taylor

Makes 9 rolls or one 9-inch coffee cake

4¼ cups all-purpose
   flour, sifted

2 (¼-ounce) packets dry yeast

¼ cup lukewarm water
   (110 to 115°F.)

½ cup granulated sugar

1 teaspoon salt

⅔ cup scalded milk

2 eggs, beaten

¼ pound (1 stick) butter,
   melted and cooled

1 teaspoon lemon zest

½ teaspoon cardamom

Place the flour in a large bowl.

In another bowl, combine the yeast, water, and 1 teaspoon of sugar. Let sit for 10 minutes.

Add the remaining sugar and salt to the scalded milk and stir. Let the milk cool to lukewarm, then stir in the yeast mixture and eggs. Add half of the flour and beat with an electric mixer set on low speed. Add the butter, zest, and cardamom. Gradually stir in all but 1 cup of the remaining flour until incorporated. Cover and let stand for 10 minutes to stiffen.

Turn the dough out onto a floured surface and knead thoroughly, at least 5 minutes. The dough will be soft. Place the dough in a lightly greased bowl, then turn once to make sure the entire surface is greased. Cover with a damp cloth and let rise in a warm place until the dough doubles in size, about 1½ to 2 hours.

Punch the dough down, turn over, cover, and let rise again until it doubles in size, about 30 minutes.

Punch the dough down and turn out onto a lightly floured surface. Cover with a bowl and let rest about 10 minutes.

Preheat the oven to 350°F.

Using your hands, shape the dough into individual rolls and place on greased pans. Alternately, spread the dough into a greased layer cake pan.

Bake for 25 to 30 minutes or until golden brown.

Cheese Scones

Makes 12

1½ cups all-purpose flour

1½ cups rolled oats

¼ cup brown sugar

1 tablespoon baking powder

1 teaspoon cream of tartar

½ teaspoon salt

2 ounces (½ cup) your choice
  cheese, finely shredded

¼ pound (1 stick) plus
  3 tablespoons butter, melted

⅓ cup milk

1 egg

Preheat the oven to 425°F. Lightly butter a baking sheet.

In a large bowl, combine the flour, oats, brown sugar, baking powder, cream of tartar, and salt. Stir in the cheese.

In a small bowl, beat together the butter, milk, and egg. Add to the dry ingredients, stirring until just mixed. Shape the dough into a ball and pat onto a lightly floured surface to form an 8-inch disk. Cut into 8 to 12 wedges and place on the prepared baking sheet. Bake for 12 to 15 minutes or until light golden brown.

Brioche

Makes about 16

1 (¼-ounce) packet dry yeast

¼ cup lukewarm water
(110 to 115°F.)

1 teaspoon plus 1 tablespoon
granulated sugar

4 cups all-purpose flour

¼ pound plus 4 tablespoons
(1½ sticks) butter, at
room temperature

¼ teaspoon salt

3 eggs

⅓ cup milk

1 egg yolk mixed
with 1 teaspoon milk

In a small bowl, proof the yeast in the water. Add 1 teaspoon of sugar and 1½ cups of flour and beat until smooth. Shape the dough into a ball and cut it in half. Place each half in a bowl, cover the bowls, and set in a warm place for 15 to 20 minutes. These are sponges.

In a separate bowl, combine 1½ cups of flour, 1 tablespoon of sugar, 6 tablespoons of butter, the salt, and 1 egg. Mix with a wooden spoon, then add the milk gradually to make a smooth paste. Add the remaining 6 tablespoons of butter, 1 egg, and the remaining 1 cup of flour, and beat until smooth. The dough shouldn't be sticky.

Form a hollow in the center of the dough and add the sponges and the remaining egg. Knead the dough in the bowl about 5 minutes, until smooth.

Place the dough in a separate greased bowl and cover. Let the dough sit in a warm place for about 1½ hours.

Turn the dough out onto a lightly floured surface and beat down with the palm of your hand. Return the dough to the bowl, cover, and put in the refrigerator overnight.

Turn the dough out onto a lightly floured surface and beat down again. Cut the dough into fourths. Keep one of the fourths in the refrigerator. Shape the remaining dough into 16 balls of equal size. Place the dough balls into well-greased brioche or muffin pans.

Take the reserved dough and cut into 16 equal sized balls. Using kitchen scissors, cut a crisscross on top of each large ball of dough. Separate the dough and place a small ball of dough in the hollow you've just created.

Cover the dough with a clean dish towel and let it rise, about 1 hour.

Preheat the oven to 425°F.

Brush the brioches with the egg yolk mixture and bake for 20 to 25 minutes until the brioches are shiny and brown. Remove them from the pans immediately and allow to cool on racks.

Diner Griddle Cakes

Makes 2 dozen

2 cups all-purpose flour

2 teaspoons baking powder

1 teaspoon baking soda

2 tablespoons
   granulated sugar

¼ teaspoons salt

2 eggs

1 cup vanilla yogurt

2 cups buttermilk

4 tablespoons butter, melted,
   plus more for cooking

In a large bowl, combine the flour, baking powder, baking soda, sugar and salt; set aside.

In a small bowl, beat the eggs, then add the yogurt and mix well. Stir in the buttermilk and melted butter. Pour the liquid ingredients into the dry ingredients and whisk until just moistened.

Heat a griddle over medium heat (300°F. for electric griddle) and melt 2 tablespoons of butter. Pour ¼ cup batter onto the griddle for each pancake. Cook for 2 to 3 minutes until bubbles form on the top and the underside is golden. Flip the pancake and cook for 3 to 4 minutes more, until the center of each pancake springs back when gently pressed. Repeat with remaining batter.

German Apple Pancake

Makes 12 servings

4 tablespoons butter

3 large (1½ pounds total)
  Granny Smith apples, peeled,
  cored, and sliced into ⅛-inch
  thick slices

¼ cup brown sugar, packed

½ teaspoon ground nutmeg

1 teaspoon cinnamon

6 large eggs,
  at room temperature

1½ cup buttermilk,
  at room temperature

1 cup all-purpose flour

¼ cup granulated sugar

1 teaspoon vanilla

½ teaspoon salt

Confectioners' sugar,
  for garnish

Preheat the oven to 375°F.

Place the butter in 13 x 9 x 2-inch glass baking pan and melt in the oven. Arrange the apple slices over the melted butter and return to the oven, baking until the apples are soft, about 10 minutes.

In a small bowl, combine the brown sugar with the nutmeg and ½ teaspoon cinnamon. Remove the pan from the oven and sprinkle the apples with the brown sugar mixture; set aside.

In a medium mixing bowl, combine the eggs, buttermilk, flour, sugar, vanilla, salt, and remaining ½ teaspoon cinnamon. Mix with an electric mixer for 1½ minutes or in a blender for about 30 seconds. Pour over the apples.

Return the pan to the oven and bake for 35 minutes or until the top is golden brown and the apples rise to the (somewhat uneven) surface. Remove from the oven, sprinkle with confectioners' sugar, and serve immediately.

Flapjacks with Apple Maple Syrup

Makes 4 servings

2 to 3 large apples,
    cored and sliced

4 tablespoons butter, plus
    more for cooking

1 cup maple syrup

2 cups buttermilk pancake mix

1⅓ cups milk

¼ cup vegetable oil

2 eggs

6 slices bacon, cooked
    and crumbled

To make the syrup, sauté the apple slices in the butter until tender. Add the maple syrup and bring to a boil. Remove from the heat and cover.

In a medium bowl, combine the pancake mix, milk, oil, and eggs; beat well. Melt some butter on a hot griddle (300°F. for electric griddle) and pour ¼ cup of batter onto the griddle for each pancake. Cook for 2 to 3 minutes until bubbles form on the top and the underside is golden. Flip the pancake and cook for 3 to 4 minutes more, until the center of each pancake springs back when gently pressed. Repeat with remaining batter.

Top the flapjacks with apple maple syrup and bacon crumbs. Serve immediately.

TIP: For an extra treat, make these Cheddar flapjacks by adding 8 ounces (2 cups) of shredded Cheddar cheese to the flapjack mix.

Basic Crepes

Makes 10 to 12

3 eggs

½ teaspoon salt

2⅛ cups all-purpose flour

2 cups milk

¼ cup melted butter

With an electric mixer, beat the eggs and salt. Add the flour alternately with the milk until smooth. Stir in the melted butter. Allow the batter to stand for 1 hour or more in the refrigerator before cooking. The flour may expand and some of the bubbles will collapse. The batter should be the same thickness as heavy cream. If the batter is too thick, add 1 to 2 tablespoons of milk and stir well.

Heat a pan coated with nonstick cooking spray over medium-high heat. Pour in 3 tablespoons of batter and lift the pan above the heating unit. Quickly rotate the pan until the batter covers the bottom, then return it to the heat. Cook until light brown. Turn and brown the other side for a few seconds.

FOR DESSERT CREPES: Follow the basic crepe recipe and add 2 tablespoons sugar with the flour and 1 teaspoon vanilla extract with the milk.

NOTE: Freeze crepes by separating with pieces of wax paper and wrap air-tight. May be stored for up to 3 months.

Cherry-Cheese Crepes

Makes 10 to 12

3 eggs

½ teaspoon salt

2⅛ cups all-purpose flour

2 tablespoons
  granulated sugar

1 teaspoon vanilla

2 cups milk

4 tablespoons butter, melted

5 ounces (1¼ cups) small curd
  cottage cheese

2 tablespoons cream cheese,
  at room temperature

¾ cup sour cream

½ cup confectioners' sugar

1 (21-ounce) can
  cherry pie filling

TIP: Freeze remaining crepes by separating them with pieces of waxed paper and wrapping air-tight. They may be stored for 3 months.

Beat the eggs and salt.

In a separate bowl, combine the flour and granulated sugar. In another bowl, combine the vanilla and milk.

Beating with electric mixer or whisk until smooth, add the flour and milk mixtures alternately to the egg mixture. Stir in the butter. Allow the batter to stand for 1 hour or more in the refrigerator. The flour may expand and some of the bubbles will collapse. The batter should be the same thickness as heavy cream. If the batter is too thick, add 1 to 2 tablespoons of milk and stir well.

Whip the cottage cheese and cream cheese until smooth. Stir in the sour cream and confectioners' sugar.

Heat a nonstick coated pan to medium-high heat. Pour 3 tablespoons of batter into the pan, then lift the pan above the heating unit. Quickly rotate the pan until the batter covers the bottom, then return it to the heat. Cook until the bottom of the crepe is light brown. Flip the crepe and brown the other side for a few seconds. Repeat with the remainder of the dough.

Fill the crepes with cheese mixture and cherry filling. Fold the crepes and top with cheese mixture.

Swiss Toast with Hot Buttered Rum Sauce

Makes 6 servings

2 eggs, beaten

¾ cup milk

½ teaspoon salt

1 tablespoon granulated sugar

¼ teaspoon vanilla

12 slices day-old white or
   wheat bread

6 slices (¾ ounce each)
   Swiss cheese

2 to 3 tablespoons butter

Hot Buttered Rum Sauce

1 cup granulated sugar

2 tablespoons cornstarch

⅛ teaspoon salt

¾ cup water

¾ cup dark rum

2 tablespoons butter

In a medium mixing bowl, combine the eggs, milk, salt, sugar, and vanilla.

Make six sandwiches of cheese and bread. Dip each sandwich into the egg mixture and fry on a well-buttered griddle until the cheese melts or until the bread is golden brown.

Meanwhile, make the Hot Buttered Rum Sauce. In a small saucepan over medium heat, combine the sugar, cornstarch, salt, and water. Heat slowly until the mixture comes to boil. Boil for 1 minute until the sauce thickens. Remove from heat, stir in the rum and butter.

Serve the Swiss Toasts with Hot Buttered Rum Sauce.

Ham and Egg Brunch Bake

Makes 8 servings

6 to 7 slices firm white bread,
  cut into ½-inch cubes

1 pound baked ham,
  cut into ½-inch cubes

½ pound (8 ounces) aged
  Cheddar cheese,
  cut in ½-inch cubes

3 large eggs

2 cups milk

½ teaspoon dry mustard

½ teaspoon salt

½ pound (2 sticks)
  butter, melted

Butter a 13 x 9 x 2-inch baking pan.

Combine the bread with the ham and spread over the bottom of the prepared baking pan. Sprinkle with cheese.

Beat the eggs until well blended; add milk, mustard, and salt and blend. Pour the milk mixture over the bread mixture. Pour the melted butter over top.

Cover the baking pan with plastic wrap and refrigerate overnight.

When you're ready to continue, preheat the oven to 325°F. Remove the plastic wrap and bake for 1 hour. Cut into serving pieces and serve while warm.

TIP: This recipe must be made the night before so the bread properly absorbs the milk mixture.

Scrambled Egg Casserole

Makes 12 servings

Cheese Sauce

2 tablespoons butter

2½ tablespoons
all-purpose flour

2 cups milk

½ teaspoon salt

⅛ teaspoon pepper

4 ounces (1 cup) medium
Cheddar cheese, shredded

Egg Layer

3 tablespoons butter, melted

1 cup (4 ounces) cubed
baked ham

¼ cup chopped green onion

1 cup (8 ounces) mushrooms,
cleaned and sliced or
1 (4-ounce) can mushroom
slices, drained

1 dozen large eggs, beaten

Topping

4 tablespoons butter

2½ cups soft breadcrumbs

To make the sauce, melt the butter in a 2-quart saucepan over medium heat. Whisk in the flour and cook for 1 minute, whisking constantly. Gradually whisk in the milk until the mixture boils and thickens, about 3 minutes. Add the salt, pepper, and Cheddar cheese, whisking until the cheese melts. Set aside.

To make the egg layer, pour the butter in a 10-inch nonstick skillet set over medium heat; add the ham, green onion, and mushrooms. Sauté until the mushrooms begin to soften, about 3 minutes.

Add the eggs and cook, lifting the cooked eggs toward the center and allowing the uncooked eggs to flow to the bottom. Avoid constant stirring. Cook until the eggs are set, about 5 minutes. Stir in the sauce and blend.

Spray a 13 x 9-inch baking dish with non-stick spray and spoon the egg mixture into the dish. Combine the topping ingredients and spread evenly over top. Cover with plastic wrap and refrigerate overnight.

To cook, bring the dish to room temperature for about 20 minutes before baking at 350°F. for 30 minutes. Serve hot.

Blue Cheese-Potato Casserole

Makes 4 servings

4 medium potatoes, washed
  and peeled

¼ cup water

8 ounces (2 cups) Brie cheese,
  at room temperature

1 cup (8 ounces) plain yogurt

2 eggs

Salt and pepper to taste

4 tablespoons butter, melted

5 ounces (1 cup) crumbled
  blue cheese

Place the potatoes and water in a covered 2-quart casserole and microwave on high for 8 to 10 minutes; drain and let cool. Dice the potatoes and place in a bowl.

Combine the Brie, yogurt, eggs, salt, and pepper in a food processor or blender. Process until smooth. Pour over the diced potatoes and mix well. Divide the potatoes into 4 individual serving dishes or 1 quart soufflé dish. Drizzle with melted butter, sprinkle crumbled cheese on top and microwave on high for 4 to 6 minutes or until the cheese is melted.

TIP: Cream cheese can be substituted for the Brie cheese and shredded Cheddar cheese for the crumbled blue cheese.

DID YOU KNOW?
Although more people use margarine than butter, that is likely due to margarine's lower price. Most people prefer the taste of butter.

Bacon, Cheese, and Onion Pie

Makes 1 (8-inch) pie

1 cup cracker crumbs (about
  26 crackers)

4 tablespoons butter, melted

6 slices bacon

1 cup chopped onion

2 eggs, slightly beaten

¾ cup sour cream

½ teaspoon salt

Dash pepper

8 ounces (2 cups) Swiss
  cheese, shredded

2 ounces (½ cup) sharp
  Cheddar cheese, shredded

Preheat the oven to 375°F.

Combine the cracker crumbs and butter, then press onto the bottom and sides of an 8-inch pie plate. Set aside.

In a medium sauté pan, cook the bacon until crisp. Drain on paper towels, then crumble. Pour off all but 2 tablespoons of bacon fat. Add the onion to the pan and cook until tender but not brown. Drain.

In a bowl, mix the onion with the crumbled bacon, eggs, sour cream, salt, pepper, and Swiss cheese. Pour the mixture into the pie shell and sprinkle with Cheddar cheese.

Bake for 25 to 30 minutes, or until a knife inserted halfway between the center and edge of the filling comes out clean. Let stand for 5 to 10 minutes before slicing.

Open-Faced Apple Omelet

Makes 6 servings

5 eggs, separated

2 tablespoons milk

¾ teaspoon salt

2 teaspoons plus ¼ cup
   granulated sugar

4 tablespoons butter

3 tart apples, cored, peeled
   and sliced

¼ teaspoon nutmeg

⅛ teaspoon ground ginger

Preheat the oven to 325°F.

In a small mixing bowl, combine the egg yolks, milk, and ½ teaspoon of salt. Beat with an electric mixer until thick and lemon-colored.

In a large mixing bowl, beat the egg whites until foamy. Add 2 teaspoons sugar and beat until stiff but not dry. Fold the beaten yolks into the whites.

Meanwhile, in an oven-proof, 10-inch skillet set over low heat, melt the butter and heat until it sizzles. Quickly pour the egg mixture into the pan, spreading it evenly. Cook until the omelet is golden brown on bottom. Move the pan to the oven and bake for 10 minutes, or until the top of the omelet is golden brown and the eggs are set, or until a knife inserted near the center comes out clean.

In a 1-quart saucepan, combine the apples, ¼ cup sugar, nutmeg, ¼ teaspoon salt and ginger. Cook over medium heat until the apples are glazed; keep warm.

Turn the omelet out onto platter and spoon the apple mixture overtop. Serve immediately.

Cranberry Scones with Cranberry Cream Cheese Butter

Makes 16

Scones

2¼ cups all-purpose flour

⅓ cup granulated sugar

1 tablespoon baking powder

¼ pound (1 stick) plus
   3 tablespoons butter,
   chilled and diced

2 eggs

⅓ cup heavy cream

1 teaspoon vanilla

½ cup chopped
   fresh cranberries

Cranberry Cream
   Cheese Butter

¼ pound (1 stick) butter, at
   room temperature

½ cup confectioners' sugar

3 ounces cream cheese,
   at room temperature

¼ cup finely chopped
   fresh cranberries

Preheat the oven to 400°F.

To make the scones, combine the flour, sugar, and baking powder in a large mixing bowl. Using your fingertips or 2 knives, cut in the butter until the mixture resembles coarse crumbs.

In a small bowl, combine the eggs, cream, and vanilla. Stir this mixture into the flour mixture and turn out onto a well-floured surface. Knead in the cranberries.

Divide the dough in half and roll or pat each half into a 7-inch disk. With a floured knife or pizza cutter, cut each circle into 8 wedges. Place the wedges on a buttered baking sheet and bake for 12 to 15 minutes or until the bottoms are light brown.

Meanwhile, make the Cranberry Cream Cheese Butter. Combine the butter, sugar, and cream cheese, mixing until well-blended. Stir in the cranberries. Chill until ready to use.

Serve the scones warm with Cranberry Cream Cheese Butter.

Makes 4 dozen

¾ pound (3 sticks) butter,
   at room temperature

4 to 4 ½ cups all-purpose flour

¼ cup warm water
   (105 to 115°F.)

2 (¼-ounce) packages active
   dry yeast

1 tablespoon plus ¼ cup
   granulated sugar

1 cup milk

1 egg, beaten

1 egg, beaten with
   1 tablespoon water

Cheese Filling

8 ounces cream cheese,
   at room temperature

2 tablespoons
   granulated sugar

1 egg yolk

1 teaspoon vanilla

½ teaspoon grated lemon zest

Cream the butter and ⅓ cup of flour until well-blended. Cover and chill until firm enough to roll, about 30 to 45 minutes.

Combine the water, yeast, and 1 tablespoon of sugar in a large mixing bowl and let stand for 10 minutes. Add the milk, remaining ¼ cup sugar, and 1 egg and beat well. Stir in the remaining flour until the dough is easy to handle.

Turn the dough out onto a lightly floured surface and knead until smooth, about 2 to 5 minutes. Shape the dough into a ball, dust it with flour, and roll it into a 16-inch square.

Turn the butter mixture out onto floured waxed paper. Roll the butter mixture and shape it into an 16 x 8-inch rectangle. Place onto half of the dough, then fold the other half of the dough over the butter mixture and press the edges together to seal. Lightly roll the dough until it is ½-inch thick.

Fold a third of the dough to the center, then fold the remaining third over top, making 3 layers. Turn the folded dough toward you so one of the narrow ends faces front. Roll out again, fold and turn. Repeat for a total of 3 times. Wrap and refrigerate the dough for

30 to 60 minutes (or freeze for 10 to 20 minutes, but do not freeze solidly). Repeat rolling, folding, and turning 3 more times. Wrap and let rest in the refrigerator for 30 to 60 minutes.

Meanwhile, to make the cheese filling, beat together all ingredients until well-blended. Cover and refrigerate until ready to use.

Roll the dough until it is ⅛-inch thick. Cut into 2- to 3-inch squares. Place about 1 teaspoon of cheese filling in center of each square. Fold the opposite corners of dough over the filling, overlapping slightly. Pinch tightly to keep the dough from opening during baking. Place on buttered baking sheets, cover lightly with a damp towel, and refrigerate for 1 to 2 hours.

Preheat the oven to 400°F. About 15 minutes before baking, brush each danish with egg and water mixture. Bake for 5 minutes, then reduce the oven temperature to 350°F. and continue baking for 10 minutes or until lightly browned. Remove from baking sheet and cool.

Cinnamon Buns

Chef Jill Prescott
Makes 12

Dough

4½ to 5½ cups unbleached
   all-purpose flour

1 (¼-ounce) packet active
   dry yeast

1 cup whole milk

¼ cup granulated sugar

4 tablespoons unsalted butter,
   cut into ½-inch cubes

2 large eggs,
   at room temperature

1 teaspoon sea salt

Filling

¼ pound (1 stick) unsalted
   butter, at room temperature

½ cup granulated sugar

1 tablespoon best-quality
   ground cinnamon

Icing

1½ cups confectioners' sugar

4 to 6 tablespoons heavy cream

1 teaspoon vanilla extract

In the bowl of a standing mixer fitted with the paddle attachment, combine 2 cups of flour with the yeast. In a saucepan, heat the milk, sugar and butter just until warm (115°F.), stirring to dissolve the sugar and melt the butter. Add the milk mixture to the flour and mix on low speed for 1 minute, scraping down the sides of the bowl once. Add the eggs with the machine off and beat on medium speed for 2 minutes.

Add the salt and the remaining flour in ½- to 1-cup increments, still on medium speed, to make a firm, pliable, but not stiff dough. Stop the machine when adding the flour. The dough will appear ragged but should not feel wet or sticky. This process should not take more than 2 minutes.

Switch to the dough hook attachment. Lift up the dough slightly and scatter about 2 tablespoons of flour underneath. Knead for 2 to 3 minutes on low speed or turn out onto a slightly floured surface and knead by hand for 7 to 8 minutes or until smooth, pliable and very elastic. Shape into a ball.

Lightly butter the same mixing bowl (no

need to wash it). Return the dough to the bowl and turn over once to lightly coat all sides with the butter. Cover the bowl with a damp towel and place over a pot containing hot (not boiling) water for about 2½ hours or until the dough doubles in size.

Punch the dough down to force out the air and shape into a rough rectangle. Place on a flat surface, cover with the damp towel and let rest for 10 minutes.

Roll the dough out into a 18 x 14-inch rectangle with one long edge parallel to the edge of the counter. With an offset spatula or the back of a large spoon, spread the stick of butter evenly over the dough. In a small bowl, mix together the sugar and cinnamon and sprinkle the mixture evenly over the butter. Starting with one long side of the dough, roll the rectangle into a log and pinch the edges to seal. With a serrated knife, cut the log crosswise into thirds, using light pressure to avoid squeezing the filling out. Cut each third into four slices to yield 12 pieces.

Arrange the buns, cut side down, into a deep 12 x 9-inch baking pan. Cover the pan with a damp towel and let the buns rise in a warm place for 30 to 60 minutes or until doubled in size.

Preheat the oven to 350°F. and place a rack in the lower third of the oven. Bake the buns for 20 to 30 minutes, until golden brown. The buns should not be doughy in the center.

While the buns are still baking, combine the confectioners' sugar, 2 tablespoons of cream and the vanilla in a bowl. Whisk the mixture briskly to remove all the lumps. Add more cream, 1 tablespoon at a time, until the mixture has a thick, fluid coating consistency. You may need slightly more than 4 tablespoons depending on the sugar.

Remove the buns from the baking pan and cool on a wire rack, bottom side up. Immediately drizzle the icing over the hot buns so that it seeps and melts into the crevices. Serve warm.

Eggnog Buttercream Coffee Cake

Makes 1 (9-inch) square cake

¼ pound plus 4 tablespoons (1½ stick) butter, at room temperature

¾ cup plus 1 tablespoon granulated sugar

2 eggs

1 teaspoon vanilla

2 cups all-purpose flour

1 teaspoon baking soda

1 teaspoon baking powder

½ teaspoon salt

1 cup sour cream

¾ cup finely chopped walnuts

2 tablespoons brown sugar

½ teaspoon cinnamon

¼ teaspoon ground nutmeg

Eggnog Buttercream Filling

¼ cup granulated sugar

2 tablespoons cornstarch

1½ cups eggnog (substitute whole milk or half-and-half)

3 tablespoons butter

1 teaspoon vanilla

½ cup heavy cream, whipped

Preheat the oven to 350°F. Line a 9-inch square baking pan with wax paper.

In a large mixing bowl, beat the butter and ¾ cup of granulated sugar until light and fluffy. Blend in the eggs and vanilla.

In a separate bowl, combine the flour, baking soda, baking powder, and salt. Add this mixture to the butter mixture alternately with the sour cream, mixing well after each addition. Pour into the prepared baking pan.

Combine the walnuts, brown sugar, cinnamon, and nutmeg and sprinkle over the batter in the pan. Bake for 35 to 40 minutes or until a toothpick inserted in the center comes out clean.

Meanwhile, prepare the Eggnog Buttercream Filling. Combine the sugar and cornstarch in a saucepan over medium heat. Gradually add the eggnog and bring to a boil, stirring constantly. Boil for 1 minute until thickened, stirring constantly. Stir in the butter and vanilla. Remove from the heat and let cool. Fold in the cream and chill.

Cool the cake in the pan for 10 minutes before removing to a wire rack to cool completely. Cut the cake in half horizontally and spread Eggnog Buttercream Filling over bottom layer. Place top layer over filling and store in refrigerator.

Yogurt Coffee Cake

Makes 1 (20 x 4-inch) bundt cake

¼ pound plus 4 tablespoons
   (1½ sticks) butter, at room
   temperature
1½ cups granulated sugar
3 eggs
1½ teaspoons vanilla
3 cups all-purpose flour
1½ teaspoons baking powder
1½ teaspoons baking soda
¼ teaspoon salt
1½ cups plain yogurt
½ cup packed brown sugar
½ cup finely chopped nuts
1½ teaspoons cinnamon

Preheat the oven to 350°F. Butter a 20 x 4-inch bundt pan.

In a large mixing bowl, combine the butter, sugar, eggs, and vanilla. Beat until well-blended.

In a separate bowl, combine the flour, baking powder, baking soda, and salt. Add the dry mixture to the butter mixture alternately with yogurt until well-blended.

In a small bowl, mix the brown sugar, nuts, and cinnamon.

Pour half of the batter into the prepared pan. Sprinkle with half the nut mixture. Repeat layers. Bake for 1 hour, or until the topping is browned. Cool slightly in pan before removing.

Blueberry Ricotta Coffee Cake

Makes 1 (8-inch) square cake

1 cup all-purpose flour

½ cup oat bran

½ cup plus 2 tablespoons
 light brown sugar

2 teaspoons baking powder

½ teaspoon baking soda

¼ teaspoon ground cinnamon

¼ teaspoon salt

8 ounces (1 cup) low-fat
 ricotta cheese

½ cup plain yogurt

2 eggs, beaten

4 tablespoons butter, melted

½ teaspoon vanilla

½ cup fresh or frozen
 blueberries

Preheat the oven to 350°F. Butter an 8-inch square baking pan.

In a large mixing bowl, combine the flour, oat bran, ½ cup light brown sugar, baking powder, baking soda, cinnamon, and salt.

In a separate bowl, combine the ricotta cheese, yogurt, eggs, butter, vanilla, and blueberries. Add the wet ingredients to the dry ingredients, stirring until just mixed. Pour into the prepared baking pan and sprinkle with the remaining 2 tablespoons of brown sugar. Bake until just firm to the touch, about 40 minutes.

Cherry Ladder Coffee Cakes

Makes 2 (8 x 4-inch) cakes

¼ pound (1 stick) butter

½ cup sour cream

1 cup all-purpose flour

1 cup canned cherry pie filling

¼ cup chopped walnuts,
  optional

½ cup sifted
  confectioners' sugar

2 teaspoons milk

In a large mixing bowl, beat the butter with an electric mixer on high speed for 30 seconds. Add the sour cream and beat until fluffy. Add the flour and mix well. Cover and chill for about 1 hour or until firm enough to handle.

Preheat the oven to 350°F.

Divide the dough in half. Working with half of the dough at a time, roll out to a 10 x 8-inch rectangle. Place the rectangle on a greased baking sheet. Spread half of the cherry pie filling lengthwise down the center third of the rectangle. Sprinkle half of the chopped walnuts over the pie filling.

Using a sharp knife, make 2½-inch-long horizontal cuts at 1-inch intervals along both long sides of the dough rectangle, forming strips. Pull the corresponding strips from each side to meet in the middle, over the filling, and pinch the ends of strips together in a narrow point at center. Repeat until all strips are connected and resemble a ladder. Tuck the top edges in to cradle the filling. Repeat with the remaining dough.

Bake for 30 minutes or until golden. Sprinkle with additional chopped walnuts.

Combine the confectioners' sugar and milk and drizzle over top.

Swedish Coffee Bread

Makes 2

Topping

2 tablespoons
  granulated sugar

½ teaspoon ground cinnamon

Bread

2 (¼-ounce) packages active
  quick rise yeast

1 teaspoon plus ½ cup
  granulated sugar

½ cup warm water
  (110°F. to 115°F.)

1 cup milk

¼ pound (1 stick)
  plus 3 tablespoons butter

7 cups bread flour

1 teaspoon salt

1½ teaspoons ground
  cardamom

3 large eggs,
  at room temperature

To make the topping, combine the sugar and cinnamon; set aside.

Combine the yeast, 1 teaspoon of sugar, and warm water, stirring until smooth. Set aside to proof for 5 minutes (yeast bubbles will form on the surface and expand).

Heat the milk and butter together in a microwave or small saucepan until warm, about 110°F. (the butter will start to melt).

Place 2 cups of flour, the remaining ½ cup of sugar, salt, and cardamom in a large mixing bowl. Add the dissolved yeast mixture and the milk and butter; blend with an electric mixer until smooth, about 3 minutes.

Beat in the eggs, one at a time, beating for 1 minute after each addition.

Add 4 cups of flour, one cup at a time, beating with heavy duty mixer until blended and dough forms a ball (dough will still be sticky). Knead in, by hand or with machine, the remaining 1 cup flour until the mixture is smooth and elastic, 5 to 8 minutes.

Place the dough in a greased bowl and turn the dough over to coat. Cover with plastic wrap and let the dough rise in a warm place until it doubles in size, about 1 hour.

Punch down the dough to remove air

bubbles, then divide the dough into six equal parts.

Grease two 16 x 12-inch baking sheets. For a traditional Swedish coffee braid, bread the dough. For each braid, roll three pieces of dough into ropes about 20 inches long and place the ropes side by side on a baking sheet. Braid the ropes until they are too short to braid. Pinch together the short ends and tuck under. Repeat for second braid.

To make loaves, form each dough piece into a loaf and place in separate greased 8 x 4-inch pans.

Cover the dough and let it rise in a warm place until it doubles in size, about 45 to 50 minutes. Sprinkle the bread with the topping mixture.

Bake at 350°F. for about 35 minutes until golden brown. Carefully remove the loaves from pans or braids from sheets and transfer to a wire rack to cool before slicing.

Indian-Spiced Pumpkin Bread

Makes 1 (9¼ x 5¼ x 3-inch) loaf

2 teaspoons cumin seeds

3 tablespoons butter

½ cup finely chopped onion

2 teaspoons curry powder

¼ teaspoon ground cumin

⅛ teaspoon cayenne pepper

¾ teaspoon salt

¾ cup all-purpose flour

¾ cup cornmeal

1 teaspoon baking powder

½ teaspoon baking soda

1 tablespoon granulated sugar

8 ounces (1 cup)
   pumpkin puree, canned
   or homemade*

1½ teaspoon finely diced
   hot chile, such as jalapeño
   or Serrano

2 eggs, lightly beaten

⅔ cup buttermilk

3 ounces (¾ cup) colby
   cheese, shredded

*To purée pumpkin: peel the pumpkin and cut in 2-inch cubes. Boil in salted water until tender, 8 to 12 minutes. Drain. Purée pumpkin in food processor or blender.

Preheat the oven to 350°F. Butter a 9¼ x 5¼ x 3-inch loaf pan.

Heat a small, heavy skillet over medium-low heat. Add the cumin seeds and toast just until aromatic. Do not scorch or brown. Pour the seeds onto a plate and set aside.

In the same skillet, heat 1 tablespoon of butter. Add the onion, curry powder, cumin, cayenne pepper, and salt. Cook, stirring frequently, until the onion is soft, about 5 minutes. Let cool and stir in the reserved cumin seeds.

Sift the flour, cornmeal, baking powder, baking soda, and sugar into a bowl.

Melt the remaining butter and set aside.

In a large bowl, whisk the pumpkin puree, chile, eggs, buttermilk, onion mixture, and melted butter. Mix just until moistened. Add the flour mixture and stir just until mixed. Fold in ½ cup colby cheese. Spoon the mixture into the prepared loaf pan. Bake for 35 minutes. Remove from the oven and sprinkle the remaining cheese over the bread. Return to the oven for 5 to 7 minutes longer, until the cheese melts and the bread is baked through.

Spicy Pumpkin Gingerbread Loaves

Makes 2 (8 x 4-inch) or 5 (6 x 3-inch) loaves

3 cups all-purpose flour

1 tablespoon baking powder

1 tablespoon ground ginger

2 teaspoons cinnamon

1 teaspoon ground cloves

1 teaspoon baking soda

¾ teaspoon salt

1¼ cups packed brown sugar

¼ pound (1 stick) butter,
  at room temperature

3 eggs

1 cup canned pumpkin

⅓ cup dark molasses

1 cup buttermilk

1 cup chopped dates

1 cup chopped pecans

Preheat the oven to 350°F. Grease two 8 x 4-inch or five 6 x 3-inch loaf pans.

Combine the flour, baking powder, ginger, cinnamon, cloves, baking soda, and salt; set aside.

In a large bowl, using an electric mixer set at medium speed, beat the brown sugar and butter until creamy. Add the eggs; continue beating until fluffy. Blend in the pumpkin and molasses.

Gradually add the flour mixture alternately with the buttermilk. Stir in the dates and pecans, then spread the batter into the pan.

Bake for 60 minutes in the 8 x 4-inch pans, 40 minutes in the 6 x 3-inch pans, or until a toothpick inserted in center comes out clean. Cool in the pan for 15 minutes before removing to wire rack.

TIP: Bake 6 x 3-inch pans on a baking sheet to easily remove the loaves from the oven.

Confetti Cornbread

Makes 8 to 10 servings

1¾ cups yellow cornmeal

3 ounces (¾ cup) Parmesan
  cheese, grated

½ cup all-purpose flour

3 tablespoons
  granulated sugar

2 teaspoons baking powder

½ teaspoon baking soda

¼ teaspoon salt

2 teaspoons butter

½ cup finely chopped
  red bell pepper

½ cup finely chopped
  green bell pepper

3 eggs

2 cups milk

1⅓ cups buttermilk

Preheat the oven to 375°F. Butter a 9-inch square or 10-inch round baking pan.

Combine the cornmeal, Parmesan cheese, flour, sugar, baking powder, baking soda, and salt in a bowl. Set aside.

Heat the butter in a small skillet. Add the red and green peppers and sauté for 3 minutes. Remove from the heat and cool slightly.

Beat the eggs, milk, and buttermilk. Add the cornmeal mixture and stir just to blend. Fold in the cooked peppers and spread into the prepared pan. Bake for 45 minutes until set and the top is golden.

TIP: For a special treat, add ¾ cup (3 ounces) shredded colby cheese to the mixture, and sprinkle a little on top before baking.

Double Corn Cornbread with Honey Butter

Makes 8 to 10 servings

Cornbread

1 cup yellow cornmeal

1 cup all-purpose flour

¼ cup granulated sugar

2 teaspoons baking powder

¾ teaspoon baking soda

¾ teaspoon salt

2 large eggs

1 cup buttermilk

4 tablespoons butter, melted
  and cooled

1 cup frozen whole kernel
  corn, thawed

Honey Butter

½ stick (¼ cup) butter,
  at room temperature

2 tablespoons honey

Preheat the oven to 400°F. Butter a 8- or 9-inch square baking pan.

In a large bowl, combine the cornmeal, flour, sugar, baking powder, baking soda, and salt; mix well.

In a medium bowl, beat the eggs. Add the buttermilk and butter; mix well. Add to the dry ingredients, mixing just until the dry ingredients are moistened. Fold in the corn.

Spread the batter into the prepared pan and bake for about 25 to 30 minutes, or until golden brown and a wooden pick inserted in the center comes out clean.

Meanwhile, prepare the honey butter by combining the butter and honey. Cut the corn bread into squares and serve warm or at room temperature with honey butter.

Onion and Olive Chive Bread

Makes 1 large loaf

¼ pound (1 stick) butter

2 cups chopped yellow onion

1 (¼-ounce) packet active
  dry yeast

2 teaspoons granulated sugar

1 cup warm water
  (110 to 115°F.)

4 cups all-purpose flour

2 tablespoons chopped chives

½ cup good quality olives,
  such as Kalamata or Gaeta,
  roughly chopped

1½ teaspoons salt

Melt the butter in a sauté pan set over medium-low heat; add the onion and cook, stirring often, until the onion is golden and soft, about 15 to 20 minutes. Set aside to let cool.

In the bowl of a stand mixer, combine the yeast, sugar, warm water, and ½ cup of flour, and let stand until foamy, about 20 minutes.

Add half of the remaining flour to the mixture along with the chives, olives, and salt.

Mix thoroughly (alternately, you can mix with a wooden spoon, but do not try using a hand mixer). Add the rest of the flour slowly and then the onion mixture to form a slightly sticky, stiff dough.

Knead the dough with the dough hook attachment for 10 minutes (or by hand on a lightly floured surface for 15 minutes). Shape the dough into a flattened disk and place on a buttered baking sheet. Cover and let rise in a warm place for about 45 to 60 minutes, until the dough doubles in size.

Bake at 400°F. for 30 minutes until brown and crisp.

Pepper-Cheese Bread

Makes 2 breads, to serve 15 to 20

5½ to 6 cups all-purpose flour

2 (¼-ounce) packages active
  dry yeast

1 cup milk

¼ pound (1 stick) plus
  3 tablespoons butter

1 tablespoon granulated sugar

1 to 2 tablespoons coarse
  black pepper

1 teaspoon salt

4 eggs

8 ounces (2 cups) sharp
  Cheddar cheese, shredded

1¼ cups unseasoned
  mashed potatoes

In a large mixing bowl, combine 2 cups of flour and the yeast.

In a small saucepan, combine the milk, butter, sugar, pepper, and salt. Cook and stir until warm (115°F. to 120°F.) and the butter is almost melted. Add to the flour mixture. Add the eggs and beat with an electric mixer on low speed for 30 seconds, scraping the sides of bowl. Beat on high for 3 minutes. Stir in the Cheddar cheese, mashed potatoes, and as much of the remaining flour as you can mix in with a spoon.

Turn the dough out onto a lightly floured surface. Knead until the dough is moderately stiff and smooth and elastic, about 6 to 8 minutes total; add as much of the remaining flour as necessary. Shape the dough into a ball and place it in a greased bowl; turn once to grease the entire surface. Cover the dough and let it rise in a warm place until it doubles in size, about 1 hour.

Grease 2 baking sheets.

Punch the dough down, then turn it out onto a lightly floured surface. Divide the dough into 6 pieces. Cover the dough and let it rest for about 10 minutes. Roll each piece into a 16-inch long rope.

On a prepared baking sheet, braid 3 ropes together. Repeat with the remaining ropes on the second baking sheet. Cover the dough and let rise in a warm place until nearly doubled in size, about 30 minutes.

Preheat the oven to 375°F.

Bake the braids at for 35 to 40 minutes or until the top is browned; cover with foil for the last 15 minutes of baking to prevent over-browning. Remove from pans; cool.

Stuffed Cheese Bread

Makes 8 to 10 (see photo on page 73)

1 loaf (1 pound) French
   baguette bread,
   24 x 4-inches
¼ pound (1 stick) butter,
   at room temperature
2 tablespoons chopped onion
1 tablespoon poppy seeds
1 teaspoon seasoned salt
½ teaspoon lemon juice
1 tablespoon
   prepared mustard
1 (4-ounce) can mushroom
   stems and pieces, drained
   and chopped
1 pound (4 cups) Swiss
   cheese, shredded

Preheat the oven to 350°F.

Slice the bread at 1½-inch intervals without cutting through the bottom crust. Cut the loaf lengthwise across the top, perpendicular to the other slices, again not slicing through the bottom loaf. Set aside.

Mix the remaining ingredients in a large mixing bowl. Spread the filling between the slices. Wrap the loaf in aluminum foil, sealing all ends, and place on baking sheet. Bake for 30 to 40 minutes. Serve warm.

Cranberry Pecan Loaf with Cheddar Streusel

Makes 1 (9 x 5 x 4-inch) loaf

Cranberry Pecan Loaf

2 cups all-purpose flour

¾ cup light brown sugar

1 tablespoon baking powder

2 teaspoons ground cinnamon
or apple pie spice mixture

½ teaspoon salt

⅔ cup buttermilk

2 large eggs, lightly beaten

4 tablespoons unsalted butter,
melted

1 cup chopped
fresh cranberries

1 cup chopped pecans,
toasted

Cheddar Streusel

1 cup whole oats

½ cup light brown sugar

½ cup all-purpose flour

2 ounces (½ cup) Cheddar
cheese, shredded

4 tablespoons unsalted
butter, melted

Preheat the oven to 350°F. Grease a 9 x 5 x 4-inch loaf pan.

In a bowl, combine the flour, brown sugar, baking powder, cinnamon, and salt; set aside.

In another bowl, combine the buttermilk, eggs, and melted butter. Stir the dry mixture into the wet mixture and mix just to combine. Fold in the cranberries and pecans.

To make the streusel, combine all of the streusel ingredients.

Pour half of the batter into the prepared pan. Spread half of the Cheddar streusel over top and pour the remaining half of the batter over the streusel. Spread the remaining half of the streusel evenly over top and bake for 1 hour or until the top is golden brown and a cake tester comes out clean. Cool in the pan for 15 minutes, then remove from the pan and cool on a wire rack.

Orange-Rosemary Pound Bread

Makes 1 (9 x 5 x 4-inch) loaf

½ pound (2 sticks) unsalted
   butter, at room temperature

1 cup granulated sugar

2 tablespoon light honey

5 large eggs

2 cups cake flour

1 tablespoon orange juice

1 tablespoon chopped fresh
   rosemary leaves

Grated zest of 1 orange

1½ teaspoons orange
   flower water

Orange flavored whipped
   cream, vanilla ice cream,
   or macerated fresh berries,
   for serving

Preheat the oven to 350°F. Grease and lightly flour a 9 x 5 x 4-inch loaf pan.

In bowl, cream the butter and sugar until very light and fluffy. Stir in the honey and add the eggs, one at a time, beating well after each addition. Add the flour, ½ cup at a time, mixing after each addition. Gently stir in the orange juice, rosemary, orange zest, and orange flower water.

Spoon the batter into the prepared pan and bake for 1 hour, or until golden brown on top and a cake tester comes out clean. Cool in the pan for 15 minutes, then remove from the pan and cool completely. Let stand overnight, wrapped, for best results.

Serve with orange flavored whipped cream, vanilla ice cream, or macerated fresh berries.

TIP: For extra zing, add 1 cup shredded Brick or Monterey Jack cheese to the dough.

Lemon Poppy Seed Bread

Makes 2 (8 x 4-inch) loaves

2½ cups all-purpose flour

½ cup poppy seeds

1 tablespoon grated
  lemon zest

1 teaspoon baking powder

1 teaspoon baking soda

½ teaspoon salt

¾ cup buttermilk

½ cup sour cream

½ pound (2 sticks) butter

1 cup brown sugar

1 cup granulated sugar

3 eggs

⅓ cup lemon juice

Preheat the oven to 350°F. Grease and flour two 8 x 4-inch loaf pans.

Combine the flour, poppy seeds, lemon zest, baking powder, baking soda, and salt; set aside.

Combine the buttermilk and sour cream; set aside.

Beat the butter, brown sugar, and ⅓ cup of sugar until light and fluffy. Blend in the eggs. Add the flour mixture alternately with the buttermilk mixture, mixing well after each addition.

Pour into the prepared pans and bake for 50 to 60 minutes or until a wooden pick inserted in the center comes out clean.

Meanwhile, combine the remaining sugar and lemon juice in a small saucepan. Bring to a boil, stirring until the sugar dissolves.

Pierce the hot loaves with a wooden pick and pour the hot lemon mixture over top the loaves. Cool for 30 minutes before removing from the pans.

Savory Bundt Loaf

Makes 1 (10-inch) bundt loaf

1 tablespoon poppy seeds

2½ cups all-purpose flour

2 tablespoons
   granulated sugar

1 teaspoon salt

2 (¼-ounce) packages dry yeast

¼ pound (1 stick) butter, at
   room temperature

¼ teaspoon marjoram

¼ teaspoon thyme

1 teaspoon dried minced onion

½ cup milk

½ cup water

1 egg

Generously grease a 10-inch bundt pan, then sprinkle with poppy seeds. Set aside.

In large mixing bowl, combine 1½ cups of flour, the sugar, salt, and yeast; mix well and set aside.

Prepare the filling by combining 4 tablespoons of butter with the marjoram, thyme, and onion; mix well and set aside.

In a small saucepan, combine the milk, water, and remaining 4 tablespoons of butter; heat until warm (butter does not need to melt). Add the warm milk mixture and egg to the flour mixture. Blend at low speed until moistened; then beat for 3 minutes at medium speed.

Gradually add the remaining flour, stirring by hand to make a stiff batter. Spoon half of the batter into the prepared pan, then cover the batter with the filling. Spoon and spread the remaining batter over the filling. (Don't worry if the filling is not entirely covered, the batter will cover it once it rises.) Cover and let rise in a warm place until the batter doubles in size, about 1 hour.

Preheat the oven to 350°F. Bake for 35 to 40 minutes or until golden brown. Invert immediately and remove the pan.

Cheddar Cheese Apple Bread

Makes 1 (9 x 5 x 3-inch) loaf

¼ pound (1 stick) butter

2 eggs, slightly beaten

2 cups all-purpose flour

⅔ cup granulated sugar

1 teaspoon baking powder

½ teaspoon baking soda

½ teaspoon salt

2 apples, peeled and shredded

1 cup chopped walnuts

2 ounces (½ cup) Cheddar
cheese, shredded

Preheat the oven to 350°F. Grease a 9 x 5 x 3-inch loaf pan.

In a large mixing bowl, combine the butter, eggs, flour, sugar, baking powder, baking soda, and salt. Blend well. Stir in the apples, walnuts, and cheese. Turn the batter into the prepared pan and bake for 55 to 60 minutes, or until the top is browned.

Pull-Apart Cheese Bread

Makes 12 servings

3 packages frozen dinner roll
dough (approximately
3 dozen total), thawed to
room temperature

5 tablespoons butter, melted

3 ounces (1 cup) Parmesan
cheese, grated

4 ounces (1 cup) provolone
cheese, shredded

Grease a 12-cup fluted tube pan.

Roll each dinner roll in butter, then in Parmesan cheese. Arrange half of the rolls in the pan. Sprinkle with provolone cheese. Top with the remaining coated rolls. Sprinkle with any remaining Parmesan cheese. Let the dough rise until it doubles in size, about 1 hour.

Preheat the oven to 375°F. Bake for 35 to 45 minutes or until golden brown. Remove from the pan and serve warm.

Cranberry Vanilla Chip Muffins

Makes 24

3 cups all-purpose flour

1 tablespoon baking powder

¾ teaspoon salt

1 teaspoon baking soda

1 cup granulated sugar

¼ pound (1 stick) plus
   3 tablespoons butter, melted

2 large eggs

¾ cup plain yogurt

¼ cup buttermilk

1 cup vanilla chips

¾ cup chopped cranberries,
   fresh or frozen

1 teaspoon almond extract

Topping

¼ pound (1 stick) butter,
   melted

½ cup granulated sugar

Preheat the oven to 375°F. Line 2 (12-cup) muffin tins with paper liners.

Whisk together the flour, baking powder, salt, and baking soda in large mixing bowl; set aside.

In separate mixing bowl and using an electric mixer, beat the sugar and melted butter until well blended, about 1 minute. Beat in the eggs, one at a time.

Combine the yogurt and buttermilk and add to the sugar mixture, along with the vanilla chips, cranberries, and almond extract. Stir to blend. Gradually add the dry ingredients to the wet; stirring just until combined. Using an ice cream scoop, drop the batter into the prepared cupcake tins, filling each cup about two-thirds full.

Bake for 15 to 20 minutes or until golden brown.

Before the muffins cool, dip the tops of each muffin into the melted butter and then into sugar for the topping.

Pumpkin Date Nut Muffins

Makes 16

¾ cup brown sugar, packed

¼ pound (1 stick) butter,
  at room temperature

¼ cup dark molasses

1 extra large egg,
  lightly beaten

1 cup canned pumpkin

¼ cup buttermilk,
  at room temperature

1¾ cups unbleached,
  sifted all-purpose flour

1 teaspoon baking soda

¼ teaspoon salt

1 teaspoon ground cinnamon

¼ teaspoon ground nutmeg

½ cup pitted, finely diced dates

⅓ cup chopped walnuts

Preheat the oven to 350°F.

Cream the brown sugar, butter, and molasses together in large mixing bowl with an electric mixer, about 3 minutes. Add the egg, scraping down the bowl as needed. Add the pumpkin and buttermilk, beating until smooth.

In a separate bowl, whisk together the flour, baking soda, salt, cinnamon, and nutmeg. Add the dates, mixing just to coat dates with flour mixture.

Add the flour-date mixture and walnuts to the pumpkin mixture, stirring just until blended (the batter will be lumpy). Spoon the batter into paper-lined muffin cups.

Bake for 20 to 22 minutes for standard muffins, or until an inserted toothpick comes out clean. Cool for 5 minutes in tins on a wire rack; remove from the tins to a rack to cool completely.

Raspberry Sour Cream Muffins

Makes 16

Streusel Topping

¼ cup chopped pecans

⅓ cup brown sugar, packed

¼ cup all-purpose flour

2 tablespoons butter, melted

Muffins

2 large eggs,
  at room temperature

1 cup granulated sugar

½ cup vegetable oil

1 teaspoon almond extract

2 cups all-purpose flour

1 teaspoon baking powder

½ teaspoon salt

½ teaspoon baking soda

1 cup sour cream,
  at room temperature

3 ounces cream cheese,
  cut into 16 pieces

1 cup fresh or
  frozen (dry pack) raspberries

Preheat the oven to 375°F.

To make the streusel topping, combine the pecans, brown sugar, flour, and butter with a fork until crumbly; set aside.

Beat the eggs in a large bowl with an electric mixer; gradually add the sugar. With the mixer running, pour in the vegetable oil and almond extract, blending until smooth.

In a separate bowl, whisk together the flour, baking powder, salt, and baking soda. Add the flour mixture to the egg mixture, alternating with the sour cream; blend until smooth and set aside.

Form each cream cheese piece into a disk the size of a quarter.

Spoon one generous tablespoon of batter into the bottom of muffin tins. Portion half of the raspberries equally among muffin cups. Top each muffin cup with a cream cheese disk. Divide the remaining batter among the muffin cups, spooning over the cream cheese. Top with the remaining equally divided raspberries. Sprinkle each muffin with streusel topping.

Bake for 20 to 25 minutes. Let stand for 5 minutes in tins on a wire rack. Remove from the tins to a rack to cool completely.

Mini Corn Gems
with Orange Honey Butter

Makes 36

6 tablespoons butter, melted

1 cup all-purpose flour

1 cup cornmeal

3 tablespoons
  granulated sugar

2¼ teaspoons baking powder

½ teaspoon baking soda

1 teaspoon salt

1 cup buttermilk

1 large egg

¾ cup frozen corn kernels,
  thawed and drained

¼ cup jarred roasted
  red peppers, drained
  and chopped

Orange-Honey Butter

¼ pound (1 stick) butter, at
  room temperature

3 tablespoons honey

1 teaspoon grated orange zest

Preheat the oven to 400°F. Lightly brush 36 mini muffin cups with melted butter; set aside the pans and remaining melted butter.

In a large bowl, combine the flour, cornmeal, sugar, baking powder, baking soda, and salt. Set aside.

In a medium bowl, combine the remaining butter, with the buttermilk, egg, corn, and peppers. Stir in the flour mixture until just combined. Spoon the batter into the prepared muffin cups. Bake for 15 to 18 minutes, or until the muffins are golden brown.

Meanwhile, make the Orange-Honey Butter: In a small bowl, using an electric mixer, cream together all the ingredients. Transfer to a small serving bowl or crock. Cover and refrigerate until ready to use.

Serve warm, or cool on a wire rack, with Orange-Honey Butter.

Cheese and Bacon Puffs

Makes 5 dozen

2 tablespoons finely chopped
  green onions or chives

¼ pound (1 stick) butter

1 cup water

⅛ teaspoon cayenne pepper

1 cup all-purpose flour

4 eggs

5 slices bacon, cooked
  and crumbled

1 cup grated sharp
  Cheddar cheese

Preheat the oven to 400°F.

Sauté the green onions in 1 tablespoon of butter over medium heat until soft, about 3 minutes. Add the remaining butter, water, and cayenne pepper and bring to a boil. Remove from the heat and stir in the flour using a wooden spoon or electric mixer set on low. Incorporate thoroughly and return to a low heat. Cool until the mixture forms a thick ball that pulls away form the sides of the pan, about 5 to 7 minutes.

Remove from the heat and add the eggs, one at a time, stirring until each egg is completely incorporated before adding the next. Stir in the bacon and the cheese.

Form teaspoon-sized mounds of pastry and place them about 1 inch apart on a lightly greased baking sheet. Bake for 15 to 20 minutes or until golden brown and puffed. Cool on wire racks.

Herbed Dinner Rolls

Makes 14

1 (¼-ounce) package active
  dry yeast

¼ cup warm water
  (110°F. to 120°F.)

2½ cups all-purpose flour

¼ cup granulated sugar

1 teaspoon oregano leaves

1 teaspoon salt

¼ pound (1 stick) butter,
  chilled and diced

8 ounces (1 cup) small curd
  cottage cheese

1 egg, beaten

Dissolve the yeast in the warm water.

In a large bowl, stir together the flour, sugar, oregano, and salt. Using 2 knives or your fingertips, cut in the butter until the mixture resembles coarse meal. Blend in the cottage cheese, egg, and yeast.

Turn the dough out onto a well-floured surface and knead for about 5 minutes. Place the dough in a well-buttered bowl and brush the top with melted butter. Cover and let rise until doubled, about 1 hour.

Punch the dough down, then shape it into rolls. Place the rolls on a buttered baking sheet, cover, and let rise again until almost doubled in size.

Preheat the oven to 375°F. Bake for 12 to 15 minutes. Serve warm.

Cottage Cheese Butter Horns

Makes 3 dozen

Horns

½ pound (2 sticks) butter,
  at room temperature

1½ cups small curd
  cottage cheese

2 cups all-purpose flour

½ teaspoon salt

Creamy Glaze

5 tablespoons butter

2 cups confectioners' sugar

1½ teaspoons vanilla or
  lemon extract

2 to 4 tablespoons hot water

In a large mixing bowl, cream all of the horns ingredients. Cover and refrigerate overnight.

Divide the dough into 3 equal parts and let it sit at room temperature until it is easy to handle.

Preheat the oven to 350°F.

Roll each piece of dough into a 10-inch diameter circle. Cut each circle into 12 pie-shaped pieces, then roll up each piece into a croissant shape, starting with wide end. Place the pieces on lightly buttered baking sheets.

Bake for 30 minutes. Cool on a wire rack. Serve plain or frost with Creamy Glaze.

To make the Creamy Glaze: Melt the butter in a small saucepan. Blend in the sugar and vanilla. Stir in the hot water 1 tablespoon at a time until the glaze is of proper consistency.

Soups and Sandwiches

French Onion Soup

Makes 6 servings

3 tablespoons butter

6 large yellow onions, peeled and sliced

8 cups beef stock

½ cup dry white wine

Salt, to taste

⅛ teaspoon white pepper

6 ounces (1½ cups) aged Swiss cheese, shredded

1 sheet (½ package) frozen puff pastry, thawed

In a large, heavy saucepan, melt the butter. Add the onions and sauté over low heat until the onions are transparent, about 30 seconds.

Add the stock, wine, salt, and pepper. Simmer for 20 minutes, then remove from the heat and cool.

Before serving, preheat the oven to 425°F. Ladle the hot soup into 6 individual soup crocks or cups (about 1½ cups in each) and top each with ¼ cup Swiss cheese.

Cut the puff pastry sheet into 6 equal squares. Place a pastry square on top of each of the bowls. Gently press the pastry to the edges of the bowls to seal. Bake until the pastry is golden, about 10 minutes.

Onion Soup with Two Cheeses

Makes 4 servings

2 tablespoons butter

5 cups onions, sliced

¾ teaspoon salt

2 (14-ounce) cans beef stock

¼ cup dry red wine (or water)

1 bay leaf

¼ teaspoon freshly ground
   black pepper

4 (¾-inch) slices French
   bread, toasted

2 ounces (½ cup) Asiago
   cheese, finely shredded

4 ounces (1 cup) part-skim
   mozzarella cheese,
   finely shredded

¾ teaspoon dried thyme

In a Dutch oven set over medium-high heat, melt the butter, then sauté the onions and ½ teaspoon salt. Lower the heat and cook for about 35 minutes or until onions are golden brown and caramelized, stirring often.

Preheat the oven to 425°F.

Add the stock, red wine, and bay leaf. Simmer gently for 15 minutes. Remove the bay leaf and add the remaining ¼ teaspoon salt and the pepper. Ladle the soup into 4 (1½-cup) ovenproof bowls. Top each with a slice of toast, pushing the toast down to saturate with stock.

In a small bowl, mix the cheeses and thyme. Divide the cheese mixture equally over the soup bowls, completely covering the bread and soup. Place the soup bowls on a baking sheet and bake for about 10 minutes, until the cheeses melt and turn lightly brown. Serve immediately.

Vidalia Onion and Wild Leek Soup

Makes 4 servings

½ pound wild leeks*

4 Vidalia onions, peeled
 and sliced

1 tablespoon olive oil

1 tablespoon butter

1½ cups Amber Beer

5 cups chicken stock

Salt and freshly ground black
 pepper, to taste

8 slices sourdough bread

3 ounces (¾ cup) Pepato
 cheese, shaved

*Wild leeks, also known as ramps, are a
member of the onion family. Both the white
root and the broad green leaves are edible.
A common description of the flavor is like a
combination of onions and strong garlic.

Trim the leeks, cutting off and reserving the leaves. Slice the leek bulbs and add to the sliced onions.

In a large heavy skillet, heat the olive oil. Add the butter and wait until the butter foams and begins to turn nutty brown. Add the onions and leeks and cook over a high heat until the onions brown. Add the beer and heat until the liquid reduces by half. Add the stock and simmer for 6 to 8 minutes. Season with salt and pepper.

Ladle half the soup, a little at a time, into a blender and puree. Combine the pureed soup with the simmered soup.

Cut the leek leaves into thin ribbons and stir into the soup. Ladle into bowls, top with bread and generous amounts of shaved Pepato cheese.

Oyster Stew

Makes 8 servings

1 quart half-and-half

1 cup heavy cream

4 tablespoons butter

1 tablespoon all-purpose flour

2 pints oysters, liquor drained
  and reserved

1 teaspoon salt

½ teaspoon pepper

Additional butter, for serving

Oyster crackers, for serving

Combine the half-and-half, cream, and butter in a 3-quart saucepan and cook over medium heat until bubbles form at the edge of the saucepan.

In a bowl, combine the flour with 2 tablespoons of oyster liquor, then add in the oysters and remaining liquor. Add the oyster mixture to the saucepan and cook over low heat, stirring occasionally, until the edges of the oysters begin to curl. Stir in the salt and pepper.

To serve, divide the oysters among 6 serving bowls and ladle stock over top. Serve each with a pat of butter and oyster crackers.

Quick Salmon Bisque

Makes 4 to 6 servings

4 tablespoons butter

¼ cup chopped onion

¼ cup finely chopped celery

¼ cup all-purpose flour

3 cups whole milk

1 teaspoon salt

1 teaspoon dried dill

1 tablespoon capers, drained

1 cup V-8 juice

1 (14.75-ounce) can pink
salmon, drained, picked over,
and flaked

Melt the butter over low heat in a large saucepan. Add the onion and celery and sauté for 5 minutes until the vegetables are soft and the onions are translucent. Add the flour and stir to blend completely. Add the milk gradually, stirring with a whisk to avoid lumps. Simmer until the mixture thickens, stirring constantly, about 10 minutes. Add the salt, dill, capers, and V-8 juice, and cook an additional 5 minutes, stirring often. Add the salmon and heat for 5 minutes until cooked through.

Salmon and Cheddar Chowder

Makes 8 servings

1 (16-ounce) can
  diced tomatoes

1½ cups carrot slices

1½ cups diced potatoes

⅓ cup chopped onion

3 tablespoons butter

2 tablespoons chopped
  bell pepper

1 (16-ounce) can pink salmon,
  drained

3 cups milk

1 (10½ ounce) can condensed
  cream of celery soup

8 ounces (2 cups) sharp
  Cheddar cheese, shredded

In a 3-quart saucepan, combine the tomatoes (with their liquid), carrots, potatoes, onion, butter, and bell pepper. Cover and simmer for 30 minutes, or until the vegetables are tender.

Meanwhile, remove the skin and bones from the salmon and break it into chunks.

In another large saucepan, combine the milk and the cream of celery soup, then stir in the salmon. Heat over low heat, stirring occasionally. Slowly add the vegetable mixture to the salmon-milk mixture. Gradually add the cheese, stirring constantly, until it melts. Serve immediately.

Quick New England Clam Chowder

Makes 4 to 6 servings

4 slices bacon, finely chopped

4 tablespoons butter

½ cup chopped celery

2 cups chopped yellow onions

2 cloves garlic, minced

1 bay leaf

¼ cup all-purpose flour

25 ounces chopped canned
   clams, drained and their
   juices reserved

3 (8-ounce) bottles clam juice

1 pound russet potatoes,
   par-boiled, peeled, and diced

1¼ cups half-and-half

Salt and pepper, to taste

Cook the bacon in the butter over medium heat in a large heavy pan until the bacon begins to brown. Add the celery, onions, garlic, and bay leaf and sauté until the vegetables are tender, about 5 minutes. Stir in the flour gradually so it doesn't clump. Be careful not to brown the flour. Whisk in the reserved juices from the canned clams and the bottled clam juice. Add the clams and potatoes. Stir and slowly add the half-and-half to incorporate all ingredients.

Simmer the chowder for about 10 minutes, being careful not to let it boil. Season with salt and pepper before serving.

Manhattan Clam Chowder

Makes 8 servings

3 slices bacon

1 large onion, minced

3 tablespoons all-purpose flour

2 (8-ounce) cans minced clams
   (about 2½ cups)

Water, as needed

3 cups canned tomatoes

2 cups diced potatoes

½ cup diced bell pepper

½ bay leaf

¼ cup ketchup

3 tablespoons butter

Parmesan cheese, grated,
   for serving

NOTE: Chowder is better if allowed to sit overnight.

In a small skillet, sauté the bacon until it is crispy. Let the bacon cool, then crumble it and set it aside. Sauté the onions in the bacon drippings until translucent, about 5 minutes. Sift the flour into the skillet and stir until well blended.

Drain the clams, reserving the liquid. Add enough water to the clam liquid to measure 3 cups. In a 2-quart saucepan, heat the clam liquid and water. Add the onion-flour mixture, stirring to combine. Add the tomatoes, potatoes, bell pepper, bay leaf, and ketchup. Cover and simmer until the potatoes are tender but firm, about 20 to 30 minutes. Add the bacon, clams, and butter. Simmer for an additional 3 minutes. Serve sprinkled with Parmesan cheese.

Beer Cheese Chowder

Inspired by Mr. G's Supper Club

Makes 6 servings

5 tablespoons butter

½ cup chopped onion

¾ cup chopped carrots

1½ cups small broccoli florets

1 cup chicken stock, boiling

¼ cup all-purpose flour

½ teaspoon dry mustard

¼ teaspoon pepper

2 cups milk

3 ounces cream cheese,
cut into cubes, at room
temperature

½ pound (8 ounces) cooked
Polish sausage, cubed

6 ounces (1½ cups) sharp
Cheddar cheese, shredded

½ cup beer, such as a lager or
light beer

In a medium saucepan, melt 1 tablespoon of butter. Add the onion, carrots, and broccoli. Sauté over medium-high heat for 5 minutes.

Add the stock; reduce the heat, cover and simmer for 8 minutes.

In a large saucepan over medium-high heat, melt the remaining 4 tablespoons of butter. Stir in the flour, mustard, and pepper. Add the milk, stirring until thickened. Stir for an additional 1 to 2 minutes. Add the cream cheese and stir until smooth.

Stir in the vegetable mixture, sausage, 1 cup of the Cheddar cheese, and beer. Heat to serving temperature. Top each serving with remaining cheese.

Pueblo Pepper Jack Corn and Crab Chowder

Makes 5 servings

2 tablespoons butter

1½ cups finely chopped onion

3 garlic cloves, minced

1 cup diced red bell pepper

1 (14-ounce) can low-fat
   chicken stock

1 cup water

1 teaspoon ground cumin

¾ teaspoon finely minced,
   canned smoked chipotle
   peppers in Adobo sauce

1½ cups small red potatoes,
   unpeeled and diced

2 cups fresh sweet corn
   kernels, cut from the cob (or
   2 cups frozen kernel corn)

1½ cups half-and-half

2 tablespoons cornstarch

6 ounces (1½ cups) Pepper Jack
   cheese, shredded

2 cups imitation crabmeat
   chunks, coarsely chopped

1 tablespoon cilantro,
   freshly chopped

Fresh cilantro, for garnish

Crusty bread, for serving

In a Dutch oven set over medium heat, melt the butter. Add the onion and garlic, sauté for 4 to 5 minutes until softened and golden. Stir in the bell pepper, stock, water, cumin, and chipotle pepper. Bring to a boil, then stir in the potatoes. Adjust the heat to maintain a gentle boil, cover and cook for 5 minutes.

Stir in the corn kernels and cover, simmering for 10 minutes or until the potatoes are tender.

In a small bowl, combine the half-and-half and cornstarch, stirring until smooth. Slowly stir into the soup and bring to a boil. Reduce the heat to low and stir in the Pepper Jack cheese, stirring until smooth and thickened.

Stir in the crabmeat and cilantro and heat through for several minutes. Garnish individual servings with fresh cilantro and serve with crusty bread.

Curried Cheddar Chowder

3 tablespoons butter

1 medium onion, chopped

1 cup chopped celery,
 with leaves

2 carrots, diced

1 cup diced red and/or green
 bell peppers

3 tablespoons all-purpose flour

1 quart chicken stock
 or bouillon

1 (8-ounce) can whole kernel
 corn, drained

1 pound (3 medium) russet
 potatoes, peeled and diced

1 cup half-and-half

10 ounces (2½ cups) aged
 Cheddar cheese, shredded

1 teaspoon curry powder

1 tablespoon chopped parsley

Salt and pepper, to taste

In a 3- to 4-quart saucepan, melt the butter over medium heat. Add the onion, celery, carrots, and bell peppers. Cook, stirring frequently, until the onion is translucent, about 3 minutes. Stir in the flour and cook, stirring, for 3 minutes. Mix in the stock, corn, and potatoes. Bring to a boil, reduce the heat, cover and simmer until the potatoes are tender, about 15 minutes.

Add the half-and-half, cheese, curry, and parsley. Cook until the cheese is melted. Purée 2 cups of soup in a food processor or blender. Return the purée to the saucepan. Heat through; season with salt and pepper.

Hearty Ham Chowder

Makes 4 servings

2 cups water

2 medium (2 cups) potatoes,
   peeled and coarsely chopped

½ cup chopped onion

1 teaspoon dried basil, crushed

1 teaspoon chicken
   bouillon granules

¼ teaspoon pepper

3 cups fresh or frozen chopped
   broccoli, thawed

2 cups chopped, cooked ham

2 cups light cream
   or half-and-half

1 tablespoon butter

Grated Parmesan cheese,
   for serving

In a large saucepan, combine the water, potatoes, onion, basil, bouillon granules, and pepper. Bring to a boil, then reduce the heat. Cover and simmer for 15 minutes, or until the potatoes are tender. Remove from the heat. Do not drain.

Using a potato masher or fork, mash the potatoes in the saucepan. Stir in the broccoli and return to boiling. Reduce the heat, cover, and simmer for 8 to 10 minutes, or until the broccoli is just tender. Stir in the ham, cream, and butter. Cook and stir until heated through. To serve, ladle into soup bowls. Sprinkle each serving with Parmesan cheese.

DID YOU KNOW?

Clarified butter (or ghee) is a purified form of butter that's been melted and has had water and milk solids separated from the clarified or clear part. Because the water has been extracted, clarified butter does not burn at high temperatures and therefore is commonly used as a fat for cooking.

Vegetable Chowder

Makes 6 servings

¼ pound (1 stick) butter

1 small onion, chopped,
  or 2 teaspoons
  dehydrated onion

½ cup sliced mushrooms

1 medium carrot, shredded

½ teaspoon basil

½ teaspoon dill weed

½ package onion soup mix,
  optional

½ cup all-purpose flour

6 cups milk

1 cup mixed vegetables,
  cooked

1 cup diced potato, cooked

Melt the butter in a large saucepan over low heat. Add the onion and mushrooms and cook, stirring, for 1 minute. Add the carrot, basil, dill, and soup mix, stirring well. Cook for 2 to 3 minutes.

Slowly stir in the flour until it is completely absorbed. Gradually stir in 2 cups of milk and stir until the soup thickens. Add the remaining milk, vegetables, and potato. Simmer over low heat until the soup thickens, but do not boil.

Italian Garden Vegetable Chowder

Makes 6 servings

4 tablespoons butter

½ pound zucchini, halved
  lengthwise and sliced across
  into ¼-inch thick half-moons

2 medium onions, diced

2 large garlic cloves, minced

1 tablespoon minced fresh
  basil, or 1 teaspoon
  dried basil

1 (16-ounce) can diced
  tomatoes, undrained

1 (15-ounce) can garbanzo
  beans, drained

2 teaspoons salt

¼ teaspoon freshly
  ground pepper

1 bay leaf

1½ cups Chablis,
  or other dry white wine

1 cup heavy cream

Melt the butter over medium heat in a heavy saucepan or Dutch oven; add the zucchini, onions, and garlic and sauté for 5 minutes, stirring occasionally. Add the basil, tomatoes, garbanzo beans, salt, pepper, bay leaf, and wine; stir to combine. Cover and reduce the heat to medium-low. Simmer gently for 20 minutes, stirring occasionally.

Reduce the heat to low. Add the cream and stir to combine. Remove the bay leaf and serve immediately.

NOTE: Adding 1 cup each of shredded fontina and grated Romano or Parmesan cheese adds a nice zing.

Poblano Chili Soup

Chef Dean Fearing

Makes 4 servings

1 tablespoon bacon fat

½ white onion, chopped

1 large shallot, chopped

1 garlic clove, chopped

½ jalapeño chili,
  seeded, chopped

1 teaspoon chili powder

1 tablespoon chopped cilantro

½ tablespoon chopped
  epazote, or ½ teaspoon
  dried, optional

Pinch of ground cumin seed

½ cup beer, such as a lager
  or light beer

4 cups chicken stock

2 tablespoons unsalted butter,
  at room temperature

2 tablespoons all-purpose flour

5 ounces (1¼ cups) aged
  Cheddar cheese, shredded

2 small poblano chilies,
  roasted, peeled, seeded and
  cut into ¼-inch dice, or 1 cup
  canned green chiles

Salt to taste

Juice of ½ lime

Heat the bacon fat in a large sauce or soup pan over medium heat. Add the onion, shallot, garlic, jalapeño, and chili powder. Sauté for 2 minutes or until the onions are soft. Add the cilantro, epazote, cumin, and beer. Bring to a boil and let boil for 5 minutes or the until liquid has reduced by half. Add the stock and bring to a boil.

Meanwhile, knead the butter and flour together until a paste forms. Slowly whisk the butter mixture into the boiling soup, mixing until smooth. Lower the heat and simmer, uncovered, for about 40 minutes.

Remove the soup from the heat and immediately stir in the cheese. Pour the soup into a blender in batches and blend until smooth.

Add the poblano chiles and season with salt and lime juice. Pour into soup bowls and serve immediately.

Roasted Tomato and Chile Soup with Gruyère Croutons

Chef Ben Berryhill
Makes 6 servings

Soup Base

1 red bell pepper, stemmed and seeded

3 jalapeño chiles, preferably red, stemmed and seeded

½ large yellow onion

1 carrot, trimmed and peeled

3 garlic cloves

10 ripe tomatoes, stemmed and halved, or 12 to 14 whole canned tomatoes, preferably roasted (two 28-ounce cans plus one 15-ounce can)

½ cup cilantro, stemmed plus 2 tablespoons for garnish, minced

2 tablespoons olive oil

4 cups chicken stock

Juice of ½ lime

Salt to taste

½ tablespoon pure maple syrup

*To toast oregano: Heat a small, heavy skillet until hot. Add the oregano and stir constantly with a wooden spoon until aromatic. Be careful not to burn.

Gruyère Croutons

2 garlic cloves, peeled and finely minced

½ tablespoon oregano, toasted*

18 (1-inch) bread cubes, cut from a country-style loaf (NOT sourdough)

1½ tablespoons olive oil

4 tablespoons butter, melted

5 ounces (1¼ cups) Gruyère cheese, grated

Preheat the oven to 375°F.

Roughly chop the bell pepper, jalapeños, onion, carrot, and garlic. Combine in a large bowl with the fresh tomatoes (if you're using canned tomatoes, set them aside for later) and ½ cup of cilantro. Add the olive oil and toss to coat.

Pour the vegetables out onto a baking sheet and roast until caramelized and tender, about 30 minutes. Cool and remove the tomato skins. (For canned tomatoes, dry them well, halve, and mix with the roasted vegetables.)

Purée the vegetables in a food processor in batches, leaving some texture. Pour into a

large pot and add the stock. Heat to a boil and lower heat; simmer for ½ hour.

Season with lime juice, salt and maple syrup.

To make the croutons, preheat the oven to 250°F.

Combine the garlic, oregano, bread cubes, olive oil, and butter. Toss until evenly coated.

Slowly toast the bread cubes in the oven until crusty and crunchy, about 30 minutes. Remove from the oven, briefly cool, and toss with 1 cup of Gruyère cheese, pressing the cheese into the crouton sides. Let cool.

Serve the hot soup with croutons. Sprinkle the reserved cilantro and Gruyère over top.

Mexican-Style Corn Soup

Makes 6 servings

Kernels from 5 large ears corn,
  or 2 (10-ounce) packages
  frozen corn, thawed
2 cups water
1 pound (2 cups) zucchini,
  coarsely shredded
1 cup thinly sliced green onion
2 garlic cloves, chopped finely
2 tablespoons butter
1 tablespoon vegetable oil
1 can (4 ounces) diced
  green chilies
2 (14-ounce) cans
  chicken stock
½ teaspoon dried thyme
½ teaspoon salt
¼ teaspoon freshly
  ground pepper
4 ounces (1 cup) Monterey Jack
  cheese, shredded, optional
½ cup chopped fresh cilantro
  or parsley
Tortilla chips, for serving
Lime wedges, for serving

Purée 3 cups of corn along with the water in a food processor or blender; reserve.

In a 3-quart saucepan, sauté the zucchini, onion, and garlic in the butter and oil until soft, about 5 minutes; stir in the chilies, remaining corn kernels, corn purée, stock, thyme, salt, and pepper. Bring to a boil, then reduce to a simmer. Cook until the corn is tender, about 10 minutes.

Stir in the cheese and cook over low heat, stirring frequently, until the cheese melts and is incorporated, about 5 minutes. Do not boil after the cheese has been added. Stir in the cilantro. Serve with tortilla chips and lime wedges.

Garden Vegetable Soup

Makes 6 servings

4 tablespoons butter

¼ cup all-purpose flour

2 cups milk

2 cups chicken stock

4 ounces (1 cup) colby cheese,
  shredded

4 ounces (1 cup) medium
  Cheddar cheese, shredded

2 medium zucchini, chopped

1 cup frozen corn, thawed

3 tomatoes,
  seeded and chopped

In a 3-quart saucepan, heat the butter until sizzling; stir in the flour. Cook over medium heat until bubbly. Gradually add the milk, stirring until smooth. Add the stock and continue cooking until the soup thickens slightly. Stir in the cheeses, allowing them to melt, then add the remaining ingredients. Cook over low heat for 4 to 5 minutes, or until the vegetables are heated through.

TIP: Try sharp Cheddar for a stronger flavor.

Broccoli Soup

2 (10-ounce) packages frozen
chopped broccoli

2 (10¾-ounce) cans cream of
mushroom soup

1 cup half-and-half

2 cups milk

¼ cup white wine

4 tablespoons butter

½ teaspoon tarragon leaves

Dash of pepper

Cook the broccoli according to package directions. Drain. Place the broccoli, along with the remaining ingredients, in a large pan and cook, stirring, until warmed through.

Broccoli and Cheddar Soup

5½ cups milk

1 (10-ounce) package frozen
chopped broccoli, or 1½ cups
chopped fresh broccoli

3 tablespoons chopped onion

2 tablespoons butter

1 tablespoon all-purpose flour

1 teaspoon salt

8 ounces (2 cups) medium
Cheddar cheese, shredded

Heat the milk to simmering in a large saucepan. Add the broccoli and onions, and cook until tender, about 10 minutes.

Melt the butter in a small saucepan. Stir in the flour and salt. Add the flour mixture to the milk. Cook and stir for 3 minutes. Gradually add the cheese, stirring until the cheese is melted. Serve immediately.

Cream of Broccoli Soup

Makes 6 servings

6 tablespoons butter

⅓ cup all-purpose flour

¼ teaspoon garlic powder

¼ teaspoon ground nutmeg

⅛ teaspoon ground
   white pepper

Dash ground thyme

1 (13¾-ounce) can
   chicken stock

1 cup milk

3 cups bite-size
   broccoli flowerets

1 cup heavy cream

¼ teaspoon
   Worcestershire sauce

⅛ teaspoon hot pepper
   sauce, optional

Melt the butter in a 3-quart saucepan over low heat. Add the flour and seasonings, stirring to combine. Gradually add the stock and milk and cook, stirring constantly, until the soup thickens. Stir in the broccoli and simmer for 10 minutes.

Remove from the heat and stir in the cream, Worcestershire sauce, and hot pepper sauce.

TIP: For Cheesy Cream of Broccoli Soup, add 1 cup of shredded Cheddar and ½ cup each of shredded Havarti and Swiss.

Zucchini Soup

Makes 4 servings

4 slices bacon

½ cup finely-chopped onion

¼ cup chopped bell pepper

2½ cups sliced zucchini

1 tablespoon chopped pimento

1 cup water

1½ teaspoons salt

4 tablespoons butter

¼ cup all-purpose flour

¼ teaspoon pepper

2½ cups milk

½ teaspoon
  Worcestershire sauce

4 ounces (1 cup) Cheddar
  cheese, shredded

In large skillet, cook the bacon until it is crisp. Drain, crumble, and set aside the bacon for garnish.

Sauté the onion and bell pepper in the bacon fat until both vegetables are tender. Add the zucchini, pimento, water, and ½ teaspoon salt. Cover and bring to a boil. Turn down the heat and simmer for about 5 minutes, or until the zucchini is tender.

Meanwhile, prepare the cheese soup base. Melt the butter in a 3-quart saucepan. Blend in the flour, remaining 1 teaspoon of salt, and the pepper. Remove from the heat; stir in the milk and Worcestershire sauce. Heat to boiling, stirring constantly. Boil and stir 1 minute. Remove from the heat. Gradually add the cheese, stirring constantly until it melts. Add the vegetables with their liquid to the soup base. Heat to serving temperature. Garnish with crumbled bacon.

Carrot Ginger Soup

Makes 4 to 6 servings

3 tablespoons butter

½ cup diced onions

2 cloves garlic, minced

¼ cup peeled and
   minced ginger

4 cups peeled, diced carrots

1 teaspoon dried thyme

1 teaspoon dried marjoram

3 cups chicken stock

1 teaspoon freshly
   grated nutmeg

Salt and pepper, to taste

Melt the butter in a large saucepan over medium high heat; add the onions, garlic, and ginger and sauté until the onions are soft and translucent, about 5 minutes. Add the carrots, thyme, marjoram, and chicken stock, and let simmer for 30 minutes, until the carrots are very soft.

Puree the soup in a blender or food processor in batches or use an immersion blender, processing until the soup is smooth. Return the soup to the heat and cook on low for 5 minutes. Stir in the nutmeg and season with salt and pepper.

Potato Soup

Makes 8 servings

6 cups diced potatoes

2 medium onions, chopped

6 cups water

4 chicken bouillon cubes

2 teaspoons salt

1 cup half-and-half

2 tablespoons butter

Dash of pepper

Chives, for garnish

Combine the potatoes, onions, water, bouillon cubes, and salt in a Dutch oven. Bring the soup to boil over medium heat, stirring frequently to prevent scorching. Reduce the heat and simmer for 30 minutes or until the potatoes and onions are tender. Add the half-and-half, butter, and pepper. Increase the heat to medium and return to boiling. Serve garnished with chopped chives.

Microwave Cheesy Potato Soup

Makes 6 servings

4 baking potatoes
(about 1½ pounds)

2 tablespoons butter

1 medium onion, sliced

2 tablespoons all-purpose flour

1 teaspoon beef bouillon
granules

2 cups water

1 (12-ounce) can
evaporated milk

4 ounces (1 cup) mild Brick
cheese* or mild Cheddar
cheese, shredded

1 teaspoon chopped parsley

¾ teaspoon
Worcestershire sauce

¾ teaspoon salt

¾ teaspoon pepper

*Brick cheese is a semi-hard, cow's milk
cheese originating in Wisconsin. For more
information, visit www.wisdairy.com.

Place the potatoes in the microwave and cook on high until they are tender, about 5 to 10 minutes, depending on your microwave. Set them aside to cool.

Place the butter and onions in a large bowl and cook them in the microwave on high until the onions are tender, about 2 minutes. Stir in the flour, bouillon granules, and water. Stir well and return to the microwave to cook on high for 2 minutes, or until the mixture is heated.

Chop the potatoes, and add them with the evaporated milk, cheese, and seasonings to the hot mixture and return the bowl to the microwave. Cook on high for 2½ to 4 minutes, or until the cheese is melted and the soup is hot.

Creamy Mushroom Soup

Makes 6 servings

1 pound fresh
  mushrooms, sliced

¼ cup chopped onion

6 tablespoons butter

2 tablespoons all-purpose flour

1 large bay leaf

½ teaspoon dried basil leaves

¼ teaspoon salt

⅛ teaspoon ground
  white pepper

1 (10¾-ounce) can beef stock

3 cups milk

Sauté the mushrooms and onion in butter until the vegetables are lightly browned. Remove the mushrooms and set them aside. Stir the flour, bay leaf, basil, salt, and pepper into the pan with the butter and onions and cook for 1 to 2 minutes. Gradually add the beef stock and milk. Cook over low heat for 10 minutes, stirring occasionally; do not boil. Remove the bay leaf. Return the mushrooms to the soup base and heat to simmering.

Country Bean Soup

½ pound (1¼ cups) dry navy
  beans or lima beans

4 ounces salt pork or cooked
  ham, chopped

¼ cup chopped onion

½ teaspoon oregano

¼ teaspoon salt

¼ teaspoon ground ginger

¼ teaspoon sage

¼ teaspoon pepper

2 cups milk

2 tablespoons butter

Rinse the beans and place them in a large saucepan with enough water to cover. Bring to a boil, then reduce the heat and simmer for 2 minutes. Remove from heat; cover and let stand for 1 hour. (Or cover the beans with water and soak overnight.)

Drain the beans and return them to the saucepan. Stir in 2½ cups water, the salt pork, onion, oregano, salt, ginger, sage, and pepper. Bring to a boil; reduce the heat. Cover and simmer for 2 to 2½ hours, or until the beans are tender. (If necessary, add more water during cooking time.)

Add the milk and butter, stirring until the mixture is heated through and the butter is melted. Season to taste with additional salt and pepper.

Cheesy Bean Soup

2 cups dried navy beans

2 teaspoons salt

2 tablespoons butter

1 large onion, chopped

1 garlic clove, chopped

1 (8-ounce) can tomato sauce

2 teaspoons brown sugar

½ teaspoon thyme

¼ teaspoon oregano

1 bay leaf

½ teaspoon
    Worcestershire sauce

8 ounces (2 cups) aged
    Cheddar cheese, cubed

Wash the beans, then cover them with water and soak overnight.

The next day, drain the beans and place in a soup pot. Add 3 cups of water and the salt. Simmer over low heat for about 3 hours.

In heavy saucepan, melt the butter. Add the onion and garlic; sauté for 5 minutes. Add the tomato sauce and sugar. Blend in the thyme, oregano, bay leaf, and Worcestershire sauce. Combine the tomato mixture with the beans during the last hour of their cooking time. When the beans are tender, add the cheese. Remove from heat and serve immediately.

Sharp Cheddar Cheese Soup

Makes 6 servings

2 tablespoons butter

½ cup chopped onion

¼ cup diced carrot

¼ cup celery

¼ cup all-purpose flour

¼ teaspoon baking soda

2 cups milk

1 (14½-ounce) can

   chicken stock

8 ounces (2 cups) sharp

   Cheddar Cold Pack cheese*

1 teaspoon crushed

   red pepper

Chopped parsley, for garnish

*Cold Pack cheese is sold in the dairy case of the grocery store, in plastic, often transparent, tubs. It is a blend of cheeses that is smooth and spreadable, but no heat is used in the process (as opposed to a cheese "spread.") For more information, visit www.wisdairy.com.

Melt the butter in a large saucepan. Add the onion, carrot, and celery; cook until tender. Stir in the flour and cook, stirring, for 2 to 3 minutes, or until bubbly. Stir in the baking soda. Gradually stir in the milk and stock. Bring to a boil, then reduce the heat and simmer, stirring, until the mixture thickens slightly, about 10 to 15 minutes. Add the cheese and red pepper; stir just until melted and well blended.

Garnish with parsley.

Double Cheese Souper Bowl

Makes 4 servings

4 tablespoons butter

½ cup onion, diced

½ cup diced celery

4 tablespoons all-purpose flour

3 cups milk, warm

4 ounces (1 cup) sharp
   Cheddar cheese, shredded

4 ounces (1 cup) Gouda
   cheese, shredded

White pepper, to taste

5 drops hot sauce

½ cup diced ham

1 tablespoon chives, minced

Over medium heat in a heavy bottomed sauce pan, melt the butter. Stir in the onion and celery, cover. Cook 3 minutes or until transparent. Stir often to prevent browning. Stir in the flour to thicken. Cook until it bubbles.

Slowly stir in the warm milk, mixing until thickened and smooth. Bring to a simmer (do not boil) and continue stirring. Reduce to very low heat and add the Cheddar and Gouda cheeses, white pepper, and hot sauce. Stir until well blended. Add the ham and chives.

TIP: Beer or non-alcoholic beer could be used instead of the milk.

Macaroni and Cheese Soup

Makes 5 servings

1 (13¾-ounce) can
  chicken stock

¾ cup elbow macaroni

2 carrots, sliced

2 tablespoons finely
  chopped onion

3 tablespoons butter

2 tablespoons all-purpose flour

2½ cups milk

6 ounces (1½ cups) Cheddar
  cheese, shredded

In a 2-quart saucepan, bring the stock to a boil. Add the macaroni and carrots and simmer for 7 minutes, stirring occasionally. Remove from the heat and set aside.

In a 3-quart saucepan, sauté the onion in the butter over medium heat. Reduce the heat to low and add the flour. Gradually add the milk, then stir in the macaroni mixture. Cook, stirring constantly, until the soup thickens. Remove from the heat and add the cheese; stir until melted.

Croque Monsieur

Makes 4 sandwiches

½ pound Gruyère cheese, shredded

2 tablespoons white wine

8 (¼-inch thick) slices French bread, crusts removed

4 tablespoons butter, melted

4 slices good quality ham

2 tablespoons Dijon mustard

Melt the cheese and wine in a saucepan set over medium heat stirring often until the cheese is completely melted. Set aside.

Dip the bread into the melted butter and fry on both sides in a skillet. Set aside on a baking sheet to keep warm.

Sauté the ham in the remaining butter.

To assemble, spread one side of bread with the cheese mixture. Spread the other side of bread with Dijon mustard. Top the cheese spread side with a slice of ham and cover with the mustard spread bread slice. Repeat with remaining bread, ham, and sauce.

DID YOU KNOW?

Butter contains no trans fatty acids, which are associated with increased LDL ("bad") and lower HDL ("good") cholesterol.

Classic Grilled Cheese Sandwich

Makes 4

6 to 8 tablespoons butter,
   at room temperature
8 slices firm-textured
   sandwich bread
8 ounces (½ pound) Cheddar
   cheese, grated, or 4 slices
   processed American cheese

Heat a large (12-inch) skillet over medium heat.

Spread a thin layer of butter over both sides of each of the bread slices. Evenly divide the Cheddar over four slices of the bread and top with the remaining four slices.

Place the sandwiches in the skillet and cover. Cook for about 3 minutes, until the underside is golden brown.

Carefully flip the sandwiches with a spatula and continue cooking, uncovered, for 2 to 3 minutes, until the cheese is melted and underside is browned. Serve immediately.

TIP: Adding a slice of ham or turkey to your sandwich can make this sandwich more of a meal.

Ultimate Grilled Cheese Sandwich

Chef Ken Oringer

Makes 4

8 slices raisin bread

¼ pound (1 stick) butter,
  at room temperature

¼ cup honey mustard

8 bread-sized slices Monterey
  Jack cheese

8 slices applewood-smoked
  bacon, fried crisp

1 large Granny Smith Apple,
  cored, quartered and
  each cut in six slices
  (24 slices in all)

4 bread-sized slices smoked
  Gouda cheese

Spread the outside of each slice of bread with butter. Generously spread the insides of the bread with honey mustard.

Heat a large heavy-bottomed sauté pan over medium heat.

Place a slice of Monterey Jack cheese on the mustard side of 4 slices of bread. Top with 2 slices of bacon. Layer 6 apple slices over the bacon. Layer the 4 slices with an additional slice of Monterey Jack and a slice of smoked Gouda. Top with the remaining 4 slices of bread and press together.

Grill the sandwiches in batches, cooking until the bread is golden brown on one side, then flipping the sandwich over and browning the other side. Repeat this process with all of the sandwiches. Serve immediately.

Monte Cristo Sandwich

Makes 4

2 eggs, beaten

⅔ cup plain yogurt

¼ teaspoon salt

7 tablespoons butter, melted

8 slices, firm white bread

4 slices ham

4 slices (1 ounce each)
  Swiss cheese

4 slices (1 ounce each)
  Cheddar cheese

2 tablespoons
  confectioners' sugar

In a shallow dish combine the eggs, yogurt, and salt.

Brush butter on the inside of all eight slices of bread. Place one slice of ham, Swiss, and Cheddar cheese on the buttered side of 4 slices of bread. Top with the remaining bread slices, buttered sides facing inward.

Pour 2 tablespoons of butter into a heavy skillet over medium heat.

Carefully dip each sandwich in the egg mixture and place in the heated skillet. Cook until both sides are golden brown and the cheese is melted, 3 to 4 minutes per side. Add additional butter as necessary.

Dust with confectioners' sugar and serve immediately.

Grilled Havarti Sandwich
with Spiced Apples

Makes 4

7 tablespoons butter,
  at room temperature
2 Granny Smith apples, cored
  and thinly sliced
4 to 6 tablespoons granulated
  sugar, to taste
½ teaspoon ground cinnamon
½ teaspoon ground cardamom
8 thick slices rustic round loaf
  bread (French or Italian)
8 slices Havarti cheese

Melt 3 tablespoons of butter in a skillet over medium heat. Add the apples, sugar, cinnamon, and cardamom and cook for about 7 minutes, stirring frequently until most of the apple juices are reduced and the fruit is coated with syrup. Remove the pan from the heat and set aside.

Place four slices of the bread on a griddle. Top each with one slice of Havarti, one-fourth of the spiced apples, another slice of Havarti and top with the remaining slices of bread. Butter the sandwich tops, turn the sandwiches over, and butter the remaining side.

Place the griddle over medium heat. Brown each side for 3 to 5 minutes, or until the bread is golden and the Havarti begins to melt. Cool for 5 minutes before serving.

Bacon and Brie Panini with Avocado Mayonnaise and Yam Fries

Chef Goose Sorensen

Makes 1

Avocado Mayonnaise

1 ripe avocado

¼ cup mayonnaise

½ tablespoon rice wine vinegar

Pinch cayenne pepper

Salt and pepper to taste

Bacon and Brie Panini

1 (4-inch) square of focaccia
  bread, split

1 tablespoon butter, melted

2 ounces (½ cup) Brie cheese,
  cut in 4 slices

3 strips applewood-smoked
  bacon, fried crisp

½ red onion, thinly-sliced

2 slices tomato

Head lettuce, shredded

Yam Fries

Oil for frying

1 small yam, peeled and cut
  into sticks

Salt and pepper to taste

To make the Avocado Mayonnaise, place the avocado, mayonnaise, vinegar, and cayenne pepper in a food processor or blender. Purée until smooth. Season to taste with salt and pepper.

To make the panini, brush all sides of the focaccia with melted butter. Place 2 slices of Brie on each slice of bread. Layer one side with as much bacon, red onion, tomato, and lettuce as you prefer. Place the other slice of focaccia on top, cheese side down. Grill the sandwich on a hot griddle or skillet until the bread is browned on both sides and the Brie is melted.

To make the Yam fries, heat enough oil to cover the fries in a small skillet to 375°F. Fry the yams until they are crispy, about 5 to 7 minutes. Drain the fries, drying them on paper towels; season with salt and pepper.

Spoon Avocado Mayonnaise into a small serving dish or ramekin. Slice the sandwich in half and serve with fries.

Grilled Applewood Smoked Bacon and Tomato Sandwiches

Makes 4

24 slices (about 1 pound)
  thick-cut applewood
  smoked bacon
4 tablespoon butter,
  at room temperature
8 slices thick-sliced rustic
  white bread
2 large vine ripened tomatoes,
  cored and sliced thinly
4 tablespoons
  mayonnaise, optional

Cook the bacon in a large sauté pan over medium heat until desired doneness. Place the bacon on paper towels to absorb the grease.

Set another large sauté pan over medium-low heat. Butter each slice of bread on one side. To build the sandwiches, place a slice of bread, butter-side down, on a work surface. Layer with desired amounts of bacon and tomato. Carefully spread the mayonnaise on the second piece of bread and place it on top so the buttered side faces up.

Place the sandwiches, two at a time, in the preheated sauté pan and allow to brown slowly on one side, before turning to brown on other side as cheese melts.

Cheese Steak Sandwich

Makes 4 to 6

Steak and Marinade

¾ cup vegetable oil

¼ cup red wine vinegar

¼ cup prepared chili sauce

2 teaspoons Worcestershire
sauce

½ teaspoon salt

2 tablespoons fresh
lemon juice

2 teaspoons seasoned salt

3 garlic cloves, minced

4½ pounds beef flank steak

Cheese Bread

¼ pound (1 stick) butter,
at room temperature

4 garlic cloves, minced

2 loaves French bread,
split lengthwise

16 ounces (4 cups) Muenster
cheese, shredded

TIP: For a traditional Philly
Cheese-steak, add Cheez Whiz
or provolone to your sandwich.

Whisk the vegetable oil, vinegar, chili sauce, Worcestershire sauce, salt, lemon juice, seasoned salt, and garlic together in a bowl. Place the steak in a glass or ceramic baking dish and pour the marinade over. Cover and marinate overnight in the refrigerator, turning occasionally.

Remove the steak from the marinade and drain off any excess. Let the steak come to room temperature before grilling.

Meanwhile, combine the butter and garlic and spread the mixture on the French bread loaves. Sprinkle each half with 1 cup of cheese.

Preheat the oven to broil.

Cut 2 sheets of heavy foil and spray with cooking spray. Completely, but loosely, wrap each sheet around 2 halves of bread, sitting side by side.

Place the steak on a broiler pan, and broil 2 to 3 inches from the top of the oven. Broil each side for 6 minutes. Remove the steak and let it rest for 10 minutes. Meanwhile, put the bread in the oven on the middle rack. Broil for 8 minutes or until the cheese melts.

Slice the steak thinly, across the grain. Top the warm bread with slices of beef. Cut each loaf into 2 or 3 pieces. Serve immediately.

Grilled Tenderloin Sandwich

Makes 6

2 to 2½ pounds center cut
  beef tenderloin

Extra virgin olive oil

Salt and pepper to taste

1 cup sour cream

3 ounces (¾ cup) Asiago
  cheese, shredded

2 tablespoons roasted
  chopped garlic

¼ teaspoon salt

¼ teaspoon pepper

1 large red bell pepper,
  sliced into rings

¼ pound (1 stick) butter,
  melted

1 loaf (16 ounces) French
  bread, sliced in half
  lengthwise and crosswise

8 ounces (2 cups) fontina or
  Gouda cheese, sliced

Preheat a gas or charcoal grill to medium heat.

Brush the tenderloin with oil and season with salt and pepper; let stand at room temperature for 20 minutes.

In a small bowl, combine the sour cream, Asiago, garlic, and salt and pepper; mix well.

Sear the beef over direct heat for 5 to 6 minutes each side. Move to indirect heat until the internal temperature reaches 140°F. Remove and let stand.

Brush the bell pepper rings with butter and grill for 5 minutes.

Brush the cut sides of the bread with butter and grill until toasted. Spread the bottom halves with the sour cream sauce and top with pepper rings.

Cut the tenderloin into ½-inch thick slices, and place them over the pepper rings. Cover with cheese and top with bread.

Wrap the sandwiches in foil and grill for 5 minutes. Unwrap and cut each in half.

Turkey Pizza Burger

Makes 4

3 tablespoons butter

1 cup diced celery

3 cups cooked turkey,
  finely chopped

1 (8-ounce) can tomato sauce

1 teaspoon salt

1 teaspoon ground oregano

½ teaspoon pepper

4 hamburger buns (8 halves)
  toasted and buttered

8 (1-ounce) slices
  provolone cheese

Preheat the oven to 300°F.

Melt the butter in a large skillet. Sauté the celery slowly until it is tender, about 5 minutes. Add the turkey and cook until warmed. Add the tomato sauce and seasonings; simmer.

Arrange the bun halves on a baking sheet. Spoon approximately ½ cup of the turkey mixture over each half. Top with a slice of cheese. Bake for 5 minutes, or until cheese melts. Assemble the sandwiches and enjoy.

Classic Reuben

Makes 4

8 slices rye or
pumpernickel bread

4 tablespoons butter, at room
temperature

½ cup Russian dressing

8 slices Swiss cheese

1 pound corned beef,
thinly sliced

½ pound Sauerkraut,
well drained

Preheat the oven to 425°F.

Spread 4 slices of bread with butter, and spread the remaining bread with Russian dressing. Over the bread slices spread with Russian dressing, layer one slice of Swiss cheese, corned beef, and sauerkraut, and a second slice of cheese. Top with the other slice of bread, buttered side down.

Wrap the sandwiches tightly in aluminum foil and bake for approximately 15 minutes, until the sandwiches are hot. Serve immediately.

THERE ARE MANY VARIATIONS TO THIS CLASSIC. HERE ARE JUST A FEW:

MIDSCALE: Top dark rye bread slices with sliced Brick or Cheddar cheese, sautéed onion slices, turkey pastrami, and another slice of cheese. Broil and serve open faced.

UPSCALE: Spread multi-grain rye with horseradish-tartar sauce; top with a slice of Gruyère, sliced smoked tenderloin of beef, sautéed onions, and another slice of Gruyère. Broil and serve open faced.

APPETIZER: Serve traditional Reuben toppings on mini party rye slices.

TO GO: Place ingredients in a whole-grain pita pocket. For cheese, use Havarti or Edam.

BREAKFAST: Top a toasted English muffin with sliced corned beef and sprinkle with shredded fontina; broil until golden.

The Dipper

Makes 10 to 12 servings

---

1 beef tenderloin (3 pounds),
   trimmed and cut into
   ¼-inch cubes

Salt and freshly ground black
   pepper, to taste

1 pound button mushrooms,
   cleaned, trimmed,
   and cut into quarters

12 whole portabella mush-
   rooms, cleaned, dark gills
   removed, cut in half

½ cup plus 1 tablespoon
   olive oil

¾ cup balsamic vinegar

2 tablespoons stemmed fresh
   rosemary, minced

3 whole heads garlic

¾ pound (3 sticks) butter,
   at room temperature

3 (1 pound) baguettes

12 ounces (3 cups) Parmesan
   cheese, shredded

12 slices (1 ounce each)
   provolone cheese

Season the tenderloin cubes with salt and pepper and place them and the mushrooms in a large plastic bag; set aside.

In a small bowl, whisk together ½ cup of olive oil, the vinegar, and rosemary. Pour over the meat mixture in the bag. Squeeze the bag to empty the bag of air and to distribute the marinade; refrigerate overnight.

Preheat the oven to 350°F.

Cut ½ inch from the top end (stem) of the garlic heads. Drizzle with 1 tablespoon of olive oil. Wrap in heavy aluminum foil and bake for 45 minutes to 1 hour, until the cloves are soft. Cool the garlic and squeeze the cloves out of their wrappers into a bowl. Whip the garlic into ½ pound (2 sticks) of butter.

Slice the baguettes in half lengthwise and spread the cut surfaces with the roasted garlic butter. Sprinkle with Parmesan cheese, then add slices of provolone. Cut each baguette into four pieces and wrap with heavy aluminum foil. Refrigerate.

Cut the remaining ¼ pound (1 stick) of butter into small pieces and add to the meat mixture. Cut 3 (12 x 8-inch) rectangles of aluminum foil; place equal amounts of meat/mushroom mixture on each sheet, and seal tightly, making sure that each foil packet is no more than 1 inch thick. Refrigerate the meat and mushroom packets for at least 1 hour, or until ready to cook.

Remove the meat and bread foil packets from the refrigerator 30 minutes before cooking.

Remove the portabella halves from the meat mixture and grill for about 6 minutes, or until tender, turning once. Place the foil-wrapped baguettes on a hot grill and heat through, about 6 minutes, turning once. Place the foil-wrapped meat mixture on the grill and cook for 2 to 3 minutes per side.

Remove the baguettes from the foil and toast as desired. Open the baguettes and place two pieces of portabella mushroom on one side of each baguette and spread the other side of each baguette with the cooked meat mixture. Close the baguettes and serve, saving the meat juices for dipping.

Three Cheese, Chicken, and Black Bean Turnovers with Cilantro Pastry

Chef Dave Friedman

Makes 6

Roasted Red Pepper Sauce

½ cup roasted red peppers

Salt and pepper

Filling

½ cup canned black beans, rinsed, drained

2 ounces (½ cup) Asiago cheese, grated

2 ounces (½ cup) Cheddar cheese, shredded

2 ounces (½ cup) Queso Jalapeño cheese, shredded

½ cup chopped and cooked chicken

½ cup frozen corn, thawed

3 tablespoons chopped tomato

1 tablespoon minced cilantro

½ teaspoon minced garlic

¼ teaspoon chili powder

Dash ground cumin

Cornmeal Cilantro Cheese Pastry

1¼ cups all-purpose flour

⅔ cup cornmeal

1 ounce (¼ cup) Cheddar cheese, shredded

2 tablespoons Parmesan cheese, grated

½ teaspoon salt

1 tablespoon minced cilantro

5 tablespoons butter, cubed

⅓ cup shortening

4 to 5 tablespoons ice cold water

To make the Roasted Red Pepper Sauce, purée the peppers in a blender, then season with salt and pepper; set aside.

Combine the filling ingredients and set aside.

To make the pastry, stir together the flour, cornmeal, Cheddar cheese, Parmesan cheese, and salt in a large bowl. Stir in the cilantro. Using 2 knives of your fingertips, cut in the butter and shortening until the mixture resembles coarse crumbs. Stir in the water with a fork. Gather the dough into a ball, wrap in plastic wrap and refrigerate for 30 minutes.

Preheat the oven to 425°F.

Roll the pastry on a floured surface to ⅛-inch thickness. Cut into six 6-inch circles. Place a rounded ¼ cup of cheese mixture on one half of each pastry circle, leaving a ¼-inch border. Fold the other side of each the pastry circle over the filling and pinch the edges to seal.

Place the turnovers on a baking tray; bake for 15 to 20 minutes or until the crust is golden brown.

To serve, place 2 tablespoons of Roasted Red Pepper Sauce on the bottom of each plate. Cut the turnovers in half and place both halves on top of the sauce. Garnish with cilantro sprigs.

Accordion Loaves

Makes 8 servings

1 loaf Italian bread

4 tablespoons butter, melted

8 (1-ounce) slices
   provolone cheese

8 (1-ounce) slices
   mozzarella cheese

1 large tomato, thinly-sliced

1 medium onion, thinly-sliced

Black olives, sliced

Preheat the oven to 350°F.

Make 15 cuts in the bread, yielding 16 equal slices. Do not cut all the way through to the bottom crust. Brush melted butter on all cut surfaces of bread. In the first cut, place 1 slice each of the cheeses, tomato, onion, and olives. Leave the second cut empty. Repeat until every other cut is filled.

Place the loaf on an ungreased baking sheet and bake for 15 to 20 minutes or until the bread is hot and the cheese is melted. To serve, cut through to the bottom crust at unfilled cuts.

Serve immediately.

Sides and Salads

Garlic Mashed Potatoes

Chef Jill Prescott

Makes 6 servings

1 pound Idaho potatoes,
   peeled and cut into
   1-inch cubes
1 pound Yukon Gold potatoes
   or Yellow Fin, peeled and cut
   into 1-inch cubes
8 large garlic cloves, peeled
1 tablespoon salt
1¼ cups heavy cream
¼ pound (1 stick) unsalted
   butter, at room temperature
¼ teaspoon freshly
   ground nutmeg
2 teaspoons sea salt
½ teaspoon freshly ground
   white pepper

Place the potatoes and garlic in a large pot and add enough water to cover 2 inches above the potatoes. Bring the water to a boil over high heat. Add the salt, reduce the heat to medium, and cook the potatoes until tender or easily pierced with the tip of a knife, about 15 to 20 minutes.

Heat the cream in a small saucepan over high heat until bubbles start to form around the edges. Keep warm, but do not boil.

Drain the potatoes, return them to the pan, and set them over medium heat for 1 minute to remove any excess water. Once the potatoes are dry, mash them and place in a mixing bowl. Add the cream gradually, mixing on medium speed, scraping bowl as needed. Add enough cream to give the potatoes a soft-mounded consistency, similar to softly whipped cream.

Mix in the butter, a few tablespoons at a time. Add the nutmeg, salt, and white pepper; beat until well blended.

Make-Ahead Mashed Potatoes

Makes 8 servings

8 medium potatoes

½ cup sour cream

4 tablespoons butter

Pepper to taste

Shredded cheese, bacon bits,
   paprika, and parsley,
   for garnish

Peel and boil the potatoes until tender, about 15 to 20 minutes. Drain and, in a large bowl, combine the potatoes, sour cream, butter, and pepper. Beat until light and fluffy. Spoon into a buttered 2-quart casserole dish; cover and refrigerate until ready to cook.

Preheat the oven to 350°F. Bake the casserole for 1 hour. Sprinkle with cheese, bacon bits, paprika, and parsley.

Horseradish Mashed Potatoes

Makes 8 to 10 servings

4 pounds large russet or Yukon
   gold potatoes, peeled and
   cut into 2-inch cubes

¼ pound (1 stick) butter

1½ cups whole milk, heated

2 tablespoons prepared
   horseradish

1 teaspoon salt

½ teaspoon pepper

Place the potatoes in a stock pot or Dutch oven with cold salted water to cover. Simmer over medium-high heat until tender, about 15 minutes. Pour the potatoes out into a colander to drain; return the potatoes to the pot. Add the butter, 2 tablespoons at a time, and the warm milk, about a ½ cup at a time, and mash until still lumpy but achieving a creamy consistency. Add the horseradish and continue mashing. Stir in the salt and pepper.

Gratin Potatoes with Aged Cheddar

Makes 6 servings

1 garlic clove, halved

1 cup diced onions

6 medium baking potatoes,
  peeled and cut into
  ⅛-inch slices

1 teaspoon salt

1 teaspoon freshly
  ground pepper

3 tablespoons butter, cut into
  small pieces

8 ounces (2 cup) aged Cheddar
  cheese, shredded

1 cup chicken stock

2 tablespoons all-purpose flour

1 cup whole milk

Preheat the oven to 425°F. Rub a shallow 3-quart baking dish with the garlic; discard garlic. Coat the dish with nonstick cooking spray.

Coat a small nonstick skillet with cooking spray and place over medium heat until hot. Add the onions and sauté for 5 minutes; set aside.

Arrange one-third of the potato slices in the prepared baking dish; sprinkle with one-third of the salt and pepper; top with one-third of the sautéed onions. Dot with one-third of the butter pieces.

Divide the cheese in fourths and sprinkle one-fourth over the onions; repeat the layers— potatoes, salt and pepper, onions. butter, cheese—ending with the butter.

Mix ¼ cup of the stock with the flour in a small saucepan set over low heat. Add the remaining stock and milk to the saucepan and bring to a boil; pour over the potato mixture. Sprinkle with the remaining cheese.

Bake uncovered for 60 minutes, or until tender. Let stand 5 minutes before serving.

Savory Stuffed New Potatoes

Makes 8 to 10 servings

3 pounds new potatoes,
   1 to 1½ inches in diameter

2 tablespoons butter

8 ounces (2 cups) Swiss
   cheese, shredded

1 cup (4 ounces) finely
   chopped pastrami
   or corned beef

¼ cup milk

¾ cup mayonnaise

2 teaspoons mustard

Fresh dill weed, for garnish

Preheat the oven to 350°F.

Boil the potatoes until tender; cool slightly. Cut each potato in half. Scoop out the centers, leaving a ¼-inch shell; reserve both.

Combine the butter, cheese, pastrami, milk, and potato flesh until smooth and blended and scoop back into the potato shells.

Place the stuffed potato shells on a greased baking sheet and bake for 15 minutes, or until the potatoes are heated through and the cheese is melted.

Combine the mayonnaise and mustard. Top each potato with a small dollop of the mustard mixture, and garnish with dill.

TIP: Using a melon baller to scoop the potatoes makes this recipe even easier to prepare.

Tangy Cheddar Cheese Stuffed Potatoes

Makes 12 servings

6 baking potatoes
  (about 3 pounds)
1 (8-ounce) container sour
  cream dip with toasted onion
4 ounces (1 cup) sharp
  Cheddar cheese, shredded
¼ pound (1 stick) butter,
  at room temperature
¼ teaspoon pepper
Paprika

Preheat the oven to 425°F.

Pierce the potatoes with the tines of a fork and bake for 40 to 60 minutes or until tender. Let the potatoes cool until you can handle them, then cut them in half them lengthwise and scoop out the flesh, reserving the shells.

In a large mixing bowl, combine the warm potato flesh, sour cream dip, Cheddar cheese, butter, and pepper. Beat with an electric mixer on high speed until fluffy. Spoon the potato mixture into the shells and sprinkle the tops with paprika. Place the stuffed shells in a 13 x 9 x 2-inch baking dish. Bake in a 350°F. oven for 25 minutes or until heated through.

Blue Cheese Potato Pancakes
with Hot Spiced Apple Compote

Makes 10 servings

1 pound (3 cups) blue cheese,
  crumbled

6 to 7 baking potatoes,
  shredded

2 eggs, beaten

½ cup all-purpose flour

1 small onion, grated

¼ cup chopped parsley

2 teaspoons cornstarch

2 teaspoons garlic powder

1 teaspoon salt

2 teaspoons white pepper

4 tablespoons butter

¼ cup vegetable oil

Hot Spiced Apple Compote

3 cups apple chunks

1 cup apple cider

¼ pound (1 stick)
  unsalted butter

⅓ cup apple brandy

¼ cup granulated sugar

2 tablespoons lemon juice

1 tablespoon ground cinnamon

1½ teaspoons ground nutmeg

½ cup heavy cream

Combine 2 cups of blue cheese with the potatoes, eggs, flour, onion, parsley, cornstarch, and seasonings; mix well.

In a large skillet set over medium-high heat, heat the butter and oil.

For each pancake, pour a scant ¼ cup of the potato mixture into the skillet, cook until golden brown, 2 to 3 minutes per side.

To serve, spoon Hot Spiced Apple Compote (recipe follows) onto each plate; top with 2 pancakes. Sprinkle the pancakes with 2 tablespoons remaining blue cheese. Garnish with apple wedges.

To make the Hot Spiced Apple Compote, combine all the ingredients except the heavy cream in a saucepan. Simmer for 30 minutes. Stir in the cream. Purée in a blender or food processor. Serve warm.

Gorgonzola Crisp Potato Pancakes

Makes 4 servings

4 large (2½ pounds total)
  baking potatoes

4 tablespoons butter, melted

¼ cup minced onions

½ tablespoon parsley, chopped

½ tablespoon kosher salt

Black pepper, to taste

1 teaspoon olive oil

½ cup (3 ounces) Gorgonzola,
  chilled and cut into
  ½-inch pieces

In a large pot, cover the potatoes with water and bring to a simmer. Cook for 10 minutes and shut off the heat. Let the potatoes cool to room temperature in the water.

Drain and peel the potatoes. Using the course side of a cheese grater, grate the potatoes into a bowl. Add the butter, onion, parsley, salt, and pepper and stir.

Heat the olive oil over medium-high heat in an 8-inch nonstick skillet. Add half the potato mixture and smooth down with the back of a spoon. Add the cold Gorgonzola slices and top with the remaining potatoes. Press and seal the edges with the back of a spoon.

Cook the potatoes until lightly browned, about 2 to 3 minutes. Slide the pancake onto a plate and turn it over into the same pan. Brown the other side, about 2 to 3 minutes. Remove from the pan and allow to cool slightly before serving.

Potato Mushroom Puff

Makes 8 servings

8 medium potatoes, peeled
  and quartered

1 garlic clove

½ pound mushrooms,
  cleaned and sliced

¼ cup chopped onion

¼ pound (1 stick) butter, at
  room temperature

1 cup half-and-half

2 egg yolks

½ teaspoon salt

Dash of pepper

¼ cup fresh parsley,
  chopped, or 4 teaspoons
  dried parsley flakes

1 cup soft breadcrumbs

Preheat the oven to 350°F. Butter a shallow 2-quart casserole dish.

Boil the potatoes and garlic in salted water until tender, about 15 to 20 minutes. Drain and discard the garlic.

Meanwhile, sauté the mushrooms and onion in 2 tablespoons of butter. Set aside.

Using an electric mixer, whip the potatoes with 4 tablespoons of butter. Add the half-and-half, egg yolks, salt, and pepper. Stir in the mushrooms, onions, and parsley. Spoon into the prepared casserole dish.

Melt the remaining 2 tablespoons of butter and toss with the breadcrumbs. Pour over the potatoes and bake for 25 to 30 minutes.

Cheesy Baked French Fries

Makes 8 servings

¼ pound (1 stick) butter

½ cup all-purpose flour

1 teaspoon salt

2½ cups milk

4 ounces (1 cup) Cheddar
  cheese, shredded

2 (16-ounce) packages
  frozen french fries

1 cup corn flakes, crushed

Preheat the oven to 375°F. Butter a 2-quart baking dish.

In a saucepan, melt the butter, then gradually add the flour and salt. Gradually add the milk, stirring constantly until the mixture thickens. Add the cheese and stir until melted.

Place the french fries in the baking dish, top with cheese sauce, then sprinkle with corn flakes. Bake for 25 to 30 minutes.

Parsley Garlic Fries

Makes 4 servings

Vegetable or canola oil
  for frying

6 large russet potatoes, cut
  into ⅛-inch-thick slices

5 cloves garlic, minced

¼ cup olive oil

2 tablespoons chopped
  fresh parsley

Kosher salt, to taste

Heat the oil in a cast iron skillet to 350°F, then add the potatoes and fry for about 3 minutes. Remove and drain on paper towels for 1 hour.

Meanwhile, sauté the garlic in 1 tablespoon of olive oil until soft, about 4 minutes. Add the remaining oil and remove the pan from the heat; let the oil sit, so the garlic infuses it.

Reheat the frying oil to 375°F. and fry the potatoes a second time until golden brown, about 4 to 6 minutes. Drain on paper towels and transfer to a bowl or platter. Pour the garlic oil over the fries and sprinkle with parsley. Toss with salt and serve.

Maple-Glazed Yams with Butter Pecan Topping

Makes 8 servings

4 pounds yams, peeled
  and cut into ¼-inch chunks

Salt

½ cup pure maple syrup

3 tablespoons plus ¼ pound
  (1 stick) unsalted butter,
  chilled and cut into
  ½-inch pieces

⅔ cup all-purpose flour

⅔ cup light brown sugar,
  packed

1 cup pecans,
  coarsely chopped

Preheat the oven to 400°F. Butter a 13 x 9 x 2-inch baking dish.

Bring a large pot of water to the boil, then add the yams. Cook about 4 minutes or until the water returns to a simmer. Drain and rinse under cold water.

Arrange the yams in the prepared baking dish. Season with salt and pour the syrup over top. Dot with 3 tablespoons of butter. Cover and bake for about 25 minutes, or until the yams are almost tender.

Mix the flour and brown sugar in a medium bowl. Using 2 knives or your fingertips, cut in the remaining ¼ pound of butter until the mixture resembles coarse meal. Add the pecans and mix.

Sprinkle the pecan mixture over the yams and bake for 20 minutes or until tender.

Sweet Potato-Pecan Soufflé

Makes 8 servings

5 cups (3 pounds) cooked,
  mashed sweet potatoes
  or yams

3 eggs, beaten

½ cup eggnog*

½ cup milk

¼ cup granulated sugar

1½ teaspoons vanilla

¼ teaspoon salt

½ cup all-purpose flour

½ cup brown sugar

¾ teaspoon ground nutmeg

4 tablespoons butter,
  at room temperature

¾ cup chopped pecans

*Substitute with ½ cup heavy cream,
1 teaspoon rum extract, 1 teaspoon
brandy extract, and 2 tablespoons
confectioners' sugar.

Preheat the oven to 375°F. Butter a 2-quart casserole dish.

Combine the sweet potatoes, eggs, eggnog, milk, sugar, vanilla, and salt, mixing well until blended. Spoon into the prepared casserole dish.

In a separate bowl, combine the flour, brown sugar, and nutmeg. Using two knives or your fingertips, cut the butter into the flour mixture; stir in the pecans. Sprinkle over the sweet potato mixture. Bake for 30 minutes or until the top is crispy.

Cheese and Bacon Stuffed Tomatoes

Makes 4 servings

4 medium-sized firm tomatoes

12 slices bacon, diced

½ cup diced green bell pepper

½ cup diced onion

6 ounces (1½ cups) Cheddar
  cheese, shredded

2 tablespoons chopped lettuce

2 tablespoons crushed
  cheese crackers

2 tablespoons butter

Preheat the oven to 400°F. Butter a 9-inch square baking dish.

Cut a thin slice from the top of each tomato and carefully scoop out the pulp; set the pulp aside. Drain the tomatoes upside down.

Meanwhile, in a skillet set over medium heat, cook the bacon until almost done. Drain off the fat from the skillet, add the bell pepper and onion, and sauté until soft. Pour the bacon and cooked vegetables into a large bowl and add the cheese, lettuce, and tomato pulp. Stir to combine.

Fill each tomato shell with one-quarter of the mixture, then sprinkle with cracker crumbs and dot with butter. Place in the prepared baking dish and bake for 25 to 30 minutes.

Swiss and Mushroom Stuffed Cornbread with Cream Sauce

Makes 6 to 8 servings

1 cup cornmeal

1 cup all-purpose flour

2 teaspoons baking powder

½ teaspoon baking soda

½ teaspoon salt

1 cup buttermilk

2 tablespoons honey

1 egg

3 tablespoons butter, melted

6 ounces (1½ cups)
  Swiss cheese, shredded

1 (3-ounce) can sliced
  mushrooms, drained

Cream Sauce

2 tablespoons butter

2 tablespoons all-purpose flour

1½ cups milk

2 egg yolks, slightly beaten

2 cups cooked and cubed
  chicken or turkey

Preheat the oven to 375°F. Butter an 8-inch square baking dish.

In a large bowl, combine the cornmeal, flour, baking powder, baking soda, and salt.

In a separate bowl, combine the buttermilk, honey, egg, butter, and ½ cup Swiss cheese. Add to the dry ingredients and mix well.

Spread half the batter into the prepared baking dish. Top with the remaining cheese and mushrooms, then cover with remaining cornbread batter. Bake for 25 to 30 minutes or until golden brown. Cool the bread for 10 to 15 minutes before cutting into squares. Top with Cream Sauce (recipe follows).

To make the Cream Sauce, melt the butter in a medium-sized saucepan set over medium-high heat. Add the flour and stir to combine. Add the milk, stirring constantly until the mixture thickens and boils. Remove from the heat.

Pour ¾ cup of the sauce into the bowl containing the egg yolks and mix. Stir the yolk mixture back into the remaining sauce. Add the chicken or turkey, stirring until heated through. Ladle the sauce over the cornbread squares.

Savory Golden Stuffing

Makes 8 servings

¼ pound (1 stick)
  plus 3 tablespoons butter

½ cup minced onion

2½ quarts (10 cups)
  soft bread cubes

2½ teaspoons salt

2½ teaspoons ground sage

¼ teaspoon pepper

Preheat the oven to 350°F. Lightly grease a 12 x 8-inch baking dish.

Melt the butter in a skillet, then add the onion and cook until transparent. Add the bread cubes and seasonings and stir.

Pour the bread mixture into the prepared pan and bake for 15 to 20 minutes, or unto the bread is browned.

Polenta with Garlic and Butter

Makes 6 to 8 servings

4 cups chicken stock

2 cloves garlic, minced

1 cup polenta

4 tablespoons butter

1 teaspoon salt

Pour the chicken stock and garlic into a large, heavy pot and stir in the polenta. Cook over medium high heat, stirring constantly. Bring the mixture to a boil, then lower the heat and cook for an additional 10 minutes, until the polenta thickens. Stir in the butter and salt and continue cooking, stirring constantly until the polenta pulls away from the sides of the pan. Serve immediately.

Terrine of Gorgonzola

Makes 8 to 10 servings

2 pounds (6 cups) Gorgonzola cheese, at room temperature

1 pound (4 sticks) unsalted butter, at room temperature

2 cups walnut halves

1 tablespoon coarsely ground black pepper

¼ cup sherry vinegar or red wine vinegar

1 egg yolk

3 teaspoons Dijon mustard

¾ cup vegetable oil

¼ cup olive oil

Salt and pepper

8 cups torn assorted greens

1 cup haricot verts or fresh thin green beans, blanched

2 cups assorted fresh fruit

6 slices bread, crusts trimmed, toasted, and quartered diagonally

Line a 9 x 5-inch loaf pan with plastic wrap.

In a large bowl, combine the cheese, butter, walnuts, and pepper; mix well. Pack the cheese mixture into the prepared pan. Chill for 4 hours or until firm.

In a small bowl, whisk the vinegar, egg yolk, and mustard. Add the oils, whisking constantly until thoroughly combined. Season to taste. Pour the dressing over the greens and the haricot vert; toss lightly.

Cut the terrine into 12 slices; place one slice at the bottom of each dinner plate. Arrange greens above the terrine; surround with fruit. Garnish with toast points.

Orange Glazed Carrots

Makes 6 servings

6 to 8 carrots, peeled and
  cut into 1-inch sticks

4 tablespoons butter

2 tablespoons granulated
  sugar

2 tablespoons brown sugar

1 tablespoon all-purpose flour

⅔ cup orange juice

Preheat the oven to 350°F.

In boiling water, cook the carrots until barely tender, about 10 to 12 minutes. Drain and transfer to a baking sheet.

In a small saucepan over medium-high heat, melt the butter, then stir in the sugars and flour. Gradually add the orange juice and cook, stirring constantly, until the mixture boils. Pour the sauce over the carrots, stirring to coat the carrots evenly. Bake for 30 minutes.

Green Beans with Garlic, Butter, and Olive Oil

Makes 6 servings

1 pound green beans

2 tablespoons olive oil

2 tablespoons butter

2 to 3 cloves garlic, chopped

1 teaspoon salt

Pepper, to taste

Red pepper flakes, optional

Wash and dry the green beans and snap off the tips. Cut them in half or leave them whole, depending on your preference.

Heat the oil and butter in a pan set over medium heat and, when butter is melted, add the garlic. Sauté gently, watching closely so the garlic doesn't burn. Add the green beans and toss until coated. Reduce the heat and cover for 5 to 8 minutes until the beans are crisp-tender. Season with salt, pepper, and red pepper flakes.

Soft "Sexy" Cheese Grits

Chef Jan Birnbaum

Makes 6 servings

5 tablespoons butter

1½ cups chicken stock

⅓ cup heavy cream

½ teaspoon chopped garlic

Salt and pepper to taste

Tabasco™ sauce to taste

½ cup grits (standard quick grits or stone ground*)

1½ cups Gouda cheese, shredded

*Fresh, stone-ground grits have the best flavor; the cooking time will be approximately twice as long. If you do use freshly ground grits, you will want to keep a little extra stock available. Because of the longer cooking time, evaporation occurs.

In a large saucepan set over medium-high heat, bring the butter, stock, cream, garlic, salt, pepper, and Tabasco to a boil. Lower the heat and simmer until the garlic is soft, about 2 minutes. Add the grits, stirring constantly. Simmer.

Continue cooking, stirring often with a wooden spoon as the mixture thickens, until the grits are soft and cooked through, about 10 to 15 minutes.

Fold in the Gouda cheese, reserving a little for garnish. Serve immediately.

NOTE: To turn this sumptuous recipe into an entrée, sauté 1 pound of medium peeled, deveined shrimp in butter with garlic. Top the grits with the shrimp.

Seafood Risotto

Makes 4 servings

4 tablespoons butter

1 medium onion, chopped

Salt and pepper to taste

2 cups Arborio rice

1 teaspoon chopped garlic

6 to 8 cups seafood stock,
very warm (substitute
with chicken stock)

1 pound white fish fillets

½ pound (8 ounces) medium
uncooked shrimp, peeled
and deveined

½ pound (8 ounces) kielbasa
or other smoked sausage,
thinly sliced

¼ cup heavy cream

2 ounces (½ cup) Parmesan
cheese, freshly grated

3 tablespoons green onion,
chopped (green part only)

2 tablespoons finely chopped
parsley, for garnish

Crusty bread, for serving

Heat 3 tablespoons of butter in a large sauté pan over medium-high heat. Add the onion and season with salt and pepper. Sauté until the onion softens but does not brown. Add the rice and garlic and cook until the rice begins to turn opaque. Add the stock 1 cup at a time, stirring almost constantly, making sure to keep the liquid at a low boil. Add more stock as the rice absorbs it.

Continue cooking for 16 minutes; then add the fish fillets. Cook for 3 minutes, stirring to break up the fillets into smaller pieces. Add the shrimp and sausage (and more stock as needed) and cook for 2 more minutes or until the shrimp turns pink.

Add the remaining butter, cream, Parmesan cheese, and green onion and cook for 2 more minutes, making sure to add enough stock to keep the rice creamy and moist. Adjust the seasoning with salt and pepper.

Spoon into serving bowls and sprinkle with parsley and more Parmesan cheese. Serve with crusty bread.

Rice with Leeks and Mushrooms

Makes 4 to 6 servings

2 cloves garlic, minced

1 medium-sized leek, chopped,
  white parts only

¼ cup chopped mushrooms

2 tablespoons butter

1 cup long grain rice

2 cups chicken stock

1 tablespoon chopped fresh
  parsley, optional

In a medium-sized saucepan set over medium heat, sauté the garlic, leek, and mushrooms in butter until the vegetables are soft and the mushrooms release their juices, about 8 minutes. Stir in the rice to coat it in butter and cook for 1 minute. Pour in the chicken stock and bring to a boil, about 5 minutes. Stir once, cover, and reduce the heat to low. Cook the rice for 20 minutes until all of the liquid is absorbed into the rice.

Fluff with a fork and garnish with parsley.

Wild Rice Casserole
with Orange Butter

Chef Jill Prescott

Makes 6 servings

Wild Rice

1½ cups wild rice

3 garlic cloves

2 bay leaves

7 cups chicken stock

2 tablespoons unsalted butter

4 shallots, finely minced

1 large or 2 small bulbs of fresh
  fennel, thinly sliced

½ teaspoon fennel seed,
  toasted and ground

½ cup brandy

½ cup orange juice

2 tablespoons chopped chives

¼ cup chopped tarragon leaves

1 cup chestnuts, freshly
  roasted, peeled and chopped

Sea salt and freshly
  ground pepper

Orange Butter

7 tablespoons unsalted butter,
  at room temperature

2 shallots, chopped

Zest of 1 orange

To make the Orange Butter, sauté 1 tablespoon butter and the shallots in a small sauté pan. Cook over medium heat until the shallots are softened, for 1 to 2 minutes, then let cool.

Combine the shallot mixture, zest, and remaining butter; form into a log, wrap in plastic wrap, and refrigerate until ready to use. The butter can be made several days ahead and stored in the refrigerator.

To make the Wild Rice, in a large saucepan set over medium heat, heat the wild rice, garlic, bay leaves, and 5 cups of chicken stock; bring to a boil, then reduce the heat to low and simmer until the rice is tender, 45 to 60 minutes. Drain the rice, discard the garlic and bay leaves, then return the rice to the saucepan, cover, and set aside.

Melt the butter in a large sauté pan.

Sauté the shallots until softened, about 1 to 2 minutes. Add the fennel and continue to sauté for about 1 minute. Add the fennel seed and sauté for 30 seconds more. Add the brandy and gently stir until the browned bits from the bottom and sides of the pan are dissolved, 1 to 2 minutes.

Add the remaining 2 cups of chicken stock and orange juice and heat until the liquid is reduced by half.

Combine the reserved wild rice, chives, tarragon, and chestnuts. Add salt and pepper to taste and mix well.

Place into a serving dish and dot the top of the casserole with the Orange Butter, allowing it to melt into the rice.

NOTE: This dish can be made 1 to 2 days in advance. Just refrigerate the cooked dish and reheat in a 350°F. oven for 20 minutes prior to serving.

Cheese and Chili Rice

Makes 8 servings

1 cup chopped onion

4 tablespoons butter

4 cups cooked rice, still hot

2 cups sour cream

1 cup cottage cheese

1 large bay leaf, crumbled

½ teaspoon salt

½ teaspoon pepper

3 (4-ounce) cans green chiles, chopped

8 ounces (2 cups) Cheddar cheese, shredded

Parsley, chopped

Preheat the oven to 375°F. Lightly grease a 12 x 8-inch baking dish.

In a 3-quart saucepan, sauté the onion in the butter until golden. Remove from the heat and stir in the hot rice, sour cream, cottage cheese, bay leaf, salt, and pepper. Mix well.

Layer half of the rice mixture in the prepared dish. Sprinkle all of the chiles and half of the cheese over top. Top with the remaining rice and cheese. Sprinkle top with parsley. Bake for 25 to 30 minutes. Serve hot.

Three Cheese Asparagus Gratin

Makes 6 servings

4 tablespoons butter

2 pounds asparagus, washed
and tough ends removed

1 cup milk

1 teaspoon cornstarch
mixed with 2 tablespoons
cold water

4 ounces (1 cup) Gouda (plain
or smoked) cheese, shredded

4 ounces (1 cup) Muenster
cheese, shredded

1 teaspoon salt

1 cup coarse breadcrumbs

2 ounces (½ cup) Asiago
cheese, grated

¼ teaspoon freshly ground
black pepper

Preheat the oven to 425°F.

Grease a 9-inch square glass baking dish with 1 tablespoon of butter. Arrange the asparagus in the baking dish.

Gently simmer the milk over medium heat. Stir in the cornstarch mixture to thicken slightly. Add the Gouda and Muenster cheeses and whisk until smooth and creamy; season with salt. Pour the cheese sauce over the asparagus.

Melt the remaining 3 tablespoons butter. Toss with the breadcrumbs, Asiago, and pepper. Sprinkle over the asparagus mixture.

Bake for 20 to 25 minutes, or until bubbly and lightly browned.

Roasted Asparagus with Parmesan Sauce

Makes 8 servings

2 pounds asparagus, trimmed

Salt and pepper

¼ cup olive oil

4 tablespoons butter

3 tablespoons all-purpose flour

½ teaspoon salt

1½ cups milk

1½ ounces (½ cup) Parmesan
  cheese, grated

Preheat the oven to 400°F.

Place the asparagus on a nonstick baking sheet and season lightly with salt and pepper. Pour the olive oil over the asparagus and mix so the asparagus is completely coated. Bake for 15 to 20 minutes.

Meanwhile, in a 2-quart saucepan, melt the butter, then stir in the flour and salt. Gradually stir in the milk and cook, stirring constantly, until thickened. Cook an additional 2 minutes. Gradually add the Parmesan cheese; stirring until cheese is melted. Pour over the asparagus and serve warm.

Broccoli Bake

Makes 6 servings

1¼ pounds broccoli, stems
   peeled, cut into 1-inch pieces

¼ cup diced red bell pepper

1 (10¾-ounce) can condensed
   cream of mushroom soup

¾ cup half-and-half

¼ teaspoon black pepper

¼ teaspoon garlic powder

4 tablespoons grated
   Parmesan cheese

¾ cup dry breadcrumbs

4 tablespoons butter, melted

Preheat the oven to 350°F.

Cook the broccoli until crisp tender; drain. Combine with the bell pepper.

Combine the soup, half-and-half, and seasonings; mix well.

In a buttered 9-inch pie plate, layer 1 cup of the soup mixture, the broccoli mixture, 2 tablespoons of cheese, and the remaining soup mixture.

Combine the remaining 2 tablespoons of cheese, the breadcrumbs, and melted butter. Sprinkle over the broccoli.

Bake for 30 minutes or until hot. Let stand 5 minutes before serving.

Broccoli Raab with Garlic

Makes 4 servings

1 bunch broccoli raab, cleaned
  and roughly chopped

2 to 4 tablespoons butter

2 tablespoons olive oil

2 cloves garlic,
  crushed or sliced

Juice of half lemon

Salt and pepper

Blanch the broccoli raab in boiling water for 2 minutes or until bright green. Remove from the boiling water and immediately place in an ice water bath to stop them from cooking.

In a large skillet set over medium heat, melt the butter in the olive oil. Add the garlic and sauté until the garlic is fragrant, about 3 minutes.

Drain the broccoli raab and add to the skillet. Sauté about 5 minutes, until the broccoli raab is cooked through and glistening. To serve, squeeze lemon over and season with salt and pepper.

Broccoli Polonaise

Makes 4 servings

1 pound fresh or
  frozen broccoli florets
¼ pound (1 stick) butter
½ cup soft breadcrumbs
1 hard-cooked egg,
  chopped very fine

Cook the broccoli in boiling salted water.

Meanwhile, melt 4 tablespoons of the butter in a skillet. Brown the breadcrumbs in the butter and set aside.

Add the remaining butter to the skillet and heat until it slightly browns.

Drain the broccoli and arrange in a serving dish. Spoon the browned butter over the broccoli, sprinkle with breadcrumbs and chopped egg.

Cheesy Cauliflower

Makes 6 servings

1 large head cauliflower
12 ounces (3 cups) your choice
  cheese, shredded
1½ cups half-and-half cream
3 egg yolks, beaten
¼ teaspoon nutmeg
¼ teaspoon pepper
4 tablespoons butter, melted
½ cup breadcrumbs

Preheat the oven to 350°F. Butter an 8-inch square baking dish.

Rinse the cauliflower and separate it into florets. Steam until just tender, about 8 to 10 minutes. Place the cauliflower in the prepared baking dish.

Stir together the cheese, half-and-half, egg yolks, nutmeg, and pepper until well blended. Pour over the cauliflower.

Mix together the butter and breadcrumbs. Sprinkle over cauliflower. Bake for 20 to 25 minutes.

Buttered Brussels Sprouts with Pancetta and Shallots

Makes 4 servings

1½ pounds Brussels
  sprouts, cleaned, trimmed,
  and quartered
½ cup diced pancetta
1 tablespoon olive oil
3 tablespoons minced shallots
1 clove garlic, minced
4 tablespoons butter
Salt and freshly ground pepper

Boil the Brussels sprouts in salted water until tender, about 6 minutes. Drain in a colander and set aside.

In a large skillet set over medium-high heat, cook the pancetta in the olive oil until the pancetta browns, about 5 minutes. Remove the pancetta from the pan and add the shallots and garlic, lowering the heat so the garlic doesn't burn. Add the butter to the pan and then the Brussels sprouts, tossing to coat. Stir in pepper and salt to taste.

DID YOU KNOW?
The United States produces more than 1.2 billion pounds of butter every year.

Creamy Elegant Artichokes

Makes 8 servings

½ cup slivered almonds

4 tablespoons butter

2 cups heavy cream

½ cup diced red bell pepper

¼ teaspoon white pepper

¼ teaspoon salt

⅛ teaspoon ground nutmeg

1 tablespoon grated
lemon zest

2 quarts broccoflower florets
(about 2 small heads),
cooked until crisp-tender,
and drained

3 carrots, peeled, sliced,
cooked until crisp-tender,
and drained

1 (14-ounce) can quartered
artichoke hearts, drained
and squeezed dry

Preheat the oven to 350°F.

In a small skillet set over medium heat, roast the almonds in 1 tablespoon of butter. Set aside.

Bring the cream and remaining butter to boil in a 3-quart saucepan over high heat. Reduce the heat to medium; continue boiling for 15 minutes.

Add the bell pepper, white pepper, salt, and nutmeg; continue boiling over medium-low heat until thick, stirring constantly. Stir in the lemon zest (sauce should yield 1⅓ cups). Pour over combined broccoflower and carrots; toss lightly.

Arrange the artichokes on the bottom of a buttered 2-quart rectangular baking dish. Top with broccoflower mixture; sprinkle with almonds. Bake for 20 minutes or until hot.

NOTE: To make this dish ahead of time, prepare it as directed, but do not top with almonds. Cool to room temperature, cover, and refrigerate up to 24 hours. Uncover; top with almonds. Bake at 350°F., 25 to 30 minutes or until hot.

Swiss Cheese Squash Bake

Makes 4 servings

1 egg

½ cup (2 ounces) Swiss
 cheese, shredded

¼ cup milk

1 teaspoon salt

¼ teaspoon dry mustard

Dash of cayenne pepper

¼ pound (1 stick) butter

1½ cups sliced yellow summer
 squash (3 small)

1½ cups cut fresh broccoli or
 1 (10-ounce) package frozen
 broccoli, thawed and cut

1 ounce (¼ cup) Parmesan
 cheese, grated

Preheat the oven to 375°F.

In a mixing bowl, beat the egg slightly, then stir in Swiss cheese, milk, salt, mustard, and cayenne pepper.

In a large skillet, melt the butter and sauté the vegetables until tender. Place the vegetables in a 1-quart baking dish and pour the egg mixture over. Sprinkle with Parmesan cheese and bake for 15 to 20 minutes.

Whipped Beets

Makes 8 servings

4½ pounds beets, cleaned and
  quartered, greens removed
2 tablespoons olive oil
4 tablespoons butter
½ cup heavy cream
1½ teaspoon freshly
  grated nutmeg
Salt and pepper

Heat oven to 375°F.

Place the beets on baking sheets and toss with olive oil. Roast the beets for about 1 to 1½ hours, or until a knife easily pierces the flesh. Remove from the oven and set aside to cool.

Peel the beets and put in a bowl.

In a medium saucepan set over medium-low heat, combine the butter, cream, and nutmeg, stirring often, until the butter melts, about 7 minutes.

Mash the beets and slowly add the heated cream mixture until the beets resemble roughly mashed potatoes. Pour the beets into a blender and beat at medium speed until the beets are smooth and creamy, about 3 minutes. Season with salt and pepper to taste.

Buttered Egg Noodles

Makes 6 to 8 servings

4 to 6 tablespoons butter

1 clove garlic, crushed

1 (6-ounce) package
  egg noodles

¼ teaspoon poppy seeds

Salt and pepper, to taste

Melt the butter in a saucepan; add the garlic and sauté until fragrant and soft, about 3 to 5 minutes. Be careful not to brown the garlic.

Cook the egg noodles according to the package instructions, drain, and add to the garlic butter. Toss in the poppy seeds and cook over low heat for 2 minutes. Season with salt and pepper.

Butter and Herb Croutons

4 tablespoons butter

¼ teaspoon dried marjoram

¼ teaspoon dried thyme

1 loaf day old French bread,
  cut into 1-inch cubes

⅛ teaspoon garlic powder

Preheat the oven to 375°F.

Melt the butter in a sauce pan set over medium heat. Add the marjoram and thyme and simmer for 2 minutes until the herbs release their aroma. Remove from the heat.

Place the bread on a baking sheet and pour the herb butter over top. Toss to coat each cube. Bake for 10 minutes, or until the cubes are golden brown.

Smoky Swiss and
Turkey Potato Crunch Salad

Makes 6 servings

5 tablespoons butter

2 cups instant mashed
  potato flakes

½ teaspoon chili powder

½ teaspoon salt

1 (6-ounce) jar marinated
  artichoke hearts, drained,
  liquid reserved

1 cup chopped celery

½ cup chopped red bell pepper

¾ cup low-fat Italian dressing

2 cups turkey, cut into
  ½-inch cubes

8 ounces (2 cups) smoked
  Swiss cheese, cut into
  ½-inch cubes

6 cups torn mixed salad greens

3 ounces (½ cup) Romano or
  Parmesan cheese, grated

Melt the butter in a 10-inch skillet over medium heat. Stir in the potato flakes, chili powder, and salt. Cook, stirring constantly, until the potato flakes turn dark brown, about 6 to 8 minutes; set aside.

Chop the artichoke hearts and place in a 2-quart saucepan. Stir in the artichoke liquid, celery, red bell pepper, and dressing; heat thoroughly over medium heat.

In a large glass serving bowl, combine the turkey, Swiss cheese, salad greens, and artichoke mixture.

Sprinkle with the browned potatoes and cheese. Serve immediately, while the salad is slightly warm.

Baby Arugula Salad with Grilled Beef Sirloin, Gruyère Gougère, and Balsamic-White Truffle Vinaigrette

Chef Louis Moskow

Makes 12 servings

Gruyère Gougère

3 cups water

¼ pound plus 4 tablespoons (1½ stick) butter

3 cups all-purpose flour

12 eggs

12 ounces (3 cups) Gruyère cheese, shredded

1 teaspoon salt

1 teaspoon pepper

¼ teaspoon freshly grated nutmeg

Sirloin

3 pounds beef sirloin

Salt and pepper, as needed

Balsamic-White Truffle Vinaigrette

6 tablespoons extra virgin olive oil

3 tablespoons aged balsamic vinegar

3 tablespoons white truffle oil

3 shallots, minced

Salt and pepper

12 ounces baby arugula

To make the Gruyère Gougère (or cheese puffs), preheat the oven to 400°F. Cover 2 baking sheets with parchment paper.

Boil the water and butter together in a large saucepan. Add the flour and mix over medium heat until the dough pulls away from the sides of the pan. Remove from the heat. Beat in the eggs one at a time until they are fully incorporated and the dough is smooth. Add the Gruyère, salt, pepper, and nutmeg.

Pour the dough into a pastry bag with a straight tip and pipe 36 bite-sized circles about 1-inch in diameter onto the parchment paper.

Space them about ½-inch apart to allow for expansion. (Form them larger, if you like. You can also drop the dough onto the baking sheets using a spoon.) Bake for 30 minutes, or until golden brown. Turn off the oven and let the puffs sit for 10 minutes.

Season the beef with salt and pepper and grill until done to your lik-ing. Cut across the grain into ¼-inch thick slices.

To make the Aged Balsamic Vinaigrette, whisk the olive oil, vinegar, truffle oil, shallots, salt and pepper together and toss with the arugula.

Arrange the salad on plate and top with beef slices. Arrange three Gougère on each plate.

Main Dishes

⸺⸙⸺

Cheese Soufflé

Makes 5 to 6 servings

4 tablespoons butter

¼ cup all-purpose flour

1 teaspoon salt

Dash dry mustard

⅛ teaspoon dried tarragon

1½ cups whole milk

½ pound sharp Cheddar
   cheese, shredded

6 eggs, separated

Preheat the oven to 300°F.

Melt the butter in a heavy saucepan set over medium heat; slowly whisk in the flour, salt, mustard, and tarragon until smooth. Gradually add the milk and cook until the mixture thickens, about 7 minutes. Add the cheese, cover, and cook, stirring often until the cheese melts and is well blended.

Beat the egg yolks then add warm cheese mixture very slowly, stirring constantly. Set aside to let cool slightly.

Meanwhile, beat the egg whites to stiff shiny peaks.

Fold the cooled cheese-egg mixture carefully into the beaten egg whites, being sure to incorporate thoroughly. Pour carefully into a 2-quart casserole dish. Place the dish in the oven on the center rack and bake for 1 hour, until puffed high and golden brown.

Potato Quiche

3 cups frozen hash brown
   potatoes, thawed

2 tablespoons butter

1½ cups mild Cheddar cheese,
   finely shredded

½ teaspoon salt, or to taste

¼ teaspoon freshly ground
   black pepper, or to taste

1 cup cooked and
   chopped ham

4 large eggs,
   at room temperature

½ cup milk

Paprika

Butter a 10-inch glass pie plate.

Combine the potatoes and butter in a microwave-safe bowl. Microwave for about 3 minutes or until the butter is melted.

Combine the potato mixture and ¾ cup of cheese and press into the bottom and up the sides of the prepared pie plate. Sprinkle with salt and pepper and cover with ham. Wrap in plastic wrap and refrigerate overnight.

The next day, remove the pie plate from the refrigerator and discard the plastic wrap.

Preheat the oven to 325°F.

Beat the eggs and milk, then pour over the potato crust and ham. Cover with the remaining ¾ cup cheese. Sprinkle with paprika.

Bake for 55 to 60 minutes. Cut into wedges while warm and serve.

Zucchini and Italian Sausage Quiche

Makes 6 to 8 servings

2 cups shredded zucchini

4 tablespoons butter

½ pound sweet Italian sausage

1 (10-inch) unbaked pie crust

4 ounces (1 cup) Swiss
  cheese, shredded

4 eggs

1 cup milk

½ cup heavy cream

1 ounce (¼ cup) Parmesan
  cheese, grated

½ teaspoon salt

¼ teaspoon white pepper

Preheat the oven to 450°F.

Sauté the zucchini in 2 tablespoons of butter for 5 minutes. Set aside.

Remove the sausage from the casings and crumble into a skillet. Fry in the remaining 2 tablespoons butter until cooked through, about 6 to 8 minutes. Drain on paper towels.

Spread the zucchini in the bottom of the pastry shell. Sprinkle with Swiss cheese and cooked sausage.

Beat the eggs in a large bowl. Add the milk, cream, Parmesan cheese, salt, and pepper. Pour into the pie crust and bake for 15 minutes, then lower heat to 350°F. and bake for 15 minutes or until firm.

Polish-Style Pierogies

Makes 4 servings

Filling

1 cup small curd cottage
  cheese, drained

1 egg yolk, beaten

1 tablespoon butter, melted

1 teaspoon granulated sugar

¼ teaspoon salt

Dough

2¼ cups all-purpose flour

½ teaspoon salt

2 tablespoons butter,
  cut in pieces

1 large egg,
  at room temperature

1 egg yolk,
  at room temperature

½ cup milk, at room
  temperature

2 tablespoons sour cream,
  at room temperature

Sour cream, for serving

Onions sautéed in butter,
  for serving

To make the filling, combine all of the filling ingredients and refrigerate until ready to assemble.

Meanwhile, combine the flour, salt, and butter in a food processor fitted with a plastic blade.

In a separate bowl, blend together the egg, egg yolk, milk, and sour cream. Add to the flour mixture and process until the dough cleans the sides of the bowl and sticks together (it will be slightly sticky). Remove, shape into a ball, wrap in plastic and chill for 3 hours or overnight.

Turn the dough out onto a floured surface and cut the dough into thirds. Roll each section out into a 12-inch round. Using a 3-inch circle biscuit cutter (or a glass), cut each round into eight circles. Moisten the outer edges of each dough circle with water; place 2 teaspoons of filling on each and fold the dough over. Seal the edges by pressing gently with the tines of a fork.

In large pot, bring 12 cups of salted water to boil. Add 12 pierogi at a time, reducing the heat to a gentle boil; cook for 5 minutes, or until the pierogi float to the surface. Remove with a slotted spoon, drain on paper towels and transfer to a serving dish. Repeat with the remaining pierogi. Serve warm topped with sour cream and sautéed onions.

Bucatini with Tomatoes, Garlic, Butter, and Olive Oil

Makes 6 servings

1 pound bucatini pasta

4 tablespoons extra virgin
   olive oil

4 tablespoons butter

2 cloves garlic, crushed

1 cup halved cherry tomatoes

¼ teaspoon red pepper flakes

Salt and pepper to taste

2 tablespoons chopped flat
   leaf parsley

Prepare the bucatini according to package directions.

Meanwhile, heat the olive oil and butter in a skillet set over medium heat. Add the garlic and sauté until soft, about 5 minutes. Add the tomatoes, red pepper flakes, and salt and pepper, and stir to combine.

When the pasta is ready, drain it and add it to the skillet, tossing to coat the bucatini. Top with parsley to serve.

Ricotta and Spinach Gnocchi with Butter Sauce

Makes 6 servings

Ricotta and Spinach Gnocchi

1 cup ricotta cheese, drained
  of all excess moisture

½ cup frozen spinach,
  thawed and drained of all
  excess moisture

¼ cup grated Parmesan cheese

1 egg

1¼ cups all-purpose flour,
  plus more as needed

⅛ teaspoon freshly
  grated nutmeg

Salt and pepper, to taste

Butter Sauce

¼ pound plus 4 tablespoons
  (1½ sticks) butter

2 cloves garlic, chopped

Red pepper flakes, optional

Seasoned breadcrumbs,
  optional

Parmesan cheese, for garnish

To prepare the gnocchi, combine the ricotta, spinach, Parmesan cheese, egg, flour, and nutmeg. Season with salt and pepper and mix into a smooth dough.

Transfer the dough to a pastry bag fitted with a large tip and pipe ropes of the dough onto a lightly floured surface. Cut the ropes into 1-inch pieces and, using your fingers, shape into gnocchi. Place the gnocchi on a lightly floured kitchen cloth and set aside until ready to use.

Meanwhile, prepare the butter sauce. In a large, heavy skillet set over medium heat, melt the butter and add the garlic, cooking until the garlic is fragrant but not brown, about 6 minutes. Remove from the heat and add the red pepper flakes.

Bring a large pot of salted water to a boil and carefully add the gnocchi in batches. The gnocchi will float to the surface when they are cooked through; it should take 3 to 5 minutes. Transfer the cooked gnocchi to the butter sauce and lightly toss. Add the breadcrumbs and toss. Garnish with Parmesan cheese.

Cheese Super Shells

Makes 8 to 10 servings

1 (10½-ounce) can condensed
  cream of celery soup
4 ounces (1 cup) Cheddar
  cheese, shredded
¼ cup breadcrumbs or
  corn flakes
1 can water-packed tuna,
  drained and flaked
1 pound large pasta shells,
  cooked, drained
4 tablespoons butter
1½ ounces (½ cup) Parmesan
  cheese, grated
½ teaspoon paprika

Preheat the oven to 350°F.

In a saucepan, heat the cream of celery soup over low heat, stirring until smooth. Add the Cheddar cheese and stir until well blended. Stir in the breadcrumbs, then remove from heat. Mix in the tuna.

Toss the cooked pasta shells with the butter. Distribute an even amount of tuna stuffing into each pasta shell. Arrange the stuffed shells on a baking sheet; sprinkle with Parmesan cheese and paprika. Bake for 10 minutes; serve hot.

Swiss Linguine Tart

Chef Michael Hove

Makes 8 servings

¼ pound (1 stick) butter

2 garlic cloves, minced

30 paper-thin French
  bread slices

3 tablespoons all-purpose flour

1 teaspoon salt

¼ teaspoon white pepper

Dash ground nutmeg

2½ cups milk

¾ ounce (¼ cup) Parmesan
  cheese, grated

2 eggs, beaten

8 ounces linguine, cooked
  and drained

8 ounces (2 cups) Swiss
  cheese, shredded

⅓ cup sliced green onion

2 tablespoons minced
  fresh basil

2 plum tomatoes

Preheat the oven to 400°F.

In a large sauté pan, melt 4 tablespoons of butter and sauté the garlic for 1 minute.

Brush a 10-inch pie plate with the butter mixture. Line the bottom and sides of the pie plate with the bread, allowing the bread to come 1 inch over the sides. Brush the bread with the remaining butter mixture. Bake for 5 minutes or until lightly browned. Set aside.

Melt the remaining butter in a saucepan over low heat. Stir in the flour and seasonings. Gradually add the milk and cook, stirring constantly, until the sauce thickens. Remove from the heat and add the Parmesan cheese.

Stir a small amount of sauce into the beaten eggs, then pour the egg mixture into the remaining sauce; stir to combine.

In a large bowl, combine the linguine, 1¼ cups Swiss cheese, green onion, and basil. Pour the sauce over and mix to combine, then pour the entire mixture into the crust.

Cut each tomato lengthwise into eight slices and arrange on the top of the tart. Sprinkle with the remaining Swiss cheese and bake at 350°F. for 25 minutes or until warm. Let stand 5 minutes before serving.

Lasagna with Onion-Parmesan Sauce
(Chicken or Vegetarian)

Makes 16 servings

1 (16-ounce) package curly
  edged dumpling egg noodles,
  cooked and drained

Onion-Parmesan Sauce

6 tablespoons butter

2 large onions, pureed

4 garlic cloves, pureed

6 tablespoons all-purpose flour

2 teaspoons salt

1½ teaspoons pepper

6 cups milk

3 ounces (1 cup) Parmesan
  cheese, grated

Vegetable Lasagna

1 red bell pepper, seeded
  and thinly sliced

4 ounces (1 cup) Swiss cheese,
  shredded

4 ounces (1 cup) provolone
  cheese, shredded

2 carrots, thinly sliced

1 cup broccoli florets

Meat Lasagna

3 skinless, boneless chicken breast halves
  (about 1 pound), cooked and chopped

1½ teaspoons dried tarragon leaves

1 cup (8 ounces) small white mushrooms, sliced

4 ounces (1 cup) sharp Cheddar
  cheese, shredded

4 ounces (1 cup) Monterey Jack
  cheese, shredded

Preheat the oven to 375°F. Lightly butter a 2-quart oven-proof casserole dish.

To make the Onion Parmesan Sauce, heat the butter in a large saucepan over low heat. Add the onions and garlic and sauté for 3 minutes. Stir in the flour, salt, and pepper and cook, stirring constantly, until the sauce is smooth and bubbly. Remove from the heat and stir in the milk. Return to the heat and bring to a boil, stirring constantly. Boil and stir for 1 minute until thickened. Remove from heat again and stir in the Parmesan. Set aside.

To make Vegetable Lasagna, layer just enough noodles to cover the bottom of the casserole. Top the noodles with slices of bell pepper, ¼ cup each of Swiss and provolone, and ¾ cup of Onion Parmesan Sauce. Top with another layer of noodles, sliced carrots, ¼ cup each of Swiss and provolone, and ¾ cup sauce. Repeat layers, finishing with sauce. Bake for 40 minutes, until bubbly and golden.

To make Meat Lasagna, layer just enough noodles to cover bottom of casserole. Top the noodles with one chopped chicken breast half. Sprinkle ½ teaspoon of tarragon over the chicken and one-third of the mushrooms. Add ¼ cup each Cheddar and Jack cheese and ¾ cup Onion Parmesan Sauce. Repeat the layers, finishing with the sauce. Bake for 40 minutes, until bubbly and golden.

NOTE: This lasagna can be frozen, just after assembly and before baking: wrap the casserole dish with plastic, then foil and freeze. Bake frozen at 400°F. for about 1 to 1¼ hours.

Four Cheese Mostaccioli Vegetable Lasagna

Makes 8 servings

1 (16-ounce) package frozen broccoli, cauliflower, and carrot blend, thawed and drained

6 tablespoons butter

1 red bell pepper, chopped

½ cup chopped onion

2 garlic cloves, minced

¼ cup all-purpose flour

¼ teaspoon nutmeg

¼ teaspoon salt

2 cups milk

16 ounces (2 cups) ricotta cheese

1½ ounces (½ cup) Parmesan cheese, shredded

¼ cup fresh basil leaves, minced, or 1 teaspoon dried basil leaves, crumbled

6 ounces (1½ cups) mozzarella cheese, shredded

4 ounces (1 cup) provolone cheese, shredded

3 cups mostaccioli pasta, cooked and drained

Preheat the oven to 350°F.

Chop the broccoli, cauliflower, and carrot blend coarsely; set aside.

Melt the butter over low to medium heat in a medium sauce pan. Stir in the bell pepper, onion, and garlic. Sauté for 4 to 5 minutes, then add the flour, nutmeg, and salt and cook for 2 minutes. Gradually add the milk and cook, stirring, until the mixture is thick and comes to a boil. Remove from heat.

In a separate bowl, combine the ricotta cheese, Parmesan cheese, and basil.

In an additional bowl, combine the mozzarella and provolone cheese.

Arrange half of the mostaccioli in a single layer in the bottom of an 12 x 8-inch baking dish. Top with half of the white sauce mixture, all of the ricotta mixture, all of the vegetable mixture and ½ of the mozzarella mixture; press down lightly. Top with the remaining mostaccioli in single layer, remaining white sauce, and remaining mozzarella mixture. Bake for 40 to 45 minutes or until hot and bubbly. Let stand 10 minutes before serving.

Cheesy Pasta with Vegetables

Makes 4 servings

4 tablespoons butter

4 cups sliced onions

3 tablespoons lemon juice

1 teaspoon hot pepper sauce

Salt, to taste

2 cups sliced mushrooms

1½ cups fresh or frozen snow
   peas, or frozen peas, thawed

1½ cups cherry tomatoes

3 cups (8 ounces) dry fusilli
   (corkscrew) pasta, cooked

5 ounces (1¼ cups) Bel Paese
   cheese or Muenster cheese,
   shredded and chilled

2 tablespoons chopped parsley

Melt the butter over medium-low heat in a 10-inch skillet. Add the onions and cook for about 2 to 3 minutes, or until the onions are soft and pale gold; do not brown. Stir in the lemon juice, pepper sauce, and salt; cover and set aside.

Add the mushrooms, peas, and tomatoes to the onion mixture. Cover and set over medium-low heat, tossing once or twice, until the vegetables are heated through.

Pour the pasta into a serving platter. Cover with the hot vegetable mixture and scatter cheese over top. Sprinkle with parsley and serve.

Farmhouse Supper

Makes 8 servings

½ cup beer

4 tablespoons unsalted butter

6 tablespoons all-purpose flour

1 teaspoon salt

½ teaspoon paprika

¼ teaspoon black pepper

¼ teaspoon cayenne pepper

2 cups milk

1 (12-ounce) can
evaporated milk

4 ounces (1 cup) sharp aged
Cheddar cheese, shredded

4 ounces (1 cup) Gouda
cheese, shredded

4 ounces (1 cup) Baby Swiss
cheese, shredded

2 tablespoons coarse
ground mustard

1 pound mostaccioli pasta,
cooked and drained

¾ pound lightly smoked ham,
julienned

1½ cups seeded,
diced plum tomatoes

Preheat the oven to 350°F. Butter a 3-quart casserole dish.

Simmer the beer in a small saucepan over medium heat for 3 minutes, or until reduced by half; set aside.

Melt the butter in a large saucepan over low heat. Stir in the flour, salt, paprika, black pepper, and cayenne pepper. Cook for 2 minutes, stirring constantly. Gradually add the milk, evaporated milk, and reserved beer. Cook, stirring constantly, until thickened. Remove from the heat, add the cheeses and mustard, stirring until the cheese melts.

In large bowl, combine the mostaccioli, ham, and tomatoes. Add the sauce and mix well. Pour into the prepared casserole dish and bake for 25 minutes or until heated through.

Vegetable Frittata

Makes 4 servings

3 tablespoons butter

1 yellow onion, thinly sliced

1 to 2 zucchini, cut into
¼-inch dice (to yield 1 cup),
blanched

1 small garlic clove, chopped

¼ cup chopped tomatoes

1 tablespoon fresh basil, torn

4 eggs

¼ cup heavy cream

Salt and pepper, to taste

¼ cup grated Parmesan cheese

Preheat the oven to 350°F.

In a skillet set over medium heat, melt 2 tablespoons of the butter and sauté the onions, zucchini, and garlic until tender, about 6 minutes. Remove from the heat and add the tomatoes and basil.

In a large bowl, whisk the eggs with the heavy cream and season with salt and pepper. Add half of the Parmesan cheese and stir to incorporate. Stir the sautéed vegetables into the egg mixture and pour into a buttered 9-inch round baking pan.

Bake for 20 minutes or until the frittata is set and golden brown. Remove from the oven and flip onto a serving platter. Garnish with the remaining parmesan cheese.

Fettuccini Alfredo

Makes 6 servings

1 (16-ounce) package
  Fettuccini noodles

1½ ounces (½ cup) Parmesan
  cheese, grated

1½ ounces (½ cup) Romano
  cheese, grated

½ pound (2 sticks)
  butter, melted

1 cup heavy cream

¼ teaspoon nutmeg

¼ teaspoon garlic powder,
  optional

Freshly ground black pepper

Grated Parmesan cheese,
  for serving

Cook the fettuccini according to the package directions.

Meanwhile, combine the remaining ingredients in a large skillet set over medium-high heat and cook for 5 to 7 minutes until thoroughly warmed and thickened.

Drain the pasta and toss with the sauce. Serve with additional Parmesan cheese.

Pasta Primavera

Makes 4 servings

6 tablespoons butter

1 cup diagonally-cut
 carrot slices

1 cup yellow summer
 squash slices

2 cups mushroom quarters

1 cup Chinese pea pod halves

¼ cup sliced green onion

1 tablespoon chopped fresh
 basil, or 1 teaspoon dried
 basil leaves

8 ounces fettuccini, cooked
 and kept warm

8 ounces (1 cup) low fat or
 small curd cottage cheese

¾ ounce (¼ cup) Parmesan
 cheese, grated

Salt and pepper, to taste

In a large skillet, melt 4 tablespoons of butter and sauté the carrots for 5 minutes. Add the squash and continue cooking for 2 minutes. Add the mushrooms, pea pods, and green onion and continue cooking until the vegetables are tender, about 5 minutes. Stir in the basil.

Combine the fettuccini and 2 tablespoons of butter; toss until butter is melted. Toss in the cottage cheese and Parmesan cheese. Place the fettuccini on a serving platter and top with the vegetable mixture. Season to taste.

Jalapeño Jack and Sausage Pasta Bake

Makes 8 servings

1 pound penne, mostaccioli,
   or rotini pasta, uncooked

¼ pound (1 stick) butter

1 green bell pepper, diced

3 garlic cloves, minced

⅓ cup all-purpose flour

4 cups milk

1 teaspoon salt

12 ounces (3 cups) Jalapeño
   Monterey Jack cheese,
   shredded

1 pound cooked kielbasa or
   summer sausage,
   cut into ½-inch chunks

½ cup dried breadcrumbs

Paprika, optional

Preheat the oven to 350°F. Butter a 13 x 9-inch baking dish.

Cook the pasta according to package directions.

Meanwhile, melt 6 tablespoons of butter in a large saucepan. Add the bell pepper and garlic and cook for 5 minutes, stirring occasionally. Add the flour and cook, stirring, for 1 minute. Add the milk and salt; bring to a simmer and simmer uncovered for 2 minutes, stirring frequently. Remove from the heat and stir in 2 cups of cheese.

Drain the pasta and return it to the pot. Add the cheese sauce and sausage; mix well. Transfer to the prepared baking dish; top with remaining 1 cup cheese. Melt the reserved 2 tablespoons of butter and toss with the breadcrumbs. Spoon over the pasta and sprinkle with paprika. Bake for 30 to 35 minutes or until the sauce is bubbly and the breadcrumbs are golden brown

---

DID YOU KNOW?
Americans consume more than 4 pounds of butter per person per year.

Polenta Fontina "Paninis" with Mushroom Sauce

Makes 4 servings

2 tablespoons unsalted butter

⅓ cup minced shallots or onion

8 ounces mixed exotic
mushrooms, sliced, or sliced
cremini or button mushrooms

1 tablespoon chopped thyme,
or 1 teaspoon dried thyme

¾ teaspoon salt

¼ teaspoon freshly ground
black pepper

4 ounces (1 cup) fontina
cheese, shredded

¼ cup sun-dried tomatoes in
oil, chopped and drained

1 (16-ounce) tube polenta,
cut crosswise into
16 (⅓-inch) slices

Melt 1 tablespoon of butter in a small skillet over medium heat. Add the shallots and cook, stirring, for 3 minutes. Stir in the mushrooms, thyme, salt, and pepper and cook, stirring continuously, for 5 minutes, or until the mushrooms are tender. Set aside.

Meanwhile, combine ½ cup of cheese with the tomatoes.

Heat the remaining 1 tablespoon of butter on a large nonstick griddle over medium heat until melted and bubbly. Arrange 8 slices of polenta on the skillet. Top each slice with some of the cheese and tomato mixture, then top with the remaining 8 slices of polenta. Cook for 3 minutes, then carefully turn the sandwiches over and continue cooking for 3 minutes, or until the cheese is melted.

Transfer the paninis to four serving plates and top with mushroom sauce and the remaining cheese.

Sauerkraut Strudel

Makes 6 servings

---

27 ounces sauerkraut, drained
and squeezed dry

1 smoked pork chop, boned
and diced

4 ounces (1 cup) Swiss cheese,
shredded

8 sheets phyllo dough, thawed,
or 1 batch of strudel dough
(recipe follows)

¼ pound (1 stick) butter,
melted

½ cup dry breadcrumbs

Sour cream, for garnish

Preheat the oven to 400°F.

Combine the sauerkraut, pork, and Swiss cheese.

Brush one sheet of phyllo dough with butter and sprinkle with 1 tablespoon breadcrumbs. Repeat layering with three more sheets of dough. Place half of the sauerkraut mixture along one short edge of the dough, and roll up into a log.

Perform these steps again with the remaining dough and sauerkraut mixture, forming another log.

Brush a 15 x 10-inch baking pan with butter. Place the strudel logs on the pan, seam side down, and brush with more butter. Bake for 30 minutes or until golden brown.

To serve, cut each log into slices and garnish with sour cream.

Feta and Mushroom Strudel with Horseradish-Tomato Salsa

Makes 6 servings

Horseradish-Tomato Salsa

2 medium tomatoes, quartered

½ yellow bell pepper, chopped

1 small onion, chopped

2 garlic cloves

3 tablespoons horseradish

¾ cup olive oil

½ cup fresh basil or
   3 tablespoons pesto

1 teaspoon salt

Feta and Mushroom Strudel

1 tablespoon olive oil

½ cup chopped onion or leek

3 cups sliced mushrooms

Salt and pepper

3 cups (5 ounces) fresh spinach

5 sheets phyllo dough, thawed

¼ pound (1 stick) unsalted
   butter, melted

4 ounces (1 cup) feta cheese

To make the Horseradish-Tomato Salsa, process all of the ingredients in a food processor until smooth. Cover, then chill until ready to serve.

To make the Feta and Mushroom Strudel, heat the oil in a large skillet, then add the onion and sauté for 1 minute. Add the mushrooms and cook on high heat until any liquid evaporates. Season with salt and pepper; cool.

Preheat the oven to 400°F.

Blanch the spinach for 30 seconds in boiling water, then douse it in ice water until cold. Drain and squeeze until dry and set aside.

Lay 1 sheet of phyllo on a towel; brush lightly with butter. Top with another sheet of phyllo; brush lightly with butter. Repeat with remaining 3 sheets phyllo.

Along the bottom of the long end of the phyllo rectangle, form a line of spinach. Next form a line of mushroom mixture; then a line of feta cheese. Use the towel to roll the dough away from you, encasing the filling. Brush the outside with butter and bake on a baking sheet for 18 to 20 minutes, or until golden and cooked through. Cool for 15 to 20 minutes before serving.

Spanokopetes

Makes 6 servings

6 green onions, chopped

4 tablespoons butter

2 (10-ounce) packages frozen
   spinach, thawed

16 ounces (4 cups) feta cheese

12 ounces (1½ cups)
   cottage cheese

2 eggs, beaten

¼ cup chopped parsley

1 tablespoon dill weed

1 pound frozen phyllo
   dough, thawed

½ pound (2 sticks) butter,
   melted

Preheat the oven to 425°F. Lightly grease a 13 x 9-inch baking dish.

Sauté the green onions in the butter until tender. Add the spinach and simmer until almost all of the liquid evaporates. Set aside.

Crumble the feta cheese into a large bowl. Add the cottage cheese, eggs, parsley, and dill. Mix well. Add the spinach mixture and mix until thoroughly blended.

Layer half of phyllo dough in the prepared baking dish, brushing each layer with melted butter. Spread the cheese mixture evenly over top the phyllo. Repeat layering with the remaining phyllo, brushing each sheet with butter. Bake for 25 minutes, then allow to stand for 10 minutes before serving.

4 ounces (½ cup packed)
  Gorgonzola cheese,
  at room temperature
3 eggs
¾ cup all-purpose flour
¼ teaspoon salt
½ cup white wine
½ cup club soda
5 tablespoons butter, melted
2 Granny Smith apples,
  cored and sliced
Melted butter, for cooking
Bacon and/or ham, for serving

Combine the Gorgonzola, eggs, flour, salt, wine, club soda and 2 tablespoons of butter in the pitcher of a blender and blend until smooth. Let the batter stand for about 1 hour.

Meanwhile, pour the remaining 3 tablespoons of butter into a large skillet set over medium-high heat. Add the apple slices and sauté until the apples are tender. Set aside.

Heat a 6-inch seasoned crepe pan or a nonstick skillet over medium heat. Brush with additional melted butter. Swirl a scant 3 tablespoons of batter in the pan to make a 6-inch crepe. Cook until lightly browned, turning once. Repeat with remaining batter, brushing the pan with butter as needed. Stack the crepes and keep warm.

Fill the crepes with apple slices and serve with crisp bacon or slivers of ham for a light supper or hearty brunch.

Fontina and Asiago Cheese Wellington

Makes 8 servings

4 ounces Shiitake mushrooms, stems removed, sliced

2 tablespoons butter

1 boneless and skinless chicken breast (2 halves)

2 eggs

1½ cups heavy cream

3 ounces (¾ cup) Asiago cheese, grated

¼ teaspoon salt

⅛ teaspoon white pepper

8 ounces spinach

2 tablespoons olive oil

1 (17½-ounce) package frozen phyllo dough, thawed

3 ounces (¾ cup) fontina cheese, cut into 4-inch wide slices

Preheat the oven to 400°F.

Sauté mushrooms in the butter and set aside.

Cut the breast into 1-inch pieces. Place the chicken pieces and 1 egg into the bowl of a food processor fitted with a steel blade and process until puréed. With the food processor still running, gradually add the cream and process until smooth. Place the mixture in a bowl and stir in the Asiago cheese, mushrooms, salt, and pepper. Cover with plastic wrap and chill.

Sauté the spinach in olive oil for 5 to 7 minutes, or until wilted. Squeeze any excess moisture from the spinach and set aside.

Beat the remaining egg.

Lay one sheet of phyllo dough on a lightly floured surface and brush with egg. Lay a second sheet of puff pastry on top and, using a rolling pin, roll the sheets to a 16 x 14-inch rectangle. Fit the pastry into a lightly greased 9 x 5-inch loaf pan, leaving a 2-inch overhang on all sides. Brush the pastry with egg, then spread one-third of the chicken mixture into the pastry-lined pan. Layer half of the spinach down the center of the chicken mixture, leaving a ½-inch border along the long sides of the pan.

Layer fontina cheese on top of the spinach and cover with the remaining spinach. Spread the remaining chicken mixture over all and brush with egg.

Fold the excess pastry over the chicken mixture, sealing completely. Brush with egg and bake for 35 minutes. Unmold onto a baking sheet, brush again with egg, and continue baking for 10 minutes or until golden brown. Let stand for 10 minutes before cutting.

Sour Cream Onion Pie

Makes 8 servings

3 medium onions, thinly sliced

6 tablespoons butter

2 tablespoons all-purpose flour

2 cups sour cream

¼ cup pitted ripe olives,
   drained and sliced,
   plus more for garnish

3 eggs, slightly beaten

1 teaspoon Worcestershire
   sauce

½ teaspoon paprika

Salt and pepper to taste

1 (9-inch) pie shell, baked

Preheat the oven to 350°F.

Sauté the onions in the butter until tender. Sprinkle the flour over the onions and cook for 1 to 2 minutes, stirring occasionally.

In a separate bowl, combine the sour cream, olives, eggs, Worcestershire sauce, paprika, and salt and pepper. Stir the sour cream mixture into the onion mixture, then pour into the baked pastry shell. Bake for 30 to 40 minutes or until the filling is firm and golden. Remove from the oven and let stand for 10 minutes. Serve garnished with olive slices.

Pronto Cheeseburger Pie

Makes 6 servings

Crust

4 tablespoons butter

1 pound frozen hash
  browns with onion and
  bell pepper, thawed

½ teaspoon salt

½ teaspoon cumin

⅛ teaspoon pepper

4 ounces (1 cup) Cheddar
  cheese, shredded

1 egg, slightly beaten

Filling

1 tablespoon butter

1 small onion, chopped

½ bell pepper, chopped

1 pound ground chuck

1 tablespoon all-purpose flour

1 tablespoon water

1 (8-ounce) can tomato sauce

½ teaspoon seasoned salt

Dash pepper

1 whole pimento, cut in strips

4 olives, sliced

Preheat the oven to 350°F.

Melt the butter in a large skillet set over medium-high heat; add the hash browns and cook, stirring occasionally, until tender and lightly browned. Remove from the heat and stir in the salt, cumin, pepper, and ¼ cup of cheese. Cool for about 3 minutes, then stir in the egg.

Press the mixture into an 8- or 9-inch pie pan to form a shell. Bake for 5 minutes.

Meanwhile, make the filling. Heat the butter in a skillet over medium heat, then add the onion and bell pepper and cook until the onion is golden brown, about 5 to 10 minutes. Stir in the beef and cook until browned, about 8 to 10 minutes.

In a small bowl, combine the flour and water, then add this mixture to the meat along with the tomato sauce, seasoned salt, and pepper. Cook and stir until thickened.

Fill the hot potato shell with the meat mixture and sprinkle the remaining cheese over top. Garnish with pimento strips and olives. Return the pie to the oven and bake until the cheese melts, about 5 to 10 minutes. Remove from the oven and let stand 2 to 3 minutes before serving.

Salisbury Steak

Makes 5 servings

1½ pounds ground beef

1½ teaspoons seasoned salt

2 teaspoons finely minced
   yellow onion

1 egg, beaten

½ teaspoon paprika

4 tablespoons butter, melted

Preheat the oven to 450°F.

In a large mixing bowl, combine the beef, salt, onion, egg, and paprika, mixing lightly. Mold the meat into an oblong or meatloaf shape on a buttered baking sheet. Brush the top and sides of the loaf with butter and bake for 10 minutes. Reduce the heat to 325°F. and bake an additional 25 minutes, brushing with butter twice during cooking.

Old-Fashioned Beef Hash

Makes 4 servings

4 tablespoons butter,
   plus more as needed

½ cup chopped onion

1 garlic clove, chopped

1 cup boiling water

2 cups cooked, chopped roast
   beef or pot roast

3 cups cooked, chopped,
   chilled potatoes

1 teaspoon salt

1 teaspoon pepper

Melt the butter in a large skillet set over medium heat and add the onion and garlic. Sauté until the onion is tender, about 5 minutes.

Add the water, meat, and potatoes, and spread them evenly in the pan. Cook, covered, for 15 minutes until the mixture is browned on the bottom. Using a large spatula, flip the hash and cook an additional 10 minutes until the bottom is browned. Add additional butter if needed. Season with salt and pepper.

Beef Stroganoff

Makes 6 servings

3 tablespoons butter

2 pounds lean sirloin steak

2 onions, sliced thin

1 pound mushrooms, sliced

1 tablespoon all-purpose flour

½ teaspoon paprika

¼ teaspoon pepper

Dash cayenne pepper

1 cup plain yogurt

Egg noodles or rice,
   cooked, for serving

Heat **2 tablespoons** of butter in a large heavy frying pan set over high heat. Cut the beef across the grain into narrow strips and add, along with the onions, to the pan. Cook a few minutes, turning the meat to brown on all sides.

Lower the heat and add the mushrooms; cook, covered, for 10 minutes. Remove the meat, onions, and mushrooms from the pan and set aside.

To the pan juices, add the remaining 1 tablespoon of butter and stir in the flour, paprika, pepper, and cayenne pepper. Slowly pour in the yogurt, stirring constantly. Add the meat mixture and heat only until hot. Serve with noodles or rice.

Hamburger Stroganoff Platter

Makes 6 servings

½ pound bacon, diced

1 pound lean ground beef

1 cup chopped onion

Salt and pepper

1 (10¾-ounce) can
  cream of chicken soup

1 (10¾-ounce) can
  cream of mushroom soup

1 (4 ounces) can
  button mushrooms, drained

1 cup sour cream

2 cups dried egg noodles

4 tablespoons butter, melted

2 tablespoons poppy seeds

In a large sauté pan set over medium heat, cook the bacon until it is crisp; drain on paper towels. Pour off the bacon drippings, leaving 1 tablespoon in the pan. Add the ground beef and onion and cook until the beef is browned, about 5 to 7 minutes. Add salt and pepper to taste, then stir in the soups and mushrooms. Cook over low heat, stirring until mixture is bubbly. Remove from the heat and stir in the sour cream and heat thoroughly, do not boil.

Cook noodles in boiling, salted water until tender. Drain. Add butter and poppy seeds to noodles, toss lightly. Place noodles around outer edge of a large heated platter. Pour meat mixture into center. Garnish with bacon.

Shish Kebabs with Blue Cheese Butter

Shish Kebabs

2 tablespoons butter

4 small onions, peeled
and halved

1 pound beef sirloin,
cut in ¾-inch cubes

2 whole small tomatoes, cored
and cut in thirds

8 whole mushroom caps

1 medium bell pepper,
cut in eighths

2 cups olive oil

¼ cup lemon juice

2 garlic cloves, minced

Blue Cheese Butter

½ pound (2 sticks) butter,
at room temperature

5 ounces (1 cup) crumbled
blue cheese

1 tablespoon grated
lemon zest

In a skillet set over medium heat, heat the butter and sauté the onions until golden brown. Alternately arrange on skewers equal amounts of onions, beef, tomatoes, mushrooms, and bell peppers. Place the skewers in a long, shallow pan.

In a small bowl, whisk together the oil, lemon juice, and garlic, then pour over the skewers, cover with plastic wrap, and let stand in the refrigerator overnight.

To make the Blue Cheese Butter, cream the butter using an electric mixer. Blend in the blue cheese and lemon zest. Do not over blend. Refrigerate until ready to use.

When you're ready to continue, grill the skewers over hot coals or underneath a broiler for 10 to 15 minutes, depending on desired doneness. Serve with blue cheese butter.

Sautéed Steak with Wild Mushroom Butter

Chef Jill Prescott
Makes 4 servings

Wild Mushroom Butter

½ pound (2 sticks) unsalted
   butter, at room temperature

6 shallots, diced

1 cup finely chopped wild
   mushrooms, such as
   shiitake, cremini, porcini,
   or white button mushrooms

1 teaspoon fresh thyme
   leaves, chopped

1 teaspoon fine sea salt

10 grinds tellicherry pepper

Steaks

4 (6- or 8-ounce) tenderloin
   filets (1½ to 2 inches thick)
   or New York strip steaks,
   at room temperature

Sea salt and freshly
   ground pepper

Clarified butter and olive oil

To make the Mushroom Butter, heat 4 tablespoons of butter in a small sauté pan over medium heat. Add the shallots and cook until softened, about 1 to 2 minutes. Add the mushrooms and thyme, and cook until the mushrooms are just beginning to brown, about 4 to 5 minutes. Remove from the heat and cool.

Blend in the remaining butter, salt, and pepper.

Place the butter mixture on a sheet of waxed paper and roll into a log approximately 8 inches long and 2 inches in diameter. Set aside if using immediately. Otherwise, chill in the freezer, in plastic freezer bags, or in the refrigerator. Before using the butter, bring it to room temperature.

To make the steaks, preheat the oven to 450°F. Pat the steaks dry with paper towels and season with salt and pepper.

Heat a large sauté pan over high heat. Add a combination of clarified butter and olive oil to cover the bottom of the pan, about ⅛-inch deep. Arrange the steaks so they are not touching one another; leaving at least 1 inch between each steak. Sear one side of the steak for approximately 1 to 2 minutes, or until browned. Repeat with the other side.

Place the steaks on a rack in a roasting pan and finish in the oven to desired doneness. For medium-rare steaks, cook them for approximately 6 to 8 minutes. Medium-well steaks take about 10 to 12 minutes.

Remove the steaks from the pan and allow to rest for 10 minutes under a piece of foil paper.

To serve, cut four 1-inch disks out of the butter log. (Refrigerate the rest.) Place the pats of butter on top of the hot, finished steaks and serve immediately.

Peppered Steak with Red Wine Butter and Gorgonzola Potato Gratin

Adapted from Chef John McReynolds,
Café LaHaye, Sonoma, California

Makes 12 servings

Red Wine Butter

2 cups beef stock

2 cups dry red wine

1 tablespoon tomato paste

½ pound (2 sticks) butter,
   at room temperature

Gorgonzola Potato Gratin

3 cups heavy cream

4 garlic cloves, chopped

3 teaspoons kosher salt

¼ teaspoon ground nutmeg

2 tablespoons butter

10 to 12 large Russet potatoes
   (4 pounds), peeled and
   sliced thin

1 pound Gorgonzola cheese,
   crumbled

Peppered Steak

12 (8-ounce) Filet Mignon steaks

Salt, as needed

2 tablespoons coarsely ground black pepper

2 tablespoons whole dried lavender
   blossoms, optional

6 tablespoons olive oil

2 tablespoons unsalted butter

To make the Red Wine Butter, combine the stock, wine, and tomato paste in a heavy saucepan. Heat to boiling and cook until reduced to ¾ cup, about 1 hour. Cool to room temperature, then whisk in the butter. Chill the mixture, wrap in plastic wrap, and shape into a log. Chill until ready to use.

To make the Gorgonzola Potato Gratin, mix the cream, garlic, salt, and nutmeg in a bowl. Let stand at room temperature for at least 1 hour, or up to 4 hours refrigerated. Strain and set aside.

Preheat the oven to 375°F. Generously butter a 13 x 9-inch baking dish.

Spread half of the potatoes into the prepared pan. Reserve ½ cup of the Gorgonzola for garnish. Sprinkle half of the remaining Gorgonzola over the potatoes. Cover with the remaining potatoes and then the remaining half of the cheese. Pour the garlic cream over and bake for 1 hour to 1 hour and 15 minutes, or until the potatoes are tender.

To make the steaks, season both sides of each steak with salt. Mix the pepper and lavender together, then press the mixture onto both sides of the steaks.

In large cast iron frying pan set over high heat, heat the oil and butter until the butter melts. Add the steaks and sear for about 2 minutes on each side. Transfer the pan to a 400°F. oven and roast for about 5 minutes for medium-rare steak, longer if desired. When the steaks are done, set them aside to rest under a tent of foil.

To serve, spoon Gorgonzola Potato Gratin onto a plate and sprinkle with reserved cheese. Place a steak on a plate and top with 1 tablespoon Red Wine Butter.

Tamale Pie

Filling

2 tablespoons butter

1 large onion, chopped

1 pound ground beef

¾ cup chopped bell pepper

¾ cup diced celery

1 cup canned corn, drained

2 teaspoons ground cumin

1 teaspoon cayenne pepper

Crust

3 egg yolks

4 tablespoons butter, melted

2 cups cornmeal

1 cup plain yogurt

Dash of salt

6 ounces (1½ cups) Asadero or
   Queso Quesadilla cheese,
   shredded

To make the filling, melt the butter in a heavy frying pan. Add the onion and ground beef, and cook, stirring, until the beef is browned. Add the bell pepper, celery, corn, cumin, and cayenne pepper. Stir well until thoroughly mixed and heated through. Set aside off the heat.

Preheat the oven to 350°F. and butter a 2-quart casserole dish.

To make the crust, beat the egg yolks with the melted butter. Stir in the cornmeal, yogurt, and salt. Spread half the mixture in the prepared casserole dish. Bake for 10 minutes, then remove from the oven and spread the filling over the baked crust. Sprinkle cheese on top, then pour over the remaining cornmeal mixture. Return to the oven and bake until the top crust is browned and the mixture is hot, about 20 to 25 minutes.

Veal Parmigiana

Makes 6 servings

5 tablespoons butter

1 medium onion, chopped

1 garlic clove, finely chopped

2 pounds tomatoes, peeled
and diced, or 1 (26-ounce)
can whole, peeled tomatoes,
drained

Salt and pepper

6 lean (4-ounce) veal cutlets

2 tablespoons all-purpose flour

Rosemary, to taste

Sage, to taste

¾ cup dry white wine

8 ounces (2 cups) provolone
cheese, shredded

6 ounces (2 cups) Parmesan
cheese, grated

Preheat the oven to 350°F.

Melt 2 tablespoons of butter in a large skillet over medium-high heat. Sauté the onion and garlic for 4 minutes, or until transparent. Add the tomatoes, season with salt and pepper, then reduce the heat and simmer for about 10 minutes.

Coat the cutlets evenly with the flour and season with the salt, pepper, rosemary, and sage.

Melt the remaining 3 tablespoons of butter in another large skillet over medium heat. Add the cutlets and cook, about 3 to 4 minutes, turning once, until browned.

Place the cutlets in a shallow 2-quart baking dish, add the wine and tomato mixture, and top with provolone and Parmesan cheese. Bake for 25 minutes or until the cheeses melt.

Stuffed Veal Rolls

Makes 5 servings

1½ pounds boneless veal
   steaks or cutlets

¼ cup flour

1 teaspoon salt

Pepper to taste

1 cup diced celery

1 small garlic clove, chopped

4 tablespoons butter

3 cups fresh breadcrumbs

1 cup chicken stock

½ teaspoon dried sage

Lightly pound out the cutlets until they are relatively thin (about ⅛ inch). Dredge one side of the veal in flour seasoned with salt and pepper. Set aside.

In a large skillet set over medium heat, sauté the celery and garlic in 2 tablespoons of butter until tender. Add the breadcrumbs, tossing to coat, and remove from the heat.

Add ½ cup of chicken stock and the sage and mix well.

Place 1½ tablespoons of stuffing on each piece of veal and roll the meat over the stuffing; secure with toothpicks. Brown the veal rolls with the remaining butter in the skillet set over medium heat. Add the remaining stock, cover the pan, and lower the heat to low. Let simmer for about 45 minutes, until the meat is tender.

Scaloppini del Pastore

Makes 4 servings

---

4 tablespoons butter

2 tablespoons all-purpose flour

1 (10½-ounce) can condensed
  beef stock

4 ounces (1 cup) Parmesan
  cheese, grated

2 tablespoons chopped parsley

8 (2-ounce) veal cutlet pieces

8 thin slices prosciutto

4 ounces (1 cup)
  fontina cheese

¼ cup oil

½ cup all-purpose flour

2 cups mushroom slices

½ cup dry white wine

In a small saucepan set over medium heat, brown 2 tablespoons of butter. Add the flour and cook for 2 minutes. Gradually add the stock and cook, stirring constantly, until thickened. Set aside.

Combine the Parmesan cheese and parsley, then sprinkle the mixture over each piece of veal. Wrap each veal piece with a slice of Proscuitto. Cut the fontina cheese into sticks just smaller than the width of the veal. Place one stick width-wise across each piece of veal and roll up the veal. Secure the ends and sides with toothpicks, enclosing the cheese.

Warm the oil in a large skillet set over medium heat. Coat the veal with the flour and brown in the oil, about 3 to 4 minutes. Remove from the skillet and drain the oil. Remove the toothpicks.

In the same skillet over medium-high heat, sauté the mushrooms in the remaining 2 tablespoons of butter. Add the wine and simmer for 2 minutes. Stir in the stock mixture and the veal and simmer for 5 minutes, stirring occasionally.

Pork Enchiladas

Makes 6 servings

4 dried Anaheim or
  New Mexico chiles,
  stemmed and seeded

½ cup boiling water

1 cup orange juice

1 teaspoon salt

½ teaspoon ground cumin

¼ teaspoon dried
  oregano leaves

2 garlic cloves

1½ pounds boneless pork,
  cut into 3 or 4 chunks

3 tablespoons butter

1 cup milk

1 (4-ounce) can diced
  green chiles

2 tablespoons all-purpose flour

8 ounces (2 cups) Asadero
  cheese or Monterey Jack
  cheese, shredded

12 burrito-size (about
  10 inches) flour tortillas

Soak the chiles in the water for 20 minutes. In a blender or food processor, purée the chiles, orange juice, salt, cumin, oregano, and garlic; set aside.

In a large saucepan, brown the pork in 1 tablespoon of butter. Add the chile sauce and heat to a boil. Cover, reduce the heat, and simmer for 1½ to 2 hours or until the pork is tender. Shred the pork and return it to the saucepan.

In a blender or food processor, purée the milk and green chiles; set aside.

In a small saucepan set over medium heat, melt the remaining 2 tablespoons butter. Stir in the flour and cook for 1 minute. Gradually stir in the milk mixture and cook, stirring, until the mixture thickens and begins to boil. Stir in 1 cup of cheese.

Preheat the oven to 350°F. Spread ½ cup of the cheese sauce in the bottom of a greased 13 x 9 x 2-inch baking pan; set aside.

Spoon ¼ cup of the pork mixture down the center of each tortilla; roll up and place seam-down in the pan. Pour the remaining cheese sauce over the filled tortillas. Sprinkle with remaining cheese. Cover with foil and bake for 30 minutes. Uncover and bake for 15 minutes more or until hot and bubbly.

Tangy Yogurt Chops

Makes 6 servings

4 tablespoons butter

6 loin pork chops

2 large onions, sliced

½ pound fresh mushrooms,
   cleaned and sliced

1 tablespoon paprika

1 (14-ounce) can
   sliced tomatoes

1½ teaspoons salt

¼ teaspoon marjoram

1 small bay leaf

2 tablespoons all-purpose flour

¼ cup water

1 cup plain yogurt

Noodles or rice, cooked,
   for serving

Melt 2 tablespoons of butter over medium heat in a large, heavy frying pan. Brown the pork chops on both sides, about 3 to 4 minutes, and remove from pan.

Add the remaining butter and the onions to the pan and cook until the onions are tender and transparent. Add the mushrooms and paprika and cook for 2 minutes. Stir in the tomatoes, salt, marjoram, and bay leaf. Return the pork chops to the sauce, raise the heat and bring the sauce to a boil.

Reduce the heat, cover the pan, and simmer for 1 hour. Remove the pork chops and keep them warm. Discard the bay leaf.

In a small bowl, combine the flour and water until smooth. Gradually stir this slurry into the sauce and cook until thickened. Remove the pan from the heat and stir in the yogurt.

To serve, spoon the sauce over the pork chops. Serve with noodles or rice.

Stuffed Pork Loin

Makes 8 servings

4 tablespoons butter

½ pound fresh mushrooms, trimmed and sliced

½ cup chopped onion

3 cups cooked long grain and wild rice

¼ cup chopped parsley

1 teaspoon salt

¼ teaspoon pepper

8 ounces (2 cups) Swiss cheese, diced

1 (5- to 7-pound) pork loin

Preheat the oven to 325°F.

In a large frying pan set over medium heat, melt the butter and sauté the mushrooms and onion. Stir in the rice, parsley, salt, pepper, and cheese. Set aside.

With a sharp knife, cut 6 to 10 deep pockets over each rib bone in the pork loin. Fill the pockets with the stuffing mixture.

Place the loin, pocket openings up, in a roasting pan. Bake for 35 minutes per pound, or until a meat thermometer registers 170°F. Carve by slicing between the rib bones. Place any leftover stuffing in a lightly buttered baking dish and bake with the roast during the last half hour of baking time.

DID YOU KNOW?
Butter is produced essentially the same way it was thousands of years ago. Made by churning fresh cream until the fats separate from the liquid (buttermilk), butter is one of the most highly concentrated forms of fluid milk.

Roasted Chicken

Makes 4 servings

5 tablespoons butter,
  at room temperature

1 tablespoon chopped
  fresh marjoram

2 tablespoons fresh thyme

2 tablespoons chopped
  fresh parsley

1½ teaspoon kosher salt

1 (4-pound) roasting chicken

4 sage leaves

Freshly ground black pepper

Preheat the oven to 425°F.

In a small bowl, combine the butter, marjoram, thyme, 1 tablespoon parsley, and 1 teaspoon salt and set aside.

Using your fingers, carefully separate the skin at the chicken breast from the flesh and spoon in a teaspoon of the butter mixture between the skin and the breast meat. Top with a sage leaf. Do the same for the thighs. Rub the remaining butter over the outside of the chicken. Season the chicken with pepper and the remaining parsley. Place any leftover butter mixture and the remaining sage leaf in the cavity of the chicken.

Tie the drumsticks together with kitchen string and place the chicken on a roasting rack in a roasting pan. Tent the chicken with foil and bake for 20 minutes.

Remove the foil and roast for an additional 30 minutes until the chicken is golden brown or until the leg bone moves easily and the juices run clear. A meat thermometer pierced in the fleshy part of the thigh should read 170°F when the chicken is done.

Grilled Gorgonzola Chicken

Gorgonzola Sauce

¾ cup plain yogurt

3 ounces cream cheese,
   at room temperature

5 tablespoons crumbled
   Gorgonzola or blue cheese

2 tablespoons chopped
   green onion

1½ teaspoons lemon-pepper

⅛ teaspoon salt

Chicken

4 boneless, skinless chicken
   breast halves

4 tablespoons butter, melted

Salt and pepper to taste

1 large red bell pepper,
   cut into ½-inch strips

Preheat a gas or charcoal grill to medium heat.

In a food processor, blend the yogurt and cream cheese until smooth. Add the Gorgonzola, green onion, lemon-pepper, and salt. Process just until mixed. Cover and chill until ready to serve.

Brush the chicken with a small amount of melted butter, then sprinkle with salt and pepper. Grill the chicken, uncovered over medium heat for 5 minutes on one side. Turn the chicken and grill for 7 to 10 minutes longer or until the chicken juices run clear.

Brush the pepper strips with butter and grill for 5 minutes or until crisp-tender.

Serve the chicken with cheese sauce poured overtop and garnished with grilled peppers.

Spicy Apple-Glazed Chicken 'N Grits with Gorgonzola

Makes 4 servings

4 chicken boneless,
  skinless breasts

¼ cup apple butter

¼ cup spicy brown mustard

¼ teaspoon ground red pepper

Salt and pepper

Gorgonzola Cheese Grits

2 (14½-ounce) cans
  chicken stock

¾ cup quick-cooking grits
  (not instant)

5 ounces (1 cup) Gorgonzola
  cheese, crumbled

⅓ cup sour cream

¼ teaspoon grated nutmeg

Freshly ground black pepper

2 tablespoons diced green
  onions, for garnish

Preheat the oven to 350°F. Coat a 13 x 9-inch pan with cooking spray.

Place each chicken breast between two sheets of plastic wrap and pound to a uniform thickness. Place into the prepared pan.

Combine the apple butter, mustard, red pepper, salt, and pepper. Brush over the chicken breasts and bake for 20 minutes, or until tender and done.

Meanwhile, in a medium-sized saucepan over medium-high heat, bring the stock to a boil; gradually stir in the grits, then return to a boil and reduce the heat to low. Let simmer, covered, stirring occasionally until the grits are creamy, about 5 minutes. Add the cheese, sour cream, nutmeg, and pepper, stirring until the cheese is melted and the mixture is well blended.

Remove the chicken to a cutting board and cut crosswise into ½-inch slices.

To serve, spoon grits into 4 large shallow serving bowls. Top with sliced chicken, dividing equally. Sprinkle with green onions and serve while hot.

Breast of Chicken Cordon Bleu

Makes 4 servings

2 whole (1 pound)
  chicken breasts, deboned

Salt and white pepper

½ cup milk

1 egg, slightly beaten

2 (1½-ounce) slices ham

2 (2½-ounce) slices aged
  Swiss cheese

½ cup all-purpose flour

2 cups finely ground
  dry breadcrumbs

¼ pound (1 stick) butter

Lightly season the breasts with salt and pepper.

Combine the milk and egg to make an egg wash. Brush the breasts completely with the egg wash and place them, skin side down, on waxed paper. Lay one slice each of ham and cheese on each breast half. Brush the ham and cheese liberally with the egg wash and fold the breast halves together and secure with a toothpick.

In three separate shallow dishes, place the flour, remaining egg wash, and breadcrumbs. Carefully dip the breasts in each flour, then the egg wash, then the breadcrumbs. Wrap the coated breasts in foil and refrigerate for 6 hours or overnight.

When you're ready to continue, remove the breasts from the refrigerator and preheat the oven to 350°F. Lightly butter a 13 x 9-inch baking pan.

In a large skillet set over medium-high heat, melt the butter and brown the breasts, about 5 to 7 minutes per side. Place the breasts in the prepared baking pan and pour any remaining butter over top. Bake for 35 to 40 minutes or until tender.

Almond Butter Chicken
with Orange Sauce

Makes 4 servings

2 boneless, skinless chicken
  breasts, split

2 tablespoons all-purpose flour

½ teaspoon salt

½ teaspoon pepper

1 egg, beaten

2¼ ounces sliced almonds

4 tablespoons butter

Orange Sauce

1 tablespoon brown sugar

2 teaspoons cornstarch

Juice from one fresh orange
  (½ cup)

2 tablespoons butter

1 teaspoon grated orange zest

Place each chicken breast between two pieces of plastic wrap and pound with a meat mallet to ¼-inch thickness. Coat the chicken with flour, then season it with salt and pepper. Dip one side of each breast into the egg and press with almonds.

In a large skillet set over medium-high heat, melt the butter and add the chicken, almond side down. Cook for 3 to 5 minutes or until the almonds are toasted. Flip the chicken breasts and lower the heat to medium-low; cook for an additional 10 to 12 minutes, or until the chicken is no longer pink.

To make the Orange Sauce, combine the brown sugar and cornstarch in a saucepan set over medium heat. Add the orange juice, butter, and zest. Cook, stirring constantly, until thickened.

Serve the chicken with the Orange Sauce spooned overtop.

Chicken Kiev

Makes 6 servings

6 boneless, skinless
   chicken breasts
6 tablespoons butter,
   at room temperature
1 teaspoon pepper
1¼ teaspoon garlic powder
2 eggs, beaten
3 tablespoons water
1 teaspoon dried dill
½ teaspoon salt
½ cup all-purpose flour
½ cup plain dry breadcrumbs
2 cups canola oil
Lemon slices, for garnish
Parsley, for garnish

Place each chicken breast between two sheets of wax paper and pound until it is about ⅛ inch thick. Wrap in plastic wrap and refrigerate.

Combine the butter, ½ teaspoon pepper, and 1 teaspoon of garlic powder and mix well. Spread the butter on aluminum foil and shape into a 4 x 2-inch rectangle. Wrap and freeze until firm.

Cut the butter into 6 equal-sized pieces and place one piece on each flattened chicken breast. Fold in the edges of the chicken and roll until the butter is completely encased in chicken. Secure with toothpicks and set aside.

In a small bowl, combine the eggs and water.

On a plate or shallow dish, combine the remaining pepper, the remaining garlic powder, and the dill, salt, and flour. Place the breadcrumbs in a separate dish.

Dip the chicken rolls in the seasoned flour, then the egg mixture, then the breadcrumbs. Place the coated chicken on a baking sheet and refrigerate for 45 minutes.

Heat the oil over medium-high heat in a large, heavy skillet. Deep fry the chicken for 5 minutes, then turn them and fry for an additional 5 minutes until golden and cooked through, with no pink showing inside. Drain on paper towels and garnish with lemon slices and parsley.

Chicken Croquettes

Mary E. Taylor

Makes 5 to 6 servings

6 tablespoons butter

½ cup all-purpose flour

1¼ cups chicken stock

2 egg yolks

¾ cup half-and-half

2½ cups cooked, diced chicken

Salt and pepper

⅔ cup fine dry breadcrumbs

1 egg, mixed with

  1 teaspoon water

Shortening, for frying

Parsley, for garnish

Melt the butter in the top of a double boiler, or in a bowl set over a pan filled with about 1 inch of slowly boiling water. Add the flour and chicken stock slowly, stirring constantly to incorporate. Cook and stir until the mixture boils and thickens. Remove from the heat.

Beat the egg yolks and half-and-half together until smooth, then add to the warm sauce. Stir in the chicken and salt and pepper; cook gently over boiling water for 10 minutes, stirring often. Remove from the heat and set the pan (or bowl) in cold water to cool.

Scoop ¼ cup of the cooled mixture onto waxed paper and spread with crumbs; repeat with the remaining mixture. Chill in the refrigerator until firm.

Shape the dough into small balls or triangles an hour before serving. Roll in the breadcrumbs, then the egg-water mixture, then breadcrumbs. Let set in the refrigerator for 30 minutes.

Heat the shortening to 375°F. Add the croquettes, being careful not to crowd them in the pan, as it will lower the temperature of the oil. Fry the croquettes in batches until golden brown, about 3 to 4 minutes. Drain on paper towels and serve with gravy. Garnish with fresh parsley.

Chicken a la King

Makes 6 servings

6 tablespoons butter

1 garlic clove, chopped

½ cup green pepper slices

⅓ cup chopped
  button mushrooms

⅔ cup all-purpose flour

1½ cups half-and-half

1½ cups chicken stock

2½ cups cooked, diced chicken

Salt and pepper

Melt the butter in a sauce pan set over medium heat, then add the garlic, bell pepper, and mushrooms. Sauté until tender, about 5 minutes.

Using a slotted spoon, remove the vegetables and set aside. Add the flour, whisking constantly to avoid lumps. Then add the half-and-half and stock and cook, stirring constantly, until the mixture thickens and begins to boil, about 5 to 7 minutes.

Add the chicken and sautéed vegetables and cook until the chicken is heated through, about 10 minutes. Season with salt and pepper.

Roast Turkey with Herb Butter and Bourbon-Butter Apples

Makes 12 servings

Turkey

1 (14-pound) turkey

½ teaspoon salt

¼ teaspoon ground pepper

Herb Butter

1 cup salted butter,
   at room temperature

1 tablespoon chopped
   fresh thyme

1 tablespoon chopped
   fresh sage

2 tablespoons chopped
   flat-leaf parsley

1 tablespoon chopped
   fresh chives

1 teaspoon chopped
   fresh rosemary

Bourbon-Butter Apples

¼ pound (1 stick) unsalted butter

3 tablespoons chopped shallots

4 large golden delicious apples, peeled and
   cut into ½-inch chunks

2 tablespoons maple syrup

3 tablespoons bourbon or apple cider

¼ cup apple cider

½ teaspoon dried sage

¼ teaspoon ground nutmeg

⅛ teaspoon ground cloves

Preheat the oven to 425°F.

Remove the giblets and neck from the cavity of the turkey; rinse and dry the turkey and fold the wing tips behind it. Season the cavity of the bird with salt and pepper.

To make the herb butter, using an electric mixer, combine the butter with the thyme, sage, parsley, chives, and rosemary. Set aside.

Starting at the neck end of the turkey, loosen the skin by sliding your fingers underneath it, being careful not to tear it. Slide your hand as far as you can toward the other end of the turkey, separating the skin from the meat.

Rub two-thirds of the herb butter over the entire breast. Tie the drumsticks in front and place the bird on a rack in a roasting pan breast-side up. Cover loosely with a foil tent, place the bird in the oven, and decrease the temperature to 350°F. Bake for 3 to 3½ hours.

Meanwhile, make the Bourbon Buttered Apples. Heat 4 tablespoons of butter in a large skillet over medium heat, then add the shallots and cook uncovered for 5 minutes or until translucent. Add the apples, maple syrup, and bourbon, and simmer uncovered for 3 minutes. Add the cider and bring to a boil over medium-high heat. Let boil until most of the liquid has evaporated. Reduce the heat and stir in the remaining 4 tablespoons of butter 1 tablespoon at a time. Stir in the sage, nutmeg, and cloves. Set aside.

Melt the remaining herb butter. During the last 45 minutes of baking, remove the foil tent from the turkey and baste with melted butter.

The turkey is done when the thigh meat reaches an internal temperature of 180°F. and the breast meat reaches an internal temperature of 170°F. When the turkey is done, remove from the oven; let stand 30 minutes before carving.

Serve the Bourbon-Buttered Apples warm with turkey.

Country Cornish Hens

Makes 4 servings

4 tablespoons butter, melted

2 tablespoons finely
  chopped onion

2 tablespoons finely
  chopped celery

2 ounces sliced mushrooms

⅓ cup uncooked long grain rice

¾ cup chicken stock

4 ounces (1 cup) Cheddar
  cheese, shredded

2 Rock Cornish hens

Salt and pepper, to taste

Preheat the oven to 375°F.

In a 1-quart saucepan over medium-low heat, heat 2 tablespoons of butter, the onion, celery, mushrooms, and rice. Cook for 8 to 10 minutes, stirring often, until the vegetables soften. Add the stock and bring the mixture to a boil. Cover and reduce heat to low; simmer for 25 minutes or until all of the liquid is absorbed, and the rice is tender. Mix in the Cheddar cheese.

Sprinkle the hens with salt and pepper and stuff with the cooked rice mixture. Place the hens breast-side-up on a rack in a shallow 17 x 11-inch baking pan. Cover loosely with aluminum foil and roast for 30 minutes. Remove the foil and brush with the remaining 2 tablespoons of butter. Continue to roast, uncovered, for 45 minutes. When the hens are cooked through, the drumstick meat will feel very soft when pressed and the skin will be crisp and golden brown.

NOTE: For a flavor variation, use 1 cup shredded Monterey Jack with pesto, or 1 cup shredded Monterey Jack with morels, or a blend of ¾ cup shredded fontina and ¼ cup crumbled blue cheese.

Florentine Game Hens

Makes 6 servings

¼ cup chopped onion

1 tablespoon minced garlic

¼ pound (1 stick) butter

½ cup sour cream

3 ounces cream cheese, cubed

2 (10-ounce) packages
  frozen chopped spinach,
  thawed and well drained

4 ounces (1 cup)
  feta cheese, crumbled

¼ cup minced parsley

2 tablespoons sliced
  green onion

1 teaspoon red pepper flakes

6 Rock Cornish game hens
  (1½ pounds each), cleaned

2 teaspoons paprika

2 teaspoons pepper

1 teaspoon salt

Preheat the oven to 375°F.

Sauté the onion and garlic in 4 tablespoons of butter. Add the sour cream and cream cheese, and cook until the cream cheese is melted. Add the spinach, feta cheese, parsley, green onion, and ¼ teaspoon red pepper flakes; mix well.

Place ½ cup of the spinach mixture in the cavity of each hen. Place the hens on a 15 x 10 x 1-inch jelly roll pan, and brush them with the remaining butter, melted.

Combine the paprika, pepper, salt, and remaining red pepper flakes, and sprinkle over the hens. Bake for 50 to 60 minutes or until tender.

Lobster Tails with
Two-Cheese Cornbread Stuffing

Chef Dave Ellis

Makes 6 servings

7 (4- to 5-ounce) lobster tails

6 tablespoons butter, melted

3 tablespoons chopped onion

3 tablespoons sliced
green onions

½ teaspoon minced garlic

⅓ cup heavy cream

1 tablespoon minced parsley

½ teaspoon seafood seasoning

1 cup cornbread stuffing mix

1 ounce (¼ cup) Cheddar
cheese, shredded

1 ounce (¼ cup) Monterey
Jack cheese, shredded

6 lemon wedges

Preheat the oven to 375°F.

Turn the lobster tails on their backs and, using kitchen shears, cut through the soft membrane on both sides of underside. Remove the meat from all of the shells and coarsely chop the meat from 1 lobster tail; set aside. Coat the remaining 6 lobster tails with 2 tablespoons of the melted butter. Return the tails to the shells and place them in a baking dish.

Sauté the onion in remaining 4 tablespoons of butter. Add the green onions and cook for 1 minute. Add the garlic and cook for 30 seconds. Add the chopped lobster and cook for 3 to 4 minutes until the lobster meat is opaque. Stir in the heavy cream, parsley, and seasoning.

In a bowl, combine the cornbread stuffing mix and the cheeses. Add the cream mixture and mix lightly until well-combined. Top each lobster tail with ¼ cup of the stuffing mixture and bake for 8 to 10 minutes, or until the lobster meat is opaque throughout. Serve with lemon wedges and additional melted butter.

Lobster Thermidor

Makes 4 servings

2 (1½ pound) Rock lobster tails

6 tablespoons butter

2 tablespoons all-purpose flour

1 teaspoon mustard

½ teaspoon salt

1 teaspoon paprika

⅛ teaspoon cayenne pepper

1½ cups half-and-half

8 ounces (2 cups) medium
  or sharp Cheddar cheese,
  shredded

1 teaspoon Worcestershire
  sauce

¼ cup chopped bell pepper

½ pound fresh
  mushrooms, sliced

2 tablespoons cracker crumbs

2 tablespoons butter, melted

1 ounce (¼ cup) Parmesan
  cheese, grated

Cook the lobster tails in rapidly boiling salted water, about 10 to 12 minutes. Remove the meat from the shells and cut into ½-inch cubes. Reserve the lobster shells and set the meat and shells aside.

Preheat the broiler.

In a saucepan, melt 2 tablespoons of butter and stir in the flour, mustard, salt, paprika, and cayenne pepper; gradually add the half-and-half, stirring constantly, until thickened. Turn off the heat and gradually add the Cheddar cheese and Worcestershire sauce, stirring until the cheese melts; set aside.

In a small sauce, pan melt the remaining 4 tablespoons of butter and sauté the bell pepper and mushrooms for about 5 minutes.

In a large bowl, combine the lobster meat, vegetables, and cheese sauce and mix thoroughly; fill the lobster shells with this mixture.

Combine the cracker crumbs and melted butter, and top each lobster tail with the cracker mixture and Parmesan cheese. Set the lobster tails on a baking sheet and broil until the sauce is bubbly and lightly browned. Serve immediately.

Butter-Poached Lobster

Makes 4 servings

¼ cup chopped garlic

½ cup chopped shallots

1 cup white wine

1 cup extra dry vermouth

3 cups chicken or
seafood stock

2 pounds (8 sticks)
butter, cubed

Salt and pepper to taste

3 tablespoons chopped
fresh thyme

3 tablespoons chopped
fresh marjoram

4 lobster tails

In a large saucepan set over medium-high heat, sauté the garlic and shallots until translucent, about 3 minutes. Add the wine and vermouth to deglaze the pan, stirring with a wooden spoon to loosen any browned bits on the bottom of the pan.

Allow the liquid to reduce completely, then add the stock and bring to a boil. Reduce the heat to low.

Slowly add the butter and mix with an immersion blender to form an emulsion. Add the salt and pepper, thyme, and marjoram and heat to 120°F. Add the lobster tails and gently poach until cooked through, about 15 to 20 minutes.

Shrimp Scampi

Makes 4 servings

Sea salt, as needed

1½ pounds medium shrimp, peeled and deveined

¼ pound (1 stick) butter

2 tablespoons extra virgin olive oil

3 cloves garlic, minced

½ cup white wine

Parsley, for garnish

Season the shrimp with sea salt and set aside.

In heavy skillet set over medium heat, heat the butter and olive oil. Add the garlic and sauté for about 5 minutes until it is fragrant, but not brown. Add the shrimp and cook for 3 minutes until they start to turn pink. Add the wine and cook an additional 5 minutes, until the alcohol cooks off and the shrimp are just cooked. Remove from the heat and garnish with parsley.

Butterflied Shrimp

Makes 6 servings

3 ounces pancetta or bacon, chopped and cooked

8 ounces (2 cups) smoked Gouda cheese, shredded

½ cup dried breadcrumbs

4 tablespoons unsalted butter, at room temperature

2 tablespoons chives, chopped

18 jumbo shrimp (13 to 15 count), deveined and butterflied, tails left on

¾ cup sour cream

Preheat the oven to 400°F.

Combine the pancetta, 1½ cups cheese, breadcrumbs, butter, and 1 tablespoon chives. Shape into a 9-inch log. Wrap in plastic wrap and freeze for 10 to 15 minutes.

Cut the cheese log into ½-inch slices. Lay the shrimp on the baking sheet and place a slice of cheese on each shrimp, pressing to cover.

Bake for 7 minutes, sprinkle the remaining cheese over top, and bake for 3 to 4 minutes more, or until the cheese is melted and the shrimp are cooked through. Serve with a dollop of sour cream and sprinkle with the remaining chives.

Linguine with Tiger Shrimp

Chef Philip Dorwart

Makes 8 to 10 servings

6 tablespoons canola oil

6 tablespoons minced garlic

6 tablespoons minced shallots

1½ pounds linguine

12 tablespoons butter

2 pounds Tiger shrimp, peeled and deveined

1½ cups white wine

1½ cups chicken stock

3 cups celery hearts, thinly cut on the bias

1 cup fresh pitted Kalamata olives, drained and quartered

4 tablespoons thyme leaves

4 tablespoons lemon juice

Salt and pepper, to taste

Parmesan cheese, shaved

Heat the oil in a large sauté pan and add the garlic and shallots. Cook over low heat for 10 minutes or until the shallots are soft.

Meanwhile, cook the linguine in boiling salted water until it is al dente. Drain and toss with butter.

Increase the heat under the sauté pan to high and add the shrimp, wine, and chicken stock; cook until the shrimp just turn pink. Remove the shrimp and keep warm. Add the celery hearts, olives, and thyme and boil to reduce liquid by one-third.

Add the linguine to the sauté pan along with the shrimp and toss with lemon juice, salt and pepper. Heat through. Serve with Parmesan cheese sprinkled on top.

Chef Anthony Lamas
Makes 10 to 12 servings

Smoked Cheddar, Chipotle, Sweet Corn, and Grits Cake

6 tablespoons olive oil

6 cups water

1½ teaspoons kosher salt

1½ pounds quick grits

¼ pound (1 stick) unsalted butter

3 ounces Chipotle chiles in Adobo sauce, chopped, to taste

1 pound (4 cups) smoked Cheddar cheese, cut into 1-inch cubes

1¼ cup shoepeg corn

Flour for dusting

Shrimp Marinade

¼ cup olive oil

Juice of 1 lemon

1 tablespoon chopped garlic

1 tablespoon kosher salt

1 teaspoon oregano

1 teaspoon ground white pepper

1 teaspoon crushed red pepper

2¼ pounds large shrimp

Roasted Onion Tomato Salsa

10 small Roma tomatoes, diced

2 medium red onions, diced

1 to 2 jalapeño peppers, seeds removed and diced

2 tablespoons olive oil

1 large avocado, diced

½ cup fresh lime juice

1 to 2 teaspoons Ancho chile powder

½ cup chopped cilantro

Salt and pepper, to taste

12 ounces (3 cups) manchego cheese, shredded, for serving

Begin by making the Smoked Cheddar, Chipotle, Sweet Corn, and Grits Cake. Generously coat a half sheet pan with 2 tablespoons of olive oil.

In large stockpot, bring the water,

2 tablespoons of olive oil, and salt to a boil. Slowly stir in the grits, about ¼ cup at a time, whisking continually. As the grits begin to thicken, add the butter and Chipotle chiles. Cook for 2 minutes.

Lower the heat, stir in the Cheddar cheese and corn, and remove from the heat.

Pour the grit mixture into the prepared pan and spread until it covers the bottom of the pan evenly. Cover with plastic wrap and refrigerate up to 24 hours or until the mixture becomes firm.

Preheat the oven to 350°F.

Using a cookie cutter, cut the corn mixture into the desired shapes or use a knife to cut it into small triangles. Dust each cut shape with flour and pan fry in 2 tablespoons of olive oil for about 2 minutes on each side, or until golden. Place on a sheet pan and finish in the oven at for 3 to 5 minutes.

To make the Shrimp Marinade, combine all of the marinade ingredients in a large bowl, cover, and refrigerate for 2 to 4 hours.

To make the Roasted Onion Tomato Salsa, cover a shallow baking pan with foil.

Toss the tomatoes, onions, and jalapeño(s) with olive oil. Spread the tomato mixture onto the prepared pan. Roast in a 450°F. oven for 10 minutes, or until the onions are tinged with brown. Remove from the oven and cool.

In a large bowl, combine the avocado, lime juice, Ancho chile powder, cilantro, and season with salt and pepper. Stir in the cooled roasted vegetables, cover with plastic wrap, and refrigerate.

Grill the shrimp until cooked through, about 4 to 6 minutes.

To serve, arrange the hot grit cakes on plates and top with two shrimp, top the shrimp with manchego cheese and spoon salsa on the side.

Broccoli and Shrimp Puff Pastries

Makes 8 servings

2 tablespoons butter

4 green onions, the white
and 1 inch of the green part
thinly sliced

3 garlic cloves, minced

1½ cups broccoli, cooked and
finely chopped

1 cup shrimp, cooked and
coarsely chopped

8 ounces (2 cups) Brick
cheese* or mild Cheddar
cheese, shredded

3 tablespoons grated
Parmesan cheese

⅓ cup roasted red peppers,
drained and chopped

½ teaspoon salt

¼ teaspoon ground allspice

¼ teaspoon white pepper

1 sheet frozen phyllo
dough, thawed

1 egg, lightly beaten

*Brick cheese is a semi-hard, cow's milk
cheese originating in Wisconsin. For more
information, visit www.wisdairy.com.

Preheat the oven to 350°F.

In a skillet set over medium heat, heat the butter, then add the green onions and garlic and cook for 3 minutes or until just softened. Set aside.

In a medium bowl, combine the broccoli, shrimp, cheeses, peppers, salt, allspice, and pepper.

Unfold the phyllo and cut into two rectangles. On a lightly floured surface, roll one rectangle out to a 15 x 7-inch square, and the other to 14 x 6-inches. Fold the larger piece in half lengthwise and cut through the folded edge to make slits about 2 inches long and ½ inch apart. Set aside.

Place the smaller rectangle on an ungreased baking sheet, then arrange the broccoli mixture down the center, leaving a ½-inch border. Brush the edges of the border with the beaten egg.

Unfold the reserved pastry; place over top, pressing edges together with tines of a fork. Brush with egg mixture. Bake for 35 minutes or until puffed and golden.

Crab Bisque Macaroni and Cheese

Makes 6 to 8 servings

2 tablespoons butter

½ medium onion, chopped

1½ tablespoons
all-purpose flour

½ cup milk

1 cup chicken stock

1 cup diced canned
tomatoes, drained

¼ teaspoon dried rosemary,
crushed

½ teaspoon salt

¼ teaspoon pepper

4 ounces (1 cup) sharp
Cheddar, shredded

4 ounces (1 cup) Monterey Jack
cheese, shredded

8 ounces canned
crabmeat, drained,
or imitation crab meat

1 tablespoon dry sherry

8 ounces penne pasta,
cooked al dente

Preheat the oven to 375°F. Lightly butter an oval 10 x 8-inch casserole dish.

In a large, deep saucepan over medium heat, melt ½ tablespoon of butter until sizzling. Add the onion and sauté about 3 minutes or until tender. Add the remaining butter. When the butter is sizzling, add the flour and cook, stirring, until the flour is golden. Gradually whisk in the milk and stock and cook, stirring constantly, for 8 to 10 minutes, or until the mixture is thick and smooth. Stir in the tomatoes, rosemary, salt, and pepper. Bring just to boiling point and remove from the heat.

Add ⅔ cup each of the Cheddar and Monterey Jack cheeses. Stir until the cheese is melted. Stir in the crabmeat and sherry. Stir in the pasta, mixing well.

Transfer the mixture to the prepared casserole dish. Sprinkle the remaining cheese over the casserole and bake until bubbly, about 20 minutes.

Smoked Salmon Salad with Dill Havarti Popovers

Makes 4 servings

Popovers

2 large eggs

1 cup milk

1 cup all-purpose flour

½ teaspoon salt

2 tablespoons unsalted butter, melted

2 ounces (½ cup) Dill Havarti cheese,* shredded

Salad

5 ounces spring greens or 8 cups mixed salad greens

1 cup peeled and thinly sliced cucumber

2 ounces (½ cup) Dill Havarti cheese, shredded

¼ cup vinaigrette dressing

4 ounces thinly-sliced, smoked salmon, cut crosswise into strips

2 tablespoons chopped fresh dill or 1 teaspoon dried dill

*If Dill Havarti Cheese is not available, use regular Havarti Cheese tossed with 1 teaspoon chopped fresh dill or ¼ teaspoon dried dill.

Preheat the oven to 450°F. Coat eight 6-ounce custard cups or ramekins** with nonstick cooking spray; dust lightly with flour.

In a medium bowl, whisk the eggs, then whisk in the milk. Add the flour and salt and whisk well. (Some small lumps of flour will remain.) Whisk in the butter. Pour the batter into the prepared cups, filling each one-third full. Divide the cheese evenly over each cup, then pour the remaining batter over the cheese, filling the cups two-thirds full.

Place the cups on a baking sheet and bake for 15 minutes. Reduce the oven temperature to 350°F. and continue baking for 20 to 25 minutes longer until the popovers are puffed and deep golden brown (do not open the oven during baking time). Immediately remove the popovers to serving plates.

While the popovers are baking, combine the greens, cucumber, cheese, and salad dressing in a large bowl. Toss well and transfer to four serving plates. Top salads with salmon and dill. Serve with warm popovers.

**Popovers can also be made in a 12-cup muffin tin (medium size with 4-ounce cups). Coat 10 of the cups with cooking spray, fill them, and bake as above.

Tuna Noodle Casserole

Makes 6 servings

1 (12-ounce) package
   wide egg noodles

¼ pound (1 stick) butter

⅓ cup all-purpose flour

1 teaspoon salt

¼ teaspoon pepper

2½ cups milk

8 ounces cream cheese,
   cut into cubes

1 (7-ounce) can water pack
   tuna, drained and flaked

¼ cup pimento-stuffed
   olives, sliced

2 tablespoons fresh chopped
   chives or 1 tablespoon
   dried chives

12 ounces Muenster
   cheese, sliced

4 slices soft white bread,
   crumbed in blender

Preheat the oven to 350°F. Grease a 3-quart shallow baking dish.

Cook the noodles according to the package directions; drain.

Meanwhile, melt 4 tablespoons of butter in a large saucepan. Blend in the flour, salt, and pepper; gradually add the milk. Cook, stirring until the sauce thickens and boils for 1 minute. Stir in the cream cheese until melted. Stir in the tuna, olives, and chives; remove from heat.

Pour ¾ cup of the tuna mixture into the prepared baking dish. Layer into the dish half of the noodles, half of the remaining sauce and half of the Muenster slices. Repeat, ending with the remaining sauce.

Melt the remaining butter in a small saucepan, then toss in the breadcrumbs lightly with a fork. Sprinkle over the casserole and bake for 30 minutes or until bubbly.

Baked Goods and Desserts

Cream Puffs

¼ pound (1 stick) butter

1 cup boiling water

1 cup all-purpose flour, sifted

4 eggs

Whipped cream, for filling

Preheat the oven to 450°F. Grease a baking sheet.

Put the butter in a sauce pan and pour the water over it. Heat to just boiling until the butter melts, about 7 minutes. Add the flour, stirring constantly until the mixture leaves the sides of the pan and forms a ball. Remove from the heat.

Immediately add the eggs, one at a time and beat after each addition to incorporate. Beat the dough until it is smooth.

Drop the dough by heaping tablespoons onto the prepared baking sheet, 3 inches apart. Bake for 15 minutes, until well puffed and golden brown.

Lower the heat to 300°F. and bake an additional 30 minutes.

Remove to a wire rack to cool.

When the puffs are cold, slice the tops off and fill with whipped cream.

Makes 84

Cookies

½ pound (2 sticks) unsalted
   butter, at room temperature

8 ounces cream cheese,
   at room temperature

1½ cups granulated sugar

1 egg

1 teaspoon vanilla

½ teaspoon almond extract

3½ cups all-purpose flour

1 teaspoon baking powder

Almond Frosting

2 cups confectioners'
   sugar, sifted

2 tablespoons unsalted butter,
   at room temperature

¼ teaspoon almond extract

4 to 5 teaspoons milk

Food coloring, optional

Using an electric mixer, cream the butter and cream cheese in a large mixing bowl until fluffy. Add the sugar and beat. Add the egg, vanilla, and almond extract and beat well.

In a medium bowl, combine the flour and baking powder. Add the flour mixture to the cream cheese mixture and beat until well mixed. The dough will be stiff—add a little milk, if necessary.

Divide the dough in half, wrap in plastic wrap, and refrigerate for at least 1½ hours.

Preheat the oven to 375°F.

On a lightly floured surface, roll out the dough to ⅛-inch thickness. Cut with desired cookie cutters and bake on greased baking sheets for 8 to 10 minutes. Remove to wire rack and cool. Spread or decorate with Almond Frosting.

To make the Almond Frosting, beat the confectioners' sugar, butter, and almond extract until fluffy. Beat in enough milk to make a spreadable consistency, adding more milk if necessary. Stir in food coloring.

Butter Spritz Cookies

Makes 9 dozen

¾ pound (3 sticks) unsalted butter, at room temperature

1 cup granulated sugar

1 large egg

1 egg yolk

1 teaspoon vanilla

½ teaspoon almond extract

3½ to 4 cups all-purpose flour, sifted

1 teaspoon baking powder

Colored sugar, decorative sprinkles, and cinnamon candies, for decoration

Preheat the oven to 400°F.

Using an electric mixer, cream the butter and sugar, beating for 2 minutes. Add the egg, egg yolk, and vanilla and almond extracts; beat well.

Sift together 3½ cups of flour and the baking powder; add gradually to the creamed mixture, mixing to form a soft, but not sticky, dough. (If the dough is sticky, add additional flour in small amounts until the dough can be handled without being sticky.)

Fill the dough into a cookie press and press the cookies onto ungreased baking sheets. Decorate with colored sugar or cinnamon candies or decorative sprinkles and bake for 8 to 10 minutes. Cool on a wire rack.

Rich Butter Bites

Makes 5 to 6 dozen

¼ pound plus 4 tablespoons
(1½ sticks) unsalted butter

½ cup brown sugar, packed

1 tablespoon granulated sugar

1 egg yolk

1 teaspoon vanilla

1¾ cups all-purpose flour

Frosting

4 tablespoons unsalted butter

2½ cups confectioners'
sugar, sifted

¼ cup heavy cream

1 teaspoon vanilla

Pecan halves or sliced
almonds, for garnish

Preheat the oven to 350°F.

In a medium mixing bowl and using an electric mixer, cream the butter for 30 seconds. Add the sugars and beat until fluffy. Add the egg yolk and vanilla and beat well. Beat in the flour to form a stiff dough.

Using your hands, roll the dough into ¾-inch balls. Place the balls on a greased baking sheet and flatten them with the bottom of a glass dipped in sugar. Bake for 9 to 11 minutes or until the bottoms are golden brown. Remove to a wire rack to cool completely.

To make the Frosting, melt the butter in a saucepan set over medium heat. Cook the butter, stirring, until it is lightly browned. Remove from the heat and stir in the confectioners' sugar until smooth. Gradually add the cream, stirring until smooth. Stir in the vanilla. Frost the cooled cookies and garnish with a pecan half or a sliced almond.

Brandy Snaps

Makes 11 dozen

¼ pound (1 stick) butter

1⅓ cup dark brown sugar

¾ cup light corn syrup

⅛ teaspoon salt

2 teaspoons ground ginger, or
  1 teaspoon fresh ginger juice

2¾ cups all-purpose flour

Grease two baking sheets and set aside.

Place the butter, sugar, corn syrup, salt, and ginger in the top of a double boiler and stir until the butter melts and all ingredients are well incorporated. Remove from the heat and let cool.

Stir in the flour gradually, being sure to blend well. Pour the dough out onto wax paper and chill in the refrigerator for about 1 hour.

Divide the dough into four portions. On a lightly floured surface and using a well floured rolling pin, roll out each portion to a thickness of about ⅛ inch. Using a 2-inch round cookie cutter, cut the dough and transfer to the prepared baking sheets, placing the cookies about ½ inch apart.

Preheat oven to 400°F. about 10 minutes before baking. Bake the cookies for 5 minutes. Let cool on the baking sheets for 2 minutes, then transfer them to a wire rack.

NOTE: These cookies keep for at least one month if stored in an airtight container.

Farm Cookies

Makes 60

2 cups all-purpose flour

1 teaspoon baking powder

1 teaspoon baking soda

½ teaspoon salt

½ pound (2 sticks)
  unsalted butter

1 cup brown sugar, packed

1 cup granulated sugar

2 eggs

1 teaspoon vanilla

2 cups quick-cooking
  rolled oats

2 cups cornflakes

1 cup flaked coconut

1 cup chopped walnuts
  or pecans

Preheat the oven to 375°F.

In a small mixing bowl, combine the flour, baking powder, baking soda, and salt. Stir to mix well and set aside.

In a large mixing bowl and using an electric mixer, cream the butter for 30 seconds. Add the sugars and beat until fluffy. Beat in the eggs and vanilla, then add the flour mixture and beat until well-combined. Stir in the oats, cornflakes, coconut, and walnuts. (The dough will be stiff.)

Roll the dough into 1-inch balls and place them on an ungreased baking sheet; flatten slightly with the bottom of a glass. Bake for 8 to 10 minutes or until done.

Fork-Print Cookies

Makes 25

1¼ cups all-purpose flour

¼ teaspoon baking powder

⅛ teaspoon salt

¼ pound (1 stick) plus
  2 tablespoons butter,
  at room temperature

½ cup plus 2 tablespoons
  granulated sugar

1 egg

1½ teaspoon vanilla

Preheat the oven to 300°F. Grease and lightly flour a jelly roll pan.

Sift the flour with the baking powder and salt and set aside.

Using an electric mixer, cream the butter and sugar until glossy. Add the egg and beat until fluffy. Stir in the vanilla and flour mixture and beat until well incorporated.

Turn the batter out onto the prepared pan and spread with a spatula to achieve an even thickness and smooth top. Using a fork, make crisscross patterns along the surface of the dough.

Bake for 30 minutes, or until the bars are a pale golden color. While the cookies are still warm, cut them into 25 bars and let cool in the pan on a wire rack.

Scottish Shortbread

Makes 3 dozen

2¼ cups all-purpose flour

¼ teaspoon baking powder

½ pound (2 sticks) butter,
   at room temperature

½ cup plus 1 tablespoon
   granulated sugar

Preheat the oven to 325°F. 10 minutes before baking. Do not grease the baking sheets.

Sift the flour with the baking powder.

Using an electric mixer, cream the butter until shiny and add the sugar slowly to incorporate well. Stir in the flour in 2 or 3 portions, mixing well after each addition. Turn the dough out onto a lightly floured surface and knead just until the ingredients are incorporated. Be careful to avoid overkneading.

Roll the dough into a rectangle of your desired thickness. Prick the dough all over with a fork, then cut it into 2-inch squares. Place the squares on ungreased baking sheets about ½-inch apart. Bake for 18 to 20 minutes, until the cookies are a light golden color. Remove from baking sheets and place on racks to cool.

Brown Butter Hazelnut Shortbread with Fleur De Sel

Makes 3 to 4 dozen

½ pound (2 sticks) unsalted
   butter, at room temperature

½ cup granulated sugar

½ cup light brown sugar,
   lightly packed

¼ teaspoon salt, plus a pinch

1 large egg, separated

1½ teaspoon vanilla

2 cups all-purpose flour

Topping

1½ cups chopped hazelnuts

2 tablespoons
   granulated sugar

½ teaspoon ground cinnamon

½ teaspoon ground nutmeg

1 heaping teaspoon coarse
   fleur de sel or sea salt

6 ounces bittersweet
   chocolate*

*For the best chocolate flavor, look for bittersweet chocolate with a minimum of 60% cocoa solids.

Melt 4 tablespoons of butter in a small saucepan set over moderate heat. Cook the butter until it stops foaming, smells toasty, and begins to brown, about 10 minutes. The browner the butter, the deeper the flavor, but don't let it blacken or burn. Set the butter aside to cool to room temperature.

Place the remaining butter in a bowl and, using an electric mixer, beat until creamy. Add the sugars and ¼ teaspoon of salt and continue to beat until light and fluffy. Add the egg yolk, vanilla, and cooled browned butter. Mix to combine. Then add the flour, 1 cup at a time, and stir with a wooden spoon to combine. Chill the batter for 20 to 30 minutes.

Preheat the oven to 350°F. with the oven rack set in the middle of the oven. Butter a 10 x 15-inch jelly roll pan.

Divide the dough into 8 rough portions and arrange them evenly in the pan. Press the dough into an even layer to fill the pan.

In a small bowl, beat the egg white with the pinch of salt. Brush evenly over the dough and sprinkle hazelnuts over the top, pressing down lightly so they stick to the dough.

In another small bowl, combine the sugar with the cinnamon and nutmeg and sprinkle over the nuts. Sprinkle sea salt over the top.

Bake, rotating the pan once halfway through baking, until golden brown and crisp, about 25 minutes. Let cool for 10 minutes and cut into 1- to 2-inch squares or diamonds. Transfer to a wire rack.

Melt the chocolate in a metal bowl set over a pan of simmering water. Using a very small tipped pastry bag or the tines of a fork, drizzle the chocolate over the tops of the shortbreads.

Vanilla-Chai Icebox Shortbread Cookies

Makes 3 to 4 dozen

2⅓ cups all-purpose flour

2 teaspoons pumpkin pie spice

2 teaspoons ground ginger

½ teaspoon ground allspice

½ teaspoon ground cardamom

½ pound (2 sticks) unsalted
  butter, at room temperature

1 cup granulated sugar

3 tablespoons honey

¼ teaspoon salt

2 large egg yolks

1 medium vanilla bean

Icing

1 cup confectioner's
  sugar, sifted

2 teaspoons vanilla

Seeds from 1 medium vanilla
  bean, optional

1 tablespoon water

In a large bowl, sift or whisk together the flour, pumpkin pie spice, ginger, allspice, and cardamom; set aside.

Using an electric mixer, cream the butter, sugar, honey, and salt until light and fluffy. Add the egg yolks, one at a time, and beat until smooth.

Using a small knife, split the vanilla bean in half lengthwise. With the tip of the knife, scrape the seeds from both sides of the vanilla pod and add them to the butter-sugar mixture. Beat to combine. Add in the flour mixture, 1 cup at a time, blending until fully incorporated.

Divide the dough in half and transfer each half to a sheet of wax paper. Using the wax paper, shape the dough into two 12-inch logs, rectangle or square. Chill the logs for at least 2 hours or overnight.

Preheat the oven to 350°F with the oven rack set in the middle of the oven. Line 2 baking sheets with parchment paper.

With a sharp knife, cut the logs of dough into ⅛-inch-thick slices and arrange them ½ inch apart on the baking sheets. Bake until the cookies are lightly browned around the edges, about 10 to 12 minutes. Transfer to a wire rack.

In a small bowl, whisk together the icing ingredients until smooth and transfer to a sealable plastic bag. Cut an ⅛-inch opening in one corner of the bag. Arrange the cookies as close together as possible on sheets of wax paper and drizzle the icing decoratively across the tops.

Golden Shortbreads

Makes 3 dozen

½ pound (2 sticks)
  unsalted butter

½ cup light brown sugar

2 cups all-purpose flour

Decorative colored sugars

Preheat the oven to 300°F.

Using an electric mixer, cream the butter and sugar until light and fluffy. Gradually add the flour, and gather the dough into a ball, wrap in plastic wrap, and chill for 4 to 5 hours or overnight.

On a lightly floured surface, roll the dough out to ¼-inch thick. Cut with a 2-inch round cookie cutter and place on an ungreased baking sheet. Prick the surface of the dough with a fork or use a bamboo skewer to create simple holiday designs. Reshape any leftover dough and roll. To decorate, sprinkle colored sugar over the cookies. Bake for 20 to 25 minutes. Cool on a wire rack.

DID YOU KNOW?
Butter was once a form of commerce. In the early days, people bartered butter in exchange for merchandise in the general stores of small country towns.

Hermits

Makes 4 dozen

1¾ cups all-purpose flour

½ teaspoon baking soda

½ teaspoon salt

½ teaspoon cinnamon

½ teaspoon nutmeg

¼ pound (1 stick) butter,
   at room temperature

1 cup dark brown sugar

1 egg

¼ freshly brewed coffee, cold

¾ cup raisins, plumped*

½ cup chopped nuts, walnuts,
   pecans or any combination

*To plump raisins, place the raisins in a bowl and cover with hot water; let soak for about 5 to 10 minutes. Alternatively, you can soak the raisins in rum, fruit juice, brandy, or water (adjust sugar if using a naturally sweet juice). Drain the raisins and use as directed.

Preheat the oven to 400°F. Lightly grease two baking sheets and set aside.

Sift together the flour, baking soda, salt, cinnamon, and nutmeg and set aside.

Using an electric mixer, cream the butter, then add the sugar and beat until creamy. Add the egg and beat until fluffy.

Add the flour mixture and coffee to the butter alternately in three portions each, mixing well to incorporate after each addition. Stir in the raisins and nuts.

Drop the dough on the prepared baking sheets in heaping teaspoons, spacing about 1 inch apart. Bake for 10 to 15 minutes until the edges are crisp and the tops no longer seem moist.

Iced Cardamom Cutouts

Makes 3 to 4 dozen

Cookies

¾ pound (3 sticks) unsalted
   butter, at room temperature

1 cup natural (raw) cane sugar*

2 large egg yolks

4 cups all-purpose flour

3 to 4 tablespoons
   ground cardamom

½ teaspoon salt

1 tablespoon grated lemon or
   orange zest

Icing

6 tablespoons unsalted butter,
   at room temperature

3 cups confectioners' sugar

Pinch salt

¾ teaspoon vanilla

2 to 3 tablespoons lime,
   orange or lemon juice,
   at room temperature

Additional colored
   sanding sugar

*Use large, granular-type cane sugars;
Turbinado or Demerara work well.

Using an electric mixer, cream the butter and sugar until light and fluffy. Beat in the egg yolks, then add the flour, cardamom, salt and zest. Blend until the dough is evenly mixed.

Divide the dough into four, flatten each quarter into a disk, and wrap tightly in plastic wrap. Chill for at least 1 hour or overnight.

Preheat the oven to 350°F. and butter or line 2 baking sheets with parchment paper.

Take 1 ball of dough from the refrigerator. (Keep the remaining dough chilled.) On a lightly floured surface with a lightly floured rolling pin, roll the dough out to ⅛- to ¼-inch thickness. Using a knife or cookie cutters, cut the dough into shapes and place on the prepared baking sheets. Bake until the cookie bottoms just begin to brown, about 8 to 10 minutes. Transfer to a wire rack to cool completely. Continue to roll, cut and bake the remaining dough.

For the icing, combine the butter, sugar, salt, and vanilla in a mixing bowl. Beat at low speed, gradually adding the juice to reach the consistency of a thick syrup. Drizzle over the cooled cookies, dip the cookies in icing, or top each cookie with icing and sand with sugar.

Gingerbread Men

Makes 2 to 3 dozen

3¼ cups all-purpose flour

1 teaspoon ground ginger

1 teaspoon baking soda

¼ teaspoon salt

1 teaspoon ground cinnamon

2 teaspoon ground cloves

½ pound (2 sticks) butter

¾ cup dark brown sugar

1 large egg

½ cup molasses

1 cup confectioners' sugar

2 tablespoon milk

In a medium bowl, whisk together the flour, ginger, baking soda, salt, cinnamon, and cloves. Set aside.

Using an electric mixer, cream the butter and sugar. Scrape the bowl, then add the egg and molasses, and beat until smooth. Scrape down the bowl again and add the reserved flour mixture. Blend on low speed until just combined. Do not over mix.

Separate the dough into three balls and flatten each ball into a disk. Wrap each disk in plastic wrap and refrigerate for 1 to 2 hours.

Preheat the oven to 350°F.

On a floured surface, roll one piece of dough out to ¼-inch thickness. Flour a gingerbread man cookie cutter and cut out the gingerbread shapes. Place on a greased baking sheet about ½-inch apart. Gather any scraps and re-roll the dough until all of it is used.

Bake the cookies for 9 to 11 minutes. Cool on a wire rack and repeat with the remaining dough.

In a small bowl, combine the confectioners' sugar and milk until smooth. Spoon the icing into a pastry bag with a small round tip and decorate the cooled cookies as desired.

Peanut Butter Cookies

Makes about 36

1¼ cups all-purpose flour

¼ teaspoon baking soda

¼ teaspoon salt

¼ pound (1 stick) butter,
   at room temperature

½ cup creamy peanut butter

½ cup granulated sugar

½ cup light brown sugar

1 egg

1 teaspoon vanilla

Preheat the oven to 375°F.

Sift together the flour, baking soda, and salt and set aside.

Cream together the butter and peanut butter until light and smooth. Add the sugars and mix until they are completely incorporated and the mixture is smooth. Beat in the egg and vanilla.

Add the flour to the peanut butter mixture in three portions, mixing thoroughly. Cover the dough with plastic wrap and chill for 1 hour.

Drop level teaspoons of dough onto wax paper and shape into balls. Press crisscross patterns on the cookies with the tines of a fork. Bake for 10 to 12 minutes, or until the cookies are light golden and crisp. Remove from the baking sheet to racks to cool.

Ginger Cookies

Makes 4 dozen

2 cups all-purpose flour

¼ teaspoon salt

1 teaspoon baking soda

1 teaspoon ground ginger

½ teaspoon ground cloves

¼ pound (1 stick) butter

1 cup granulated sugar,
  plus more for sprinkling

1 egg

¼ dark molasses

1 tablespoon white vinegar

Preheat the oven to 375°F. Grease two baking sheets and set aside.

Sift together the flour, salt, baking soda, ginger, and cloves; set aside.

Cream the butter until glossy, add the sugar gradually, and mix until incorporated. Add the egg and beat until fluffy. Stir in the molasses and vinegar. Add the flour in two portions, mixing well after each addition.

Drop the dough by level teaspoons onto the prepared baking sheets, sprinkle with sugar, and bake for about 12 to 13 minutes, until lightly browned.

Snappy Star Anise Thins

Makes 5 dozen

2 cups all-purpose flour

1 teaspoon baking soda

1 tablespoon ground ginger

1 teaspoon ground star anise

½ teaspoon salt

½ pound (2 sticks) unsalted
   butter, at room temperature

½ cup dark brown sugar,
   firmly packed

½ cup granulated sugar

2 tablespoons honey

1 large egg

½ cup finely chopped
   crystallized ginger
   (about 3 ounces)

½ cup Demerara sugar

In a large bowl, whisk together the flour, baking soda, ginger, ground star anise, and salt; set aside.

Combine the butter and sugars in a medium bowl and cream together until light and fluffy. Add the honey and beat to combine. Add the egg and beat to combine. Add the chopped ginger and mix, then spoon in the dry ingredients and mix just to combine.

Cover the bowl with plastic wrap and chill for 30 to 45 minutes.

Preheat the oven to 350°F. Butter 2 baking sheets or line them with parchment paper.

Place the Demerara sugar in a shallow dish.

Shape the chilled dough into 1-inch balls, rolling between the palms of your hands to make them even. Roll the dough balls in the sugar, and place them, 3 inches apart, on the prepared baking sheets. Bake until the cookie tops are evenly browned and the edges appear firm, about 10 minutes. Remove from the oven and let stand for 3 to 4 minutes. Transfer to a wire rack to cool completely.

Orange Five-Spice Sugar Cookies

Makes 3 to 4 dozen

¾ pound (3 sticks) unsalted butter, at room temperature

1 cup granulated sugar

2 large egg yolks

2 tablespoons Chinese five-spice powder*

1 tablespoon finely grated orange zest

¼ teaspoon salt

4 cups all-purpose flour

Decorative sugar, for dusting

*Five-spice powder is available in Asian markets and the spice aisle of most supermarkets.

Using an electric mixer, cream the butter and sugar until light and fluffy. Beat in the egg yolks, one at a time, then stir in the five-spice powder, orange zest, and salt. Then stir in the flour. Continue to blend just until the dough comes together and is evenly mixed.

Divide the dough into three flattened disks, wrap in plastic wrap, and chill for at least 3 hours or overnight.

Preheat the oven to 350°F. with the oven racks set in the lower and upper thirds of the oven. Butter two baking sheets.

Work with one ball of dough at a time; roll out to ⅛-inch thickness between two sheets of lightly floured wax or parchment paper. Using a knife or cookie cutters, cut the dough into shapes and place on the baking sheets. Work in batches, keeping the remaining dough chilled until you're ready to use it. For the best defined shapes, chill the cookies on the baking sheets for about 5 minutes before baking.

Sprinkle the tops of the cookies with decorative sugar and bake for about 8 minutes, just until the bottoms begin to brown. Transfer the cookies to a wire rack to cool.

Frosted Cashew Cookies

Makes 5 dozen

Cookies

¼ pound (1 stick) unsalted butter, at room temperature

1 cup brown sugar

1 large egg,
   at room temperature

½ teaspoon vanilla

2 cups all-purpose flour

¾ teaspoon baking powder

¾ teaspoon baking soda

¼ teaspoon salt

⅓ cup sour cream

1½ cups chopped cashews

Frosting

2 tablespoons unsalted butter

2 to 3 tablespoons heavy
   cream, as needed

¼ teaspoon vanilla

2 cups confectioners' sugar

About 60 whole cashews

Preheat the oven to 350°F.

Using an electric mixer, cream the butter and brown sugar, then beat in the egg and vanilla.

Whisk together the flour, baking powder, baking soda, and salt. Add to the butter mixture alternately with the sour cream; blend until combined. Mix in the cashews. Drop the dough, 2 inches apart, onto greased baking sheets, and bake for 8 to 10 minutes. Do not over bake. Remove from sheets to a wire rack and allow them to cool completely before frosting.

To make the frosting, cook the butter in a small saucepan on medium high until the butter turns golden brown. Remove from the heat and add the cream and vanilla. Whisk in the confectioners' sugar, and add more cream as needed to achieve the right consistency. Frost the cookies, decorating tops with one whole cashew.

Butterscotch Cookies
with Brown Butter Icing

Makes 5 dozen

¼ pound (1 stick) unsalted
  butter, at room temperature

1½ cups brown sugar, packed

2 eggs

1 teaspoon vanilla

2½ cups all-purpose flour

1 teaspoon baking soda

½ teaspoon salt

1 cup sour cream

1 cup finely chopped walnuts

Brown Butter Icing

6 tablespoons unsalted butter

2 cups confectioners'
  sugar, sifted

1 teaspoon vanilla

2 to 3 tablespoons hot water

Using an electric mixer, cream the butter and sugar until light and fluffy. Blend in the eggs and vanilla, mixing well.

In a separate bowl, combine the flour, baking soda, and salt, and add the mixture to the butter mixture alternately with the sour cream, mixing well after each addition. Stir in the walnuts, wrap in plastic wrap, and chill for 4 hours or overnight.

Preheat the oven to 400°F.

Drop rounded teaspoonfuls of dough, 3 inches apart, onto a well-buttered baking sheet, and bake for 8 to 10 minutes, or until lightly browned. Cool on a wire rack.

Meanwhile, make the Brown Butter Icing. Melt the butter in a small saucepan over medium heat; continue heating until golden brown. Cool the butter, then stir in the sugar and vanilla. Add enough water to reach a spreading consistency, then ice the cookies.

Latin Lace Florentines

Makes 4 dozen

¾ cup quick-cooking oats

¾ cup all-purpose flour

¾ cup granulated sugar

1 teaspoon ground cinnamon

¾ teaspoon chili powder

½ teaspoon baking soda

½ teaspoon salt

1½ cups sliced almonds

¼ pound plus 2 tablespoons
   (1¼ sticks) unsalted
   butter, melted

¼ cup half-and-half
   or whole milk

¼ cup light corn syrup

1 teaspoon vanilla

4 ounces fine-quality
   bittersweet chocolate,
   chopped*

*For the best chocolate flavor, look for bittersweet chocolate with a minimum of 60% cocoa solids.

Preheat the oven to 350°F. with the oven rack set in the middle of the oven. Line a baking sheet with a silicone baking mat or heavy-duty aluminum foil buttered generously.

In a large bowl, whisk together the oats, flour, sugar, cinnamon, chili powder, baking soda, and salt. Stir in the almonds, then add the butter, half-and-half, corn syrup, and vanilla. Stir to combine.

Scoop heaping teaspoons of batter onto the prepared sheet at least 3 inches apart, 6 cookies per sheet. Bake one sheet at a time until the cookies are flat and browned around the edges, about 7 to 9 minutes. Cool the cookies on the sheet for about 5 minutes, or until firm enough to transfer to a wire rack.

When all of the cookies are baked, melt the chocolate in a metal bowl set over a pan of simmering water. Using a very small tipped pastry bag or the tines of a fork, drizzle the chocolate in a zigzag pattern over the tops of the cookies.

Lace Cookies

Makes 5 dozen

1 cup all-purpose flour

1 teaspoon cinnamon

⅛ teaspoon nutmeg

½ teaspoon baking soda

¼ teaspoon salt

¼ teaspoon ground ginger

¾ teaspoon baking powder

¼ pound (1 stick) butter

½ cup granulated sugar

½ cup light molasses

1 teaspoon lemon extract

Preheat the oven to 325°F. Grease and flour two baking sheets and set aside.

Sift together the flour, cinnamon, nutmeg, baking soda, salt, ginger, and baking powder.

In a medium-sized saucepan set over low heat, combine the butter, sugar, and molasses, stirring until it bubbles, about 10 minutes. Remove from the heat and let it cool a minute. Add the lemon extract and whisk in the flour mixture until the dough is completely mixed.

Place the saucepan over larger pan that is partially filled with hot water; let it sit for 5 minutes, and then remove from the heat.

Drop the dough by level teaspoons onto the prepared baking sheets about 3 inches apart. These cookies spread, so you want to give them room. Bake for 10 minutes, or until the cookies become reddish brown in color. Cool on the baking sheet for 2 minutes, then remove quickly to wire racks. While the cookies are still warm, drape them over a rolling pin or paper roll tube, so they form into half moon shapes. Let cool completely before serving.

Monster Whole Wheat Cookies

Makes 18

1¼ cups all-purpose flour

1 cup whole wheat
  all-purpose flour

1 teaspoon baking soda

Large pinch salt

¼ pound plus 4 tablespoons
  (1½ sticks) unsalted butter,
  at room temperature

¾ cup granulated sugar

¾ cup light brown sugar,
  packed

1½ teaspoon vanilla

2 eggs

2 cups toasted walnut pieces*

Maple Glaze

½ cup confectioners' sugar

2 teaspoons milk

1 teaspoon maple flavoring

*To toast walnuts, place the nuts in a single layer on an ungreased shallow pan. Bake at 350°F. for 5 to 10 minutes or until golden brown. Remove from the pan to cool.

Preheat the oven to 350°F. with the oven racks set in the upper and lower thirds of the oven.

Combine the flours, baking soda, and salt; set aside.

Using an electric mixer, cream the butter and sugars until light and fluffy. Add the vanilla, then add one egg at a time. Add the flour mixture into the butter mixture and thoroughly blend. Fold in the walnut pieces.

Using ¼ cup dough for each cookie, roll the dough into balls and space them 4 inches apart on buttered baking sheets. Using your fingers, flatten each ball to about 3 inches in diameter. Bake until the cookies are lightly browned around the edges, about 12 minutes. Remove from the oven and cool about 2 minutes on the baking sheets, then transfer to a wire rack to cool completely.

To make the glaze, thoroughly mix the sugar, milk, and maple flavoring until smooth. Add a drop or two more milk, if necessary to achieve drizzling consistency. Using a spoon, drizzle each cookie with glaze. Let the glaze set.

Caramel Sandies by the Sea

Makes 2 to 3 dozen

2 cups all-purpose flour

¼ teaspoon salt

½ pound (2 sticks) unsalted
   butter, at room temperature

⅔ cup light brown sugar,
   firmly packed

1 large egg

1 teaspoon vanilla

1 cup pecans, lightly toasted
   and finely ground*

20 caramel candies

3 tablespoons heavy cream
   or whole milk

2 to 3 tablespoons large crystal
   sea salt or fleur de sel**

1 cup chopped bittersweet
   chocolate or chocolate
   morsels (at least 60% cocoa)

*To toast pecans, place the nuts in a single
layer in an ungreased shallow pan. Bake at
350°F. for 5 to 10 minutes or until golden
brown. Remove from the pan to cool.

** Sea salt and fleur de sel are found at specialty food markets and most supermarkets.
For this recipe, choose a white or pink variety with large crystals.

Combine the flour and salt in a bowl and
set aside.

In a mixing bowl, cream the butter and
sugar until light and fluffy. Add the egg and
vanilla; beat to blend. Add the flour mixture in
batches, mixing in between each addition. Stir
in the pecans, cover the bowl with plastic wrap,
and chill until firm, about 1 to 2 hours.

Preheat the oven to 350°F. Butter or line
2 baking sheets with parchment paper.

With floured hands, roll the dough into
1-inch balls. Place the balls on the prepared
baking sheets, at least 1 inch apart. Lightly
press your thumb into the center of each ball,
forming a small cavity. Bake for 13 to 15 minutes or until the bottoms are brown and set.
Cool the cookies briefly on the baking sheets,
then transfer them to a wire rack set over a
piece of parchment paper.

In a saucepan set over low heat, melt the
caramel candies and cream together, stirring
frequently. Fill the center of each cookie with
approximately ½ teaspoon of caramel sauce.
Sprinkle the warm centers evenly with sea salt,
and let sit until firm.

Place the chocolate in a bowl and

microwave on medium for 30-second intervals. Mix the chocolate between each interval until it is thoroughly melted. Dip a spoon into the melted chocolate and drizzle chocolate across each cookie; add additional salt and allow the cookies to sit until the chocolate has become firm.

Chewy Chocolate-Chocolate Chunk Cookies

Makes 3 dozen

1⅓ cups unsalted butter

1 cup brown sugar, packed

1 cup granulated sugar

2 eggs

2 teaspoons vanilla

2¼ cups all-purpose flour

⅔ cup cocoa

¾ teaspoon baking soda

¼ teaspoon salt

8 ounces sweet baking
  chocolate, coarsely chopped

1 cup chopped pecans,
  optional

Preheat the oven to 350°F.

Using an electric mixer at medium speed, cream the butter and sugars until light and fluffy. Beat in the eggs and vanilla.

In a separate bowl, combine the flour, cocoa, baking soda, and salt, then gradually add to the egg mixture, stirring to combine well. Stir in the chocolate and pecans.

Drop rounded tablespoonfuls of dough, 2 inches apart, onto ungreased baking sheets and bake for 12 to 14 minutes or until set. Let stand 2 minutes before removing to a wire rack.

Chocolate-Covered Cherry Cookies

Makes 4 dozen

¼ pound (1 stick) unsalted
butter, at room temperature

1 cup granulated sugar

1 egg

1½ teaspoons vanilla

1½ cups all-purpose flour

¼ cup cocoa

¼ teaspoon baking powder

¼ teaspoon baking soda

¼ teaspoon salt

42 maraschino cherries,
drained

6 ounces semi-sweet
chocolate pieces

½ cup sweetened
condensed milk

4 to 5 teaspoons maraschino
cherry liquid

Preheat the oven to 350°F.

Using an electric mixer, cream the butter and sugar until light and fluffy. Blend in the egg and vanilla.

In a separate bowl, combine the flour, cocoa, baking powder, baking soda, and salt. Add to the butter mixture and mix well. Shape the dough into 1-inch balls, and place on an ungreased baking sheet.

Using your thumbs, make an indentation in the center of each ball; fill each indentation with one cherry.

In small saucepan set over low heat, combine the chocolate and condensed milk, stirring until smooth. Add enough cherry juice to make the mixture a nice spreading consistency. Drop 1 teaspoon of this chocolate mixture over each cherry, spreading to cover the cherry. Bake the cookies for 12 minutes or until set.

Chocolate Sour Cream Cookies

Makes 4 dozen

2 squares
  unsweetened chocolate

1¾ cups all-purpose flour

½ teaspoon baking soda

1 teaspoon baking powder

½ teaspoon salt

¼ teaspoon cinnamon

¼ pound plus 4 tablespoons
  butter, at room temperature

1⅓ cups granulated sugar

2 tablespoons vanilla

1 egg

½ cup sour cream

½ cup chopped pecans

Lightly grease two baking sheets and set aside.

Melt the chocolate in the microwave for about 15 to 20 seconds. Set aside to cool slightly.

Sift together the flour, baking soda, baking powder, salt, and cinnamon, and set aside.

Using an electric mixer, cream the butter, then add the sugar and beat until glossy. Stir in the vanilla and egg to incorporate. Stir in the chocolate and sour cream and mix thoroughly.

Add the flour in three portions, being sure to mix well after each addition. Stir in the pecans.

Preheat the oven to 425°F. about 10 minutes before baking.

Drop the dough onto the prepared baking sheets in heaping teaspoons about 2 inches apart. Bake for 9 to 10 minutes or until they look until barely done. Let the cookies cool on the baking sheet for 2 minutes before removing them to a wire rack to cool.

Noche Buena (Christmas Eve) Chocolate Sandwich Cookies

Makes 2 dozen

1½ cups all-purpose flour

¼ cup cocoa

1 teaspoon chili powder

1 teaspoon ground cinnamon

½ teaspoon salt

¼ pound plus 4 tablespoons (1½ sticks) unsalted butter, at room temperature

⅔ cup granulated sugar

2 large egg yolks

2 tablespoons coffee liqueur, such as Kahlúa® (or 2 tablespoons brewed coffee)

1 teaspoon vanilla

4 ounces bittersweet chocolate, finely chopped, melted, and cooled*

½ cup dulce de leche**, or very thick, spreadable caramel

Ground almonds, for garnish

Additional cocoa, cinnamon, and/or chili powder, for garnish

Preheat the oven to 350°F. with the oven racks set in the upper and lower thirds of the oven.

Sift or whisk together the flour, cocoa, chili powder, cinnamon, and salt in a bowl until combined. Set aside.

Using an electric mixer, cream the butter and sugar in a bowl until light and fluffy. Add the egg yolks, coffee liqueur, and vanilla and beat well, scraping down the sides after each addition. Mix in the cooled chocolate.

Reduce the mixer speed to low and add the flour mixture ½ cup at a time, mixing until combined well.

Drop the batter by rounded teaspoons 1 inch apart on ungreased baking sheets. Sprinkle the dough with ground almonds and bake, rotating the baking sheets halfway through baking, until the cookies are puffed up and dry looking around the edges, 8 to 10 minutes. Transfer the cookies to racks to cool. Continue with the remaining dough, making sure to let the baking sheets cool between batches.

To fill the cookies, spread ½ teaspoon of dulce de leche on the flat side of a cookie, then

* For the best chocolate flavor, look for bittersweet chocolate with a minimum of 60% cocoa solids.

**Dulce de leche is available near the canned milk at Latin markets and many supermarkets. To make your own from condensed milk, visit www.milk.com/recipes/dessert/dulce-de-leche.html

top with a second cookie to form a sandwich. Fill remaining cookies in the same manner. Dust the sandwiches with additional cocoa powder and a sprinkle of cinnamon, ground almonds, and/or chili powder.

Chocolate Macadamia Clusters

Clusters

1 cup granulated sugar

¼ pound (1 stick) unsalted
butter, at room temperature

1 large egg

6 to 8 ounces unsweetened
chocolate, melted and cooled

⅓ cup buttermilk

1 teaspoon vanilla

1¾ cups all-purpose flour

½ teaspoon baking soda

½ teaspoon salt

1 cup coarsely chopped
macadamia nuts or hazelnuts

Chocolate Frosting

2 ounces
unsweetened chocolate

2 tablespoons unsalted butter

3 tablespoons buttermilk

2 cups confectioners' sugar

Preheat the oven to 400°F.

Using an electric mixer, cream the sugar, butter, and egg. Mix in the chocolate, buttermilk, and vanilla until blended.

In a separate bowl, combine the flour, baking soda, salt, and nuts, then add it to the chocolate mixture. Drop the batter by rounded teaspoonfuls about 1 inch apart onto buttered baking sheets. Bake for 8 to 10 minutes, or until almost no imprint remains when a cookie is touched lightly in center. Remove at once from the baking sheet to a wire rack.

To make the Chocolate Frosting, melt the chocolate and butter together over low heat or in the microwave. Stir in the buttermilk and sugar until smooth. Frost the cooled cookies.

Dark Chocolate Candy Cane Crackles

Makes 4 dozen

1¼ cups all-purpose flour

½ cup unsweetened cocoa
   powder, sifted

½ teaspoon baking soda

½ teaspoon salt

½ cup (1 stick) unsalted butter,
   at room temperature

⅓ cup light brown sugar,
   firmly packed

⅓ cup granulated sugar

1 large egg

1 teaspoon vanilla

8 ounces candy canes or hard
   peppermint candies, crushed

4 ounces bittersweet
   chocolate, chopped into bits*

*For best chocolate flavor, look for good-
quality dark or bittersweet (not unsweetened) chocolate with a minimum of 70%
cocoa solids.

Preheat the oven to 350°F. Line a baking
sheet with a silicon baking mat or lightly
butter sheet.

Combine the flour, cocoa powder,
baking soda, and salt in a medium bowl. Whisk
to combine.

In a separate bowl, using an electric mixer,
cream together the butter and sugars until light
and fluffy. Scrape down the sides of bowl, add
the egg and vanilla, and beat to combine. With
the mixer on low, spoon in the flour mixture
and mix to combine. Add the crushed candy
and chocolate bits, mixing until evenly incorporated. Shape dough into 1-inch balls. Place
3 inches apart on baking sheet and flatten
slightly. Bake for 10 to 12 minutes.

Remove the baking sheet from the oven
and, using a metal spatula, immediately
neaten any edges where a piece of candy may
have melted. Let the cookies cool for about
5 minutes on the sheet, then transfer to a wire
rack to cool completely.

Candy Cane Cookies

Makes 2 dozen

Cookies

½ pound (2 sticks)
  unsalted butter

½ cup confectioners' sugar

¼ teaspoon salt

1 teaspoon almond flavoring

1 cup chopped almonds

2 cups all-purpose flour

Icing

2 cups confectioners' sugar

2 to 3 tablespoons milk

4 to 6 candy canes, crushed

Preheat the oven to 350°F.

Using an electric mixer, cream the butter, sugar, salt, and flavoring until light and fluffy. Stir in the almonds and flour until well blended.

Roll a heaping tablespoon of dough into a rope and form into a candy cane shape. Place on a well-buttered or parchment-lined baking sheet and repeat, using all of the dough, to make 20 to 24 candy-cane-shaped cookies. Bake until slightly browned, about 15 to 17 minutes. Cool on the pan until slightly firm, then carefully remove to a wire rack and cool completely.

To make the icing, stir the sugar and milk together. Drizzle on the cookies and sprinkle with crushed candy canes.

Festive Eggnog Wreath Cookies

Makes 2 dozen

3 to 3 ½ cups all-purpose flour

½ teaspoon salt

1 teaspoon ground nutmeg

½ pound (2 sticks) unsalted
   butter, at room temperature

¾ cup granulated sugar

1 egg, beaten

⅓ cup eggnog, substitute with
   heavy cream

2 teaspoons vanilla

1 teaspoon rum extract

¼ teaspoon red paste
   food coloring*

¼ teaspoon green paste
   food coloring*

1 egg white, beaten, optional

¼ cup coarse sugar, optional

1 tube prepared
   white decorator frosting

24 cinnamon candies, the small
   red circular kind, optional

*Traditional liquid food colors may be used,
however they will require a larger amount to
achieve the same vibrant colors.

Preheat the oven to 350°F.

Combine 3 cups of flour with the salt and nutmeg and set aside.

Using an electric mixer, cream the butter and sugar until fluffy. With the mixer on low, add the egg, eggnog, vanilla, and rum extract, and combine well, scraping down the sides as necessary. Gradually add the flour mixture, mixing until combined. Divide the mixture in half, placing each half in a separate bowl.

Cover your work surface with plastic wrap or wax paper, dust the surface, and put on some rubber gloves. (These food colorings can stain surfaces and hands, so be forewarned!) Put one half of the dough on your work surface and make a well in the center. Add the red food coloring paste and knead the dough until the color is evenly distributed in the dough. Add more flour as necessary.

Roll the into a 12-inch log, wrap in plastic wrap or waxed paper, and refrigerate for at least 30 minutes. Repeat with the remaining dough and green coloring paste.

Cut each log into 24 pieces and roll each piece into a 6- to 8-inch-long rope. Place a red and green rope side-by-side, then twist one rope over the other, like a braid, ending by gently pressing the ends together into a circular wreath. Repeat with the remaining red and green ropes.

Place the wreaths on parchment-lined or ungreased baking sheets about 2 inches apart. Brush the wreaths with egg white and sprinkle with sugar. Bake for 10 to 12 minutes, or until lightly browned. Cool the cookies on the baking sheets until they can be handled, then remove them to a wire rack to cool completely.

Pipe frosting bows on the wreaths and top with a cinnamon candy.

Pomegranate Almond Thumbprints

Makes 4 to 5 dozen

2 cups all-purpose flour

½ teaspoon salt

1½ cup slivered almonds

⅔ cup granulated sugar

½ pound (2 sticks) unsalted
   butter, at room temperature

1½ teaspoons vanilla

2 large eggs, separated

⅓ cup sliced or slivered
   almonds, finely chopped,
   for garnish

¾ cup pomegranate jelly*

Confectioners' sugar,
   for garnish

*Pomegranate jelly may be found in
specialty food stores or ordered online
at www.pomegranatejelly.com.

Preheat the oven to 350°F. Line 2 baking sheets with parchment paper or leave them ungreased.

Combine the flour and salt in a bowl and set aside.

Combine the almonds and ⅓ cup of sugar in a food processor fitted with a metal blade. Pulse until finely ground. (Be careful not to grind to a paste).

In a medium bowl, cream together the butter and remaining sugar until light and fluffy. Add the almond mixture and combine. Add the vanilla and egg yolks and mix to combine. Mix in the flour.

Roll the dough into 1-inch balls and place them 2 inches apart on the baking sheets. Dip your thumbs in flour and use them to make deep indentations in the center of each cookie.

Lightly whisk the egg whites. Brush each cookie with egg white and scatter a few chopped almonds on the outer edge of each cookie. Fill the centers with ½ teaspoon of jelly.

Bake until the edges of the cookies are golden brown, about 15 to 18 minutes. If needed, add more jelly to each cookie. Let stand for 3 to 4 minutes. Transfer to a wire rack and dust with confectioners' sugar.

Chewy Cranberry Oatmeal Cookies

1½ cups all-purpose flour

1 teaspoon baking soda

½ teaspoon salt

½ teaspoon cinnamon

2½ cups old-fashioned oats

½ pound (2 sticks) unsalted
   butter, at room temperature

1 cup light brown sugar,
   packed

½ cup granulated sugar

2 large eggs

1 tablespoon honey

2 teaspoons vanilla

1⅓ cups dried cranberries

1 cup white chocolate chunks

Preheat the oven to 350°F. Cover 2 baking sheets with parchment paper.

In a medium bowl, mix the flour, baking soda, salt, and cinnamon; stir in the oats and set aside.

Using an electric mixer, cream the butter and sugars until light and fluffy. Beat in the eggs, one at a time. Add the honey and vanilla and beat until blended. Add the flour mixture in two additions, beating until well combined. Stir in the cranberries and chocolate chunks.

Drop the dough by heaping tablespoons onto the baking sheets, about 2 inches apart. Bake about 9 to 11 minutes; the centers of the cookies will be soft. Let the cookies cool on the sheets for 5 minutes, then transfer to a wire rack to cool completely.

Coconut-Lime Thai Snowballs

Makes 4 to 5 dozen

½ pound (2 sticks) unsalted
   butter, at room temperature

1 cup confectioners' sugar

1 teaspoon lime oil or
   2 tablespoons lime juice

1½ teaspoon finely grated
   lime zest

¼ teaspoon salt

2 cups all-purpose flour

1 cup unsweetened shredded
   coconut (medium shred)

Coating

1 cup unsweetened shredded
   coconut (medium shred)

1 cup confectioners'
   sugar, sifted

1½ teaspoon finely grated
   lime zest

2 tablespoons cornstarch,
   sifted

Preheat the oven to 350°F. with the racks set in the lower and upper thirds of the oven.

Using an electric mixer, cream the butter and sugars until light and fluffy. Add the lime oil and beat to combine. Gently fold in the lime zest, salt, flour, and coconut. Blend well.

Lightly flour your hands and roll the dough into 1-inch balls. Place the balls about 1½ inches apart on an ungreased baking sheet and bake for about 15 minutes, until the cookies are puffy, not browned, and the bottoms are golden. Allow the cookies to cool on baking sheets for about 5 minutes.

Meanwhile, combine the coating ingredients in a quart- or gallon-size plastic bag. While the cookies are still warm, carefully toss them in the coating. Place the cookies on a wire rack to cool completely.

Mojito Jammies

Makes 2 dozen

¾ cup granulated sugar

1 tablespoon grated lime zest

¼ teaspoon salt

2½ cups all-purpose flour

½ pound (2 sticks) unsalted
  butter, chilled (but not too
  firm) and cut into cubes

2 tablespoons cream cheese

1 large egg yolk

2 teaspoons rum, or
  1½ teaspoons vanilla

¼ teaspoon peppermint
  extract

Filling

¾ cup mint jelly

1 tablespoon rum or water

1 teaspoon granulated sugar

Confectioners' sugar,
  for dusting

In a food processor fitted with the metal blade, combine the sugar and lime zest. Add the salt and flour, mixing to combine. Add the butter and cream cheese and mix until the dough resembles coarse sand. Add the egg yolk, rum, and peppermint extract. Mix until the dough clumps together.

Transfer the dough to a large mixing bowl and knead with your hands until it holds together in a ball. Divide the dough into two disks, wrap in plastic wrap, and refrigerate for 20 to 30 minutes.

Preheat the oven to 350°F. with the oven racks set in the upper and lower thirds of the oven. Butter or line two baking sheets with parchment paper.

Working with one disk at a time, roll out the dough between sheets of lightly floured wax or parchment paper to ⅛-inch thickness. Slide the dough, still between the sheets of paper, onto a baking sheet, and chill for 10 to 20 minutes. Remove the top paper, carefully turn the dough over and remove the remaining paper.

Using a 2- to 2½-inch cookie cutter, cut the dough into shapes and place about

1½ inches apart on the prepared baking sheets. Cut a hole out of the center of half the cookies to make a window for the filling. Gather the remaining dough scraps into a ball, re-roll and cut into shapes. Do this only once.

Bake the cookies for about 10 to 15 minutes, rotating the baking sheet about halfway through the baking time, until lightly golden. The cookies with the cutout centers will bake more quickly. Let the cookies cool on a wire rack.

Combine the mint jelly, rum, and sugar in a small saucepan set over medium heat. Simmer for 2 to 3 minutes, the cool to room temperature. Using a small strainer or sugar shaker, dust the top halves of the cookies (the ones with the holes in the centers) with confectioners' sugar. Place about ¾ teaspoon of mint jelly onto a cookie bottom, smearing it lightly around the whole cookie leaving a small mound in the center. Top with a sugar-dusted half.

Meyer Lemon Ricotta Cookies

Makes 4 dozen

Cookies

½ pound (2 sticks) unsalted
  butter, at room temperature

2 cups granulated sugar

2 large eggs

15 ounces whole milk
  ricotta cheese

½ teaspoon lemon extract,
  or 1 teaspoon lemon and/or
  tangerine baking oil

3 tablespoons Meyer lemon
  zest, freshly grated*

1 tablespoon Meyer
  lemon juice

2½ cups all-purpose flour

1 teaspoon baking powder

1 teaspoon salt

Glaze

6 tablespoons unsalted butter

3 cups confectioners' sugar

3 to 4 tablespoons Meyer
  lemon juice

Decorating sugar,
  silver dragées

Preheat the oven to 350°F. and line 2 baking sheets with parchment paper.

In a large bowl, using an electric mixer, cream the butter and sugar until light and fluffy. Add the eggs, ricotta, lemon extract, zest, and juice; blend well. Add 1 cup of flour, the baking powder, and salt; blend to combine. Add the remaining flour in two parts, blending to combine between each, until a dough forms.

Drop by rounded tablespoons onto the baking sheets, about 2 inches apart. Bake until the cookie edges are very light golden, about 12 to 15 minutes. Let the cookies rest on the baking sheet for a few minutes, then transfer to a wire rack.

Meanwhile, prepare the glaze by creaming together the butter and sugar. Continue to mix, gradually adding the lemon juice until the glaze reaches the consistency of syrup. Drop a small amount of glaze on top of each cookie and spread so it almost reaches the edges. Decorate with silver dragées before the icing sets.

*Meyer lemons are available mid-November through early spring in specialty food stores. You will need 2 to 3 medium-sized lemons. Regular lemons can be substituted.

Lemon Cream Cheese Cookies

Makes about 3 dozen

½ pound (2 sticks) butter,
  at room temperature

¼ teaspoon salt

3 ounces cream cheese

1 cup granulated sugar

2 egg yolks

2 teaspoon vanilla

1½ teaspoon lemon zest

2¼ cups all-purpose
  flour, sifted

Lightly grease 2 baking sheets. Preheat the oven to 400°F. about 10 minutes before baking.

Using an electric mixer, cream the butter, salt, and cream cheese until smooth. Add the sugar in 2 or 3 portions, mixing well to incorporate after each addition.

In a separate bowl, beat the yolks until fluffy, then stir in the vanilla and lemon zest. Stir in the flour in 3 portions, mixing well after each addition. Cover and chill dough for an hour.

Using only one-third of the dough at a time, roll out the dough on a lightly floured surface. Cut out the cookies with a 2½-inch cookie cutter, and place them 1-inch apart on the prepared baking sheets. Bake for 10 to 12 minutes, until the tops are a light golden color. Remove from the baking sheets and place on racks to cool. Repeat with remaining dough.

Chocolate Walnut Biscotti

Makes 2 to 3 dozen

2 cups all-purpose flour

½ cup unsweetened
cocoa powder

1 teaspoon baking soda

1 teaspoon salt

6 tablespoons unsalted butter,
at room temperature

1 cup granulated sugar

2 large eggs

1 cup chopped walnuts

1 cup semisweet
chocolate chips

Confectioners' sugar,
as needed

Preheat the oven to 350°F. Grease and flour a large baking sheet.

Whisk together the flour, cocoa, baking soda, and salt; set aside.

Using an electric mixer, cream the butter and sugar until light and fluffy, about 2 minutes. Add the eggs and beat until well blended. Add the flour mixture and mix to form a stiff dough. Stir in the walnuts and chocolate chips.

With floured hands, form the dough into two flattened logs, about 12 inches long and 2 inches wide. Place the logs on the baking sheet and sprinkle each with confectioners' sugar. Bake the logs for 35 minutes or until the tops are slightly firm. Cool on the baking sheets for 5 minutes.

Carefully transfer the logs to a cutting board. With a very sharp serrated knife, slice the logs diagonally into ¾-inch wide slices. Place the slices, cut sides down, on the baking sheet and return to the oven and bake until crisp, about 10 minutes. Cool on a wire rack.

Sour Cream Brownies with Mascarpone Topping

Makes 9

Sour Cream Brownies

5 tablespoons unsalted
  butter, melted

1½ tablespoons instant coffee

2 tablespoons boiling water

1 (21- to 24-ounce) package
  brownie mix

¾ cup sour cream

2 eggs

Mascarpone Topping

8 ounces mascarpone cheese,
  at room temperature

½ cup heavy cream, whipped

2 tablespoons
  confectioners' sugar

½ teaspoon vanilla

Cocoa or bittersweet
  chocolate shavings,
  for garnish

Preheat the oven to 350°F. Using only about 1 tablespoon of the butter, butter the bottom only of a 9-inch square baking pan.

In a large bowl, dissolve the coffee in the water, then add the brownie mix, sour cream, remaining butter, and eggs; mix well. Spread the batter into the prepared pan. Bake for 25 to 30 minutes, or until the brownies begin to pull away from the sides of the pan and the center is just set (do not over bake). Transfer the pan to a wire rack to cool completely.

Meanwhile, make the Mascarpone Topping. Stir the mascarpone cheese until soft, then add the cream, sugar, and vanilla. Continue stirring until the mixture is smooth.

Cut the cooled brownies into 3-inch squares and pipe or spoon on the mascarpone topping. Garnish with cocoa or chocolate shavings. Cover lightly and refrigerate until serving time.

Decadent Chocolate Brownies

Makes 18

2 ounces unsweetened
  chocolate

¼ pound (1 stick)
  unsalted butter

1 cup granulated sugar

2 eggs

½ cup all-purpose flour

Pinch of salt

½ teaspoon vanilla

White chocolate, melted,
  for decoration

Heat oven to 350°F. Butter a 9-inch square pan.

Melt the chocolate and butter together in a small saucepan set over low heat, stirring occasionally. When the chocolate is melted, remove from the heat and stir until smooth. Transfer the mixture to a bowl, add the sugar, and stir. Beat in the eggs one at a time. Stir in the flour, salt, and vanilla. Pour the dough into the prepared pan and bake for 20 to 25 minutes, or until the sides are set and the center is soft. Cool before cutting into 1½-inch squares. Drizzle with melted white chocolate.

Cocoa Brownies

Makes 16

¾ cup all-purpose flour

¼ teaspoon salt

¼ cup cocoa

1 cup granulated sugar

¼ pound (1 stick) butter,
  at room temperature

2 eggs

2 teaspoons vanilla

½ cup chopped nuts, your choice

Preheat the oven to 350°F. Butter a 9-inch square baking pan.

Sift together the flour, salt, cocoa, and sugar into a mixing bowl. Add the butter, eggs, and vanilla, and beat with an electric mixer for 2 minutes on medium speed until well blended. Stir in the nuts until just incorporated. Pour into the prepared pan and bake for 20 to 24 minutes, or until just done. Cool in the pan on a wire rack before cutting into squares.

Black Forest Brownie Bars

Makes 24

Bars

4 ounces unsweetened
  chocolate

¼ pound (1 stick)
  unsalted butter

¾ cup all-purpose flour

¼ teaspoon salt

2 large eggs

I cup light brown sugar, packed

2 teaspoons vanilla

½ cup chopped walnuts

½ cup mini semi-sweet
  chocolate chips

Cherry Cream Cheese
Topping

¼ pound (1 stick)
  unsalted butter

4 ounces cream cheese,
  at room temperature

1 teaspoon vanilla

1¼ cups confectioners' sugar

1 cup dried cherries,
  finely chopped

Chocolate Drizzle

2 ounces semi-sweet chocolate chips

1 tablespoon heavy cream

Preheat the oven to 325°F. Butter a 13 x 9-inch baking pan.

To make the bars, melt the chocolate and butter in a small saucepan or in the microwave, stirring until smooth; set aside to cool.

Combine the flour and salt in a bowl; set aside.

In a mixing bowl, beat the eggs until fluffy, about 1 minute. Gradually beat in the brown sugar. Add the cooled chocolate mixture and vanilla, then stir in the flour mixture until blended. Stir in the walnuts and chocolate chips.

Spread the batter in the prepared pan and bake for 20 to 22 minutes, or until a toothpick inserted in the center comes out clean. Cool in the pan on a wire rack.

Meanwhile, make the Cherry Cream Cheese Topping. Using an electric mixer, cream the butter and cream cheese until light and fluffy. Gradually beat in the vanilla and confectioners' sugar. Stir in the cherries.

When the brownies have cooled, spread this filling evenly over the top and refrigerate until set.

To make the Chocolate Drizzle, melt the chocolate chips and cream over low heat or in the microwave. Cool slightly, then dip a fork into the mixture and drizzle over the cherry layer. Chill until firm.

Peppermint Cream Brownies

Makes 18

⅔ cup all-purpose flour

¼ teaspoon baking powder

⅛ teaspoon salt

6 tablespoons butter,
  at room temperature

2 teaspoons vanilla

¾ cup granulated sugar

2 eggs

2 squares unsweetened
  chocolate, melted

1 tablespoon milk

½ cup chopped pecans
  or walnuts

Peppermint Cream

2 tablespoons butter,
  at room temperature

1 cup confectioners'
  sugar, sifted

1 tablespoon hot milk

2 tablespoons light corn syrup

Pinch of salt

⅛ teaspoon peppermint
  extract

Red food coloring, optional

Preheat the oven to 350°F. 10 minutes before baking. Grease two 8 x 8 x 2-inch pans, and line the bottoms with waxed paper.

Sift together the flour, baking powder, and salt, and set aside.

Cream the butter and vanilla until smooth, then slowly add the sugar while continuing to mix. Beat in the eggs one at a time creaming well after each addition. Stir in the chocolate, then the milk, and mix until well blended. Stir in the flour and mix well, then add the nuts and mix lightly.

Divide the dough into each of the prepared pans and bake for 20 minutes.

Cool for about 3 minutes, then turn the brownies out onto the rack, loosening the paper and inverting, leaving paper underneath.

Meanwhile, prepare the Peppermint Butter Cream. Cream the butter until it appears glossy, then add the sugar gradually with the milk. Stir in the syrup, salt, peppermint extract, and food coloring. Beat until it is a smooth consistency.

When the brownies are just cool, turn them over and remove the paper.

Spread one layer of brownies with the Peppermint Butter Cream. Top with the other layer and press together gently. Cut into bars.

Blondies

Makes 16

¾ cup all-purpose flour

¼ teaspoon baking powder

½ teaspoon salt

¼ pound (1 stick) butter

1 cup light brown sugar, packed

2 eggs, beaten

1 teaspoon vanilla

¾ cup chopped walnuts or pecans

Preheat the oven to 350°F. Grease a 9-inch square pan and set aside.

Sift together the flour, baking powder, and salt; set aside.

Melt the butter in a 1-quart saucepan over low heat and add the sugar, stirring with a wooden spoon until smooth. Remove from the heat and allow to cool slightly.

Beat in the eggs until well incorporated, then add the vanilla and flour mixture, mixing until well incorporated.

Spread the batter into the prepared pan and sprinkle with nuts. Bake for 20 to 25 minutes, or until the blondies look barely done and lightly golden.

Caribbean Coco-Almond Bars

Makes 16

Cookie Crust

¾ cup all-purpose flour

⅓ cup light brown sugar,
   firmly packed

¼ teaspoon salt

1½ teaspoon ground cinnamon

½ teaspoon ground allspice

½ cup (1 stick) unsalted
   butter, chilled and cut into
   small pieces

¾ cup toasted and finely
   chopped almonds*

1 tablespoon dark rum**

Coconut Filling

1½ cups medium shred
   unsweetened coconut

½ cup sweetened
   condensed milk

2 tablespoons unsalted butter

2 tablespoons dark rum

¼ teaspoons salt

*To toast almonds, place the nuts in a single layer in an ungreased shallow pan. Bake at 350°F. for 5 to 10 minutes, or until golden brown. Remove from the pan to cool.

**Fruit juice (such as orange juice) may be substituted for dark rum.

Chocolate Layer

3 tablespoons unsalted butter

4 ounces bittersweet chocolate
   (at least 60% cocoa), chopped

2 tablespoons heavy cream or evaporated milk

1 cup shredded coconut, for garnish

Sliced almonds, for garnish

Preheat the oven to 350°F. Line an 8-inch square pan with heavy-duty foil that extends over edges of pan; butter the foil.

In a food processor fitted with a metal blade or in a large bowl and using a pastry blender, combine the flour, brown sugar, salt, cinnamon, and allspice; add the butter in small intervals until the texture resembles coarse cornmeal. Mix in the almonds and rum.

Press the dough firmly and evenly into the prepared pan, and bake until the crust deflates (it will puff at first) and the edges are barely firm to the touch, about 15 minutes. Cool slightly on a wire rack.

As the crust cools, blend the filling ingredients together in a bowl. When the crust is firm and still warm, spoon in the filling, spreading it evenly. Return the pan to the oven and bake until the edges turn golden, about 15 minutes. Cool on a wire rack.

Make the chocolate layer by combining the butter, chocolate, and cream in a small saucepan over low heat. Heat while whisking until the mixture is melted and smooth. Pour the hot topping over the cooled filling and spread evenly.

Sprinkle with coconut and almonds while the chocolate layer is still hot. Refrigerate for 4 hours or overnight before bringing to room temperature and cutting into bars

Buttery Oatmeal
Turtle Bars

Makes 48

Caramel Topping

¼ pound (1 stick) unsalted
  butter, at room temperature

⅔ cup brown sugar, packed

½ teaspoon vanilla

Bars

1 cup all-purpose flour

1 cup rolled oats

¾ cup brown sugar, packed

¼ pound (1 stick)
  unsalted butter,
  at room temperature

1½ cup whole pecans

8 ounces sweet
  baking chocolate

Preheat the oven to 350°F.

Combine the butter and brown sugar in a heavy saucepan over medium heat, stirring constantly until the entire surface of the mixture is boiling. Boil for 1 minute, then remove from the heat and add the vanilla. Set aside.

Combine the flour, oats, brown sugar, and butter. Mix until well-blended. Pat firmly into an ungreased 13 x 9 x 2-inch baking pan. Sprinkle with the pecans and pour the caramel topping evenly over top. Bake until the caramel is bubbly, about 15 to 18 minutes.

Break the chocolate into small chunks and sprinkle evenly over the caramel layer. Bake for 1 minute longer to allow the chocolate to melt. Swirl the chocolate for a marbled effect. Cool slightly, then chill to set chocolate. Cut into bars.

Triple Chocolate Caramel Peanut Bars

Makes 2 to 3 dozen

1 (14-ounce) package caramels

⅔ cup chocolate milk

1 (18-ounce) package German chocolate cake mix

¼ pound (1 stick) unsalted butter, melted

2 cups salted peanuts

1½ cups semi-sweet chocolate pieces

Preheat the oven to 350°F.

In a 4-cup measuring cup or bowl, microwave on high power the caramels and ⅓ cup of chocolate milk for 3 to 4 minutes or until smooth when stirred.

In a large bowl, thoroughly mix together the remaining ⅓ cup chocolate milk, cake mix, and butter. Reserve 1 cup of this mixture, then pour the remaining cake mixture into the bottom of an ungreased 13 x 9-inch baking pan. Bake for 10 minutes, then sprinkle 1½ cups of the peanuts and 1 cup of the chocolate pieces over top.

Drizzle the top with the caramel mixture, then top with spoonfuls of the remaining cake mixture, flattening them with a spatula, pressing into the caramel.

Sprinkle overtop the remaining ½ cup peanuts and ½ cup chocolate pieces, and press down lightly. Continue baking for 18 minutes. Cool before cutting into bars.

Cranberry Cream-Cheese Bars

Makes 15 to 20

3 cups cranberries

1½ cups granulated sugar

½ cup water

2 tablespoons cornstarch

1 cup all-purpose flour

½ cup ground pecans

¼ pound (1 stick)
  unsalted butter

16 ounces cream cheese,
  at room temperature

1 cup confectioners' sugar

2 tablespoons lemon juice

½ teaspoon grated lemon zest

1½ cups heavy cream,
  whipped, plus more
  for serving

Preheat the oven to 350°F.

In a 2-quart saucepan set over high heat, combine the cranberries, sugar, water, and cornstarch. Bring to a boil and cook, stirring constantly, until the cranberry skins pop. Cool.

Combine the flour and pecans and, using 2 knives or a pastry cutter, cut in the butter until the mixture resembles coarse crumbs. Pour into a 13 x 9 x 2-inch pan, and pat down. Bake for 15 minutes, then cool on a wire rack.

Combine the cream cheese, confectioners' sugar, and lemon juice, mixing until well-blended. Add the lemon zest and fold in the whipped cream. Spread this mixture over the cooled crust, then top with the cooled cranberry mixture. Chill for several hours before serving with additional whipped cream.

Old-Fashioned Steamed Pudding

Makes 12 servings

2½ cups all-purpose flour

¼ cup granulated sugar

1 teaspoon baking powder

1 teaspoon ground cinnamon

½ teaspoon baking soda

¼ teaspoon salt

¼ teaspoon ground cloves

2 eggs, beaten

¾ cup molasses

¾ cup milk

¼ pound (1 stick) unsalted
   butter, melted

½ cup chopped pecans

Hard Sauce

¼ pound (1 stick)
   unsalted butter

2 cups confectioners' sugar

2 tablespoons heavy cream

½ teaspoon shredded
   lemon zest

½ teaspoon vanilla

In large mixing bowl, combine the flour, sugar, baking powder, cinnamon, baking soda, salt, and cloves. Stir to mix well.

In a small mixing bowl, combine the eggs, molasses, milk, and butter; mix well. Stir the egg mixture into the flour mixture, then gently fold in the pecans. Pour the batter into a greased and floured 8-cup fluted tube pan. Cover the pan with foil, tying the foil securely in place with string, if necessary.

Place the pan on a wire rack in a deep pot and add boiling water to a depth of 1 inch. (Water should not touch the pan.) Cover the pot and adjust the heat so the water boils gently for 75 minutes, or until a wooden toothpick inserted near the center comes out clean. (Add more hot water as necessary to maintain the 1 inch depth.)

Remove the pudding pan and let stand for 10 minutes. Invert the pudding over a wire rack and carefully unmold the pudding. Let the pudding stand for 30 to 40 minutes before serving.

Meanwhile, make the Hard Sauce. In a medium mixing bowl, combine the butter, 1 cup of confectioners' sugar, the cream, lemon zest, and vanilla. Beat with an electric mixer on medium speed until thoroughly combined. Add the remaining 1 cup confectioners' sugar and beat until smooth.

To serve, place the pudding on a serving platter. With a pastry bag, pipe Hard Sauce on the platter around the pudding.

Creamy Chocolate Pudding

Makes 4 servings

¾ cup granulated sugar

2 tablespoons cornstarch

¼ teaspoon salt

2 cups milk

2 ounces unsweetened
   chocolate, chopped

2 egg yolks, beaten

2 tablespoons unsalted butter

1½ teaspoons vanilla

In a heavy-bottomed medium-sized saucepan set over medium heat, combine the sugar, cornstarch, and salt. Stir in the milk and chocolate and cook, stirring, until the mixture is thickened and bubbly. Cook and stir for 2 minutes more, then remove from the heat.

Gradually stir 1 cup of the sugar mixture into the egg yolks, then return the yolk mixture to the saucepan. Cook and stir for 2 minutes, then remove from the heat.

Add the butter and vanilla, and stir until the butter melts. Pour the mixture into a medium bowl and cover with clear plastic wrap. Chill until the pudding sets.

Chocolate Fig Pudding

Makes 6 servings

6 tablespoons unsalted butter

½ cup granulated sugar

2 eggs

1 teaspoon vanilla

½ cup unsweetened
cocoa powder

⅓ cup semi-sweet
chocolate chunks

1⅓ cups all-purpose flour

½ teaspoon salt

¼ teaspoon cream of tartar

¼ teaspoon baking soda

1 cup buttermilk

1 cup dried figs, diced

1¼ cups heavy cream,
whipped, for serving

Preheat the oven to 325°F. Butter 6 individual molds or 1 (1½-quart) pudding mold.

Using an electric mixer, cream the butter and sugar. Beat in the eggs and vanilla, then add the cocoa powder and mix until light and fluffy.

In a separate bowl, stir together the chocolate chunks, flour, salt, cream of tartar, and baking soda. Add the dry ingredients to the chocolate mixture alternately with the buttermilk; mix well. Fold in the figs.

Pour the batter into the prepared mold(s). Place the pudding(s) on the center rack of the oven, and place a roasting pan filled halfway with boiling water on the rack below.

Bake individual molds for 35 minutes or the large mold for 1 hour, or until a toothpick inserted in the center comes out nearly clean. Cool for 10 minutes before unmolding. Serve warm with whipped cream.

Plum Pudding
with Supreme Sauce

Makes 8 to 10 servings

Plum Pudding

1 cup soft white breadcrumbs

½ pound (2 sticks) unsalted
   butter, chilled and
   cut in cubes

1 medium apple,
   peeled and chopped

¾ cup brown sugar,
   firmly packed

1 cup raisins

½ cup finely chopped dates

½ cup finely chopped figs

½ cup chopped walnuts

½ cup diced citron, substitute
   with chopped dried cherries

½ cup all-purpose flour

½ teaspoon ground cinnamon

½ teaspoon ground nutmeg

½ teaspoon salt

2 teaspoons baking powder

2 large eggs, well beaten

1 cup milk

Supreme Sauce

1 cup granulated sugar

½ cup water

2 large egg yolks, beaten

1 tablespoon vanilla

1 cup heavy cream,
   stiffly beaten

To make the Plum Pudding, combine the breadcrumbs, butter, apple, brown sugar, raisins, dates, figs, walnuts and citron (or dried cherries) in a large bowl and mix with your hands.

In a separate bowl, whisk together the flour, cinnamon, nutmeg, salt, and baking powder. Combine this mixture with the fruit mixture, then add the eggs and milk, and stir until blended.

Pour the dough into a well-buttered 6-cup mold and cover with aluminum foil. Place the mold on a wire rack in the bottom of large pan that contains 1 inch of water. (Be sure the water does not touch the mold.) Bring the water to a simmer, then cover the pan with a lid and steam on low for 3 hours. Remove the mold from the pan and let cool for 30 minutes on a wire rack before inverting onto a serving platter.

Meanwhile, make the Supreme Sauce. Combine the sugar with the water in a small saucepan. Bring to a boil, stirring constantly. Place a thermometer in the pan and boil until the syrup reaches 250°F. to 255°F.

Carefully and gradually add the hot syrup to the egg yolks, beating constantly until the mixture is creamy; then add the vanilla. Just before serving, fold in the whipped cream.

Serve the warm pudding with sauce poured overtop.

DID YOU KNOW?
Butter is graded by letter code, AA, A or B, according to flavor, texture, aroma and body, with AA being the supreme quality. Most butter sold in supermarkets is AA.

Bread Pudding with Dried Cherries and Caramel Sauce

Makes 8 servings

Bread Pudding

4 cups cubed cinnamon swirl
bread (about 8 slices)

⅔ cup dried cherries
or cranberries

4 large eggs

¾ cups granulated sugar

1 teaspoon vanilla

½ teaspoon salt

2½ cups half-and-half
or whole milk

Caramel Sauce

¾ cup granulated sugar

6 tablespoons unsalted butter

⅓ cup corn syrup

1½ cups heavy cream

¼ teaspoon salt

Preheat the oven to 350°F. Butter an 11 x 7-inch baking dish or oval 1½-quart casserole dish.

Place the bread cubes in the prepared dish and sprinkle the cherries overtop.

In a large bowl, beat together the eggs, sugar, vanilla, and salt. Stir in the half-and-half until well blended. Pour the egg mixture over the bread mixture, pressing down on the bread to coat. Let stand for 15 minutes, then bake for 40 to 45 minutes or until the bread is puffed and golden brown.

Meanwhile, make the Caramel Sauce. Combine the sugar, butter, corn syrup and ½ cup of cream in a heavy-bottomed saucepan. Bring to a boil over medium-high heat, then reduce the heat to medium-low and boil, uncovered and stirring frequently, until the sauce is thickened and golden brown, about 10 to 12 minutes. Gradually stir in the remaining 1 cup of cream and salt. Return to a boil, stirring constantly.

Serve the bread pudding warm or at room temperature with warm or room temperature caramel sauce.

Chocolate Bread Pudding
with Vanilla Custard Sauce

Makes 8 servings

2 cups chocolate milk

6 ounces semi-sweet
  chocolate pieces

2 tablespoons unsalted butter

2 egg yolks

⅓ cup granulated sugar

2 egg whites, stiffly beaten

6 cups day-old French
  bread cubes

Vanilla Custard Sauce

2 cups milk

1 teaspoon vanilla

4 egg yolks

⅓ cup granulated sugar

Combine the milk, chocolate, and butter in a microwavable bowl. Microwave on high for 4 to 5 minutes or until the milk is steamy but not boiling. Stir to melt the chocolate and butter.

In another bowl, beat the egg yolks and sugar. Add some of the chocolate to the egg mixture and mix. Gradually pour the egg mixture into the chocolate, mixing well. Fold in the egg whites, then stir in the bread cubes. Let stand for 1 hour.

Preheat the oven to 325°F. Butter a 2-quart casserole dish. Pour the bread mixture into the prepared casserole dish and bake for 1 hour or until set.

Combine the milk and vanilla in a microwavable bowl and microwave on high for 4 to 5 minutes or until steamy but not boiling.

In a separate bowl, beat the egg yolks and sugar. Add a small amount of the milk to the egg mixture and mix. Gradually pour the egg mixture into the rest of the milk mixture, mixing well. Microwave on high for 1½ minutes, then stir. Continue microwaving 1½ to 2 minutes or until thickened, stirring every 30 seconds. Strain and cool.

Serve warm, topped Vanilla Custard Sauce.

Rustic Cherry-Apple Pie

Makes 8 servings

Crust

2 cups all-purpose flour

2 tablespoons
confectioners' sugar

1 teaspoon salt

¼ pound plus 4 tablespoons
(1½ sticks) unsalted butter,
chilled and cut into cubes

1 teaspoon vinegar

5 to 6 tablespoons ice water

Filling

½ cup light brown
sugar, packed

¼ cup cornstarch

1 teaspoon cinnamon

3 cups Fuji, Gala, or Granny
Smith apples, peeled
and sliced

1 cup dark sweet or
tart cherries*

1 tablespoon lemon juice

5 tablespoons unsalted butter,
chilled and cut into cubes

*Fresh, pitted, cherries; frozen cherries,
thawed and drained; or canned cherries,
drained all work in this recipe.

Streusel Topping

¼ cup all-purpose flour

¼ cup light brown sugar, packed

2 tablespoons unsalted butter, chilled and cut
into cubes

To make the pie crust, stir together the flour, sugar, and salt. Using a pastry blender, cut the butter cubes into the flour mixture until the butter pieces are about the size of a pea. Sprinkle vinegar over the flour mixture, and toss with a fork. Sprinkle cold water over the flour mixture, 1 tablespoon at a time, and toss with a fork until the dough is moistened and crumbly.

Gather the dough into a ball, flatten into a disk, wrap in plastic wrap, and refrigerate for at least 4 hours.

Preheat the oven to 375°F.

In a bowl, stir together the brown sugar, cornstarch, and cinnamon. Add the apples and mix thoroughly. Add the cherries and lemon juice and mix thoroughly.

On a floured surface, roll the dough out into a 12-inch circle. Place on a large baking sheet that has been lined with parchment paper or a silicone baking sheet.

Pour the filling into the center of the dough circle and dot with butter. Bring the pastry up and over the filling, overlapping or pleating and gathering folds in the dough. Gently press together where necessary. There should be a circle of exposed filling in the center.

To make the topping, combine the flour and brown sugar, then cut in the butter until the mixture is crumbly. Sprinkle over the exposed apples and butter.

Bake the pie for 40 to 50 minutes, or until the crust is golden. Remove to a wire rack to cool.

Sour Cream Lemon Pie

Makes 1 (9-inch) pie

1 cup granulated sugar

3½ tablespoons cornstarch

1 tablespoon grated
   lemon zest

½ cup fresh lemon juice

1 cup milk

3 large egg yolks,
   slightly beaten

4 tablespoons unsalted butter

1 cup sour cream

1 (9-inch) pie shell, baked

1 cup heavy cream, whipped

Lemon twists, for garnish

In a 2-quart saucepan set over medium heat, combine the sugar, cornstarch, lemon zest, lemon juice, and milk. Beat in the egg yolks and cook, stirring constantly, for 3 to 5 minutes or until the mixture comes to a full boil and thickens. Remove from the heat and stir in the butter. Cover and refrigerate for 2 to 3 hours or until completely cooled, mixing occasionally.

Stir in the sour cream. Spoon the filling into the pie shell, cover with whipped cream, and garnish with lemon twists. Store in the refrigerator until the pie sets.

Double Chocolate Peppermint Pie

Makes 8 servings

Crust

2 cups all-purpose flour

2 tablespoons
  confectioners' sugar

1 teaspoon salt

¼ pound plus 4 tablespoons
  (1½ sticks) unsalted butter,
  chilled and cut into cubes

1 teaspoon vinegar

5 to 6 tablespoons ice water

*Note: Pasteurized egg products are available in the supermarket dairy aisle (Egg Beaters® is the best known). This is called for in this recipe because the filling is not cooked and there is a salmonella risk associated with eating raw eggs.

Filling

¼ pound (1 stick) unsalted butter,
  at room temperature

8 ounces cream cheese, at room temperature

¾ cup granulated sugar

½ cup pasteurized egg substitute*

½ cup heavy cream

1 cup white chocolate chips, melted and cooled

½ cup (20) peppermint candies, crushed

½ cup semi-sweet chocolate chips,
  melted and cooled

To make the pie crust, in a bowl, stir together the flour, sugar, and salt. Using a pastry blender, cut the butter cubes into the flour mixture until the butter pieces are about the size of a pea. Sprinkle vinegar over the flour mixture, and toss with a fork. Sprinkle cold water over the flour mixture, 1 tablespoon at a time, and toss with a fork until the dough is moistened and crumbly. Gather the dough into a ball, flatten into a disk, wrap in plastic wrap, and refrigerate for at least 4 hours.

Preheat the oven to 400°F.

Roll the dough out to a 12-inch circle. Gently fold the crust into quarters, center over a 9-inch pie plate, and unfold. Ease the crust into the plate. Trim the dough, leaving a 1-inch overhang beyond the plate edge. Fold the crust edge under and crimp or flute the edge using a fork or your fingers.

Prick the pastry with a fork, line the bottom and sides of the crust with foil, and add dried beans or pie weights. Bake for 15 minutes, then remove the foil. Bake an additional 10 to 15 minutes, until the crust is golden. Remove to a wire rack and let the crust cool completely.

Meanwhile, make the pie filling. In a bowl, cream the butter, cream cheese, and sugar together. Combine the egg substitute and cream, then gradually add it to the butter mixture while beating, scraping the bowl as often as necessary. Beat until the mixture is light and fluffy, about 5 minutes.

Reserve half of mixture in a small bowl.

Add the white chocolate to the remaining half of mixture; beat well. Stir in the crushed candy, then spread the mixture in the baked pie crust; chill for 10 minutes.

Add the cooled semi-sweet chocolate to the remaining butter mixture and beat well. Spread over the white chocolate layer. Refrigerate at least 2 hours.

Chocolate Hazelnut Ricotta Pie

Chef Andrea Curto-Randazzo
Makes 12 servings

Crust

2½ cups all-purpose flour

¼ cup hazelnuts, finely ground

3 egg yolks

⅓ cup granulated sugar

6 tablespoons unsalted butter,
  cut into cubes

7 to 8 tablespoons cold water

Filling

4 egg yolks

⅓ cup granulated sugar

2 tablespoons all-purpose flour

¾ cup plus 1 tablespoon milk

¼ cup heavy cream

3 ounces bittersweet
  chocolate, roughly chopped

¼ cup Frangelico
  hazelnut liqueur

8 ounces ricotta cheese

Pinch of salt

1 egg white, beaten stiff

Whipped cream, for garnish

To make the crust, combine the flour, hazelnuts, egg yolks, sugar, butter, and water in the bowl of a food processor. Pulse until the dough forms a ball. Shape the dough into a disk, wrap it in plastic wrap, and refrigerate.

Meanwhile, make the filling. Beat 3 of the egg yolks with the sugar until light in color. Add the flour, ¾ cup of the milk, and the cream. Cook the mixture in a double boiler, stirring constantly until thick. Stir the chocolate and Frangelico into the mixture until the chocolate melts. Remove from the heat and allow to cool.

Add the ricotta and salt to the mixture, then fold in the egg white. Mix well and set aside for 10 minutes.

Preheat the oven to 350°F. Butter and flour a 10-inch pie pan.

Roll out three-quarters of the dough into a 12-inch circle and line the pie pan. Pour in the filling.

Roll out the remaining dough to a 12-inch circle and cover the pie. Press the overlap of the crusts together, crimping the edges with your fingers or a fork.

Beat the remaining egg yolk with the remaining 1 tablespoon of milk and brush the top of the pie with the mixture.

Bake the pie until golden brown, approximately 35 to 45 minutes.

Cool the pie before serving with whipped cream.

Hazelnut Pumpkin Pie

Crust

2 cups all-purpose flour

2 tablespoons confectioners' sugar

1 teaspoon salt

¼ pound plus 4 tablespoons (1½ sticks) unsalted butter, chilled and cut into cubes

1 teaspoon vinegar

Filling

1 (15-ounce) can pumpkin purée

¾ cup light brown sugar

2 teaspoons pumpkin pie spice

2 tablespoons all-purpose flour

3 eggs, beaten

2 tablespoons Frangelico liqueur, optional

½ cup sour cream

Topping

2 tablespoons all-purpose flour

¼ cup light brown sugar, packed

1 tablespoon Frangelico liqueur, optional

3 tablespoons unsalted butter, chilled and cut into cubes

½ cup hazelnuts, peeled and chopped

To make the pie crust, in a bowl, stir together the flour, sugar, and salt. Using a pastry blender, cut the butter cubes into the flour mixture until the butter pieces are about the size of a pea. Sprinkle vinegar over the flour mixture, and toss with a fork. Sprinkle ice water over the flour mixture, 1 tablespoon at a time, and toss with a fork until the dough is moistened and crumbly. Press the dough firmly onto the bottom and up the sides of a 9-inch pie plate.

Preheat the oven to 375°F. Combine the filling ingredients and pour into the pie crust. Bake for 30 minutes.

Combine the topping ingredients and sprinkle onto the pie.

Bake for another 15 to 20 minutes or until a knife inserted near the center of the pie comes out clean. Cool on a wire rack.

Sour Cream Raisin Meringue Pie

Makes 8 to 10 servings

1 cup raisins

1 cup boiling water

1 cup granulated sugar

6 tablespoons all-purpose flour

⅛ teaspoon salt

2¼ cups milk

3 eggs, separated

½ cup sour cream

4 tablespoons unsalted butter,
   cut into small pieces

1 (9-inch) pie shell, baked

½ teaspoon vanilla

¼ teaspoon cream of tartar

6 tablespoons
   granulated sugar

Preheat the oven to 350°F.

In a bowl, cover the raisins with the water. Let stand for 5 minutes, then drain.

In a large saucepan, combine the sugar, flour, and salt. Gradually stir in the milk. Cook and stir over medium heat until thickened and bubbly. Reduce the heat and continue to cook and stir for 2 more minutes. Remove from the heat.

In a small mixing bowl, lightly whisk the egg yolks. Add about 1 cup of the sugar mixture into the yolks and stir well. Pour the yolk mixture into the saucepan and cook, stirring, for 2 minutes more. Remove from the heat and add the sour cream, butter, and drained raisins. Stir just until mixed; do not over mix. Pour into the baked pie shell.

In a small mixing bowl and using an electric mixer on medium speed, beat the egg whites, vanilla, and cream of tartar until soft peaks form. Gradually add the sugar, beating at high speed until stiff peaks form. Spread the meringue over the hot filling, sealing to the edge. Bake for 12 to 15 minutes or until the meringue is golden. Cool on a wire rack before serving.

Grandma's Holiday Pie

Chef Bill Rowling

Makes 2 (9-inch) pies

5 eggs

½ cup all-purpose flour, sifted

1½ cups granulated sugar

2 cups buttermilk

½ pound (2 sticks) unsalted
   butter, melted

½ teaspoon vanilla

½ teaspoon almond extract

Zest of one lemon

8 ounces mascarpone cheese

2 (9-inch) unbaked pie shells

1 pinch nutmeg

1 cup heavy cream

1 tablespoon granulated sugar

Preheat the oven to 350°F.

Beat the eggs in a large bowl, then add the flour and sugar.

In a separate bowl, combine the buttermilk, butter, vanilla, almond extract, zest, and mascarpone cheese. Add this mixture to the egg mixture, beating until smooth. Pour the filling into the two pie shells; sprinkle the tops lightly with nutmeg. Bake for 20 minutes, then reduce the heat to 325°F. and loosely tent the pies with foil. Bake for 20 minutes more or until the surface of the pies are golden brown and the centers are set.

Whip the cream to soft peaks, stir in the sugar, then whip to stiff peaks. Serve atop pie slices.

Banana Split Pie

Makes 10 servings

1 large banana, sliced,
plus more for garnish

10 maraschino cherries,
halved, plus more for garnish

1 (9-inch) baked pie shell

½ cup chopped walnuts

1 quart vanilla ice cream,
softened

½ cup semi-sweet
chocolate pieces

½ pound plus 4 tablespoons
(2½ sticks) unsalted butter

1 cup confectioners'
sugar, sifted

¾ cup half-and-half

½ teaspoon vanilla

1 cup heavy cream

1 tablespoon
confectioners' sugar

Place the banana slices and cherry halves alternately in the bottom of the pie shell. Sprinkle with walnuts, then spread the ice cream over top. Freeze for several hours.

In a heavy saucepan, melt the chocolate and butter. Add the confectioners' sugar and half-and-half and cook, stirring, until thick. Add the vanilla, and remove from the heat to cool. Pour over the ice cream layer and freeze for at least 4 hours.

When you're ready to serve the pie, whip the cream, and gradually add the sugar, whipping until stiff.

To serve, garnish the pie with whipped cream, cherries, and banana slices.

Chocolate Swirl Cheesecake

Makes 12 to 16 servings

Crust

20 plain chocolate
   wafer cookies

4 tablespoons
   unsalted butter, melted

3 tablespoons
   granulated sugar

Filling

24 ounces cream cheese, at
   room temperature

1 cup sour cream

1 cup granulated sugar

2 tablespoons all-purpose flour

3 large eggs

2 tablespoons crème de cacao
   liqueur, optional

6 ounces semi-sweet chocolate
   chips, melted

Glaze

6 ounces bittersweet chocolate, chopped

4 tablespoons unsalted butter

¼ cup confectioners' sugar

⅓ cup water

Garnish

1 cup heavy cream

Granulated sugar, to taste

To make the crust, process the cookies in a food processor. Add the butter and sugar and process for 30 seconds. Press the crumb mixture evenly on the bottom of an 8½- or 9-inch springform pan and chill.

Meanwhile, prepare the filling. Preheat the oven to 350°F.

In a large mixing bowl, beat together the cream cheese, sour cream, sugar, and flour for 1 minute. Add the eggs, one at a time, beating after each addition. Fold in the liqueur, then pour the filling into the springform pan. Drop the melted chocolate by spoonfuls on top of the filling. Draw a knife through the cheesecake batter, swirling the chocolate throughout. Bake for about 55 minutes, or until the top is puffed and cracked around the edges and the center moves just slightly when pan is moved. Cool the cake in the pan on a wire rack. Cover the cooled cake with plastic wrap and chill overnight in the refrigerator.

The next day, remove the sides from the cheesecake pan and place the cheesecake on a wire rack set over waxed paper.

To make the glaze, melt the chocolate and butter together in a small saucepan over low heat. Whisk in the sugar and water until smooth. Pour the warm glaze over the cheesecake, smoothing with a knife to cover completely. Chill for 2 hours.

In a chilled, non-plastic bowl, whip the cream for 2 to 3 minutes until stiff peaks form; add sugar to taste. Using a pastry tube, pipe a frill around the base of the cake. Refrigerate until serving time.

Cranberry Cheesecake with Creamy Butter Sauce

Makes 12 servings

2 large eggs

1 cup granulated sugar

1 cup sour cream

1 teaspoon vanilla

2 cups fresh
or frozen cranberries

1 cup sliced almonds, toasted

1¾ cups all-purpose flour

¼ teaspoon baking soda

1½ teaspoon baking powder

½ cup mascarpone cheese,
at room temperature

1 teaspoon orange zest

Creamy Butter Sauce

1½ cups granulated sugar

1 cup heavy cream

2 tablespoons whiskey,
optional

1 teaspoon vanilla

8 tablespoons unsalted butter,
cut into cubes

Preheat the oven to 350°F. Grease and flour a 13 x 9-inch pan.

Using an electric mixer, cream the eggs and sugar. Add the sour cream and vanilla.

In a small bowl, combine the cranberries, almonds, and 2 tablespoons of flour. Toss to coat.

In a separate bowl, combine the remaining flour, baking soda, and baking powder. Blend into the sour cream mixture, then fold in the cranberry mixture.

Spread the batter into the prepared pan.

In a small bowl, combine the mascarpone and orange zest. Drop by spoonfuls over the batter, then bake for 40 minutes, or until a toothpick inserted in the center comes out clean. Let cool.

Meanwhile, make the Creamy Butter Sauce. Combine the sugar, cream, and whiskey in a medium saucepan set over high heat. Boil for 2 minutes, then remove from the heat, add the vanilla and let cool for 5 minutes. Stir in the butter, one piece at a time until all of the butter has been incorporated.

Serve the cake at room temperature with sauce poured overtop.

Pecan Pound Cake

Makes 12 servings

½ pound (2 sticks) unsalted
  butter, at room temperature

2¾ cups granulated sugar

2 teaspoons vanilla

6 eggs

3 cups all-purpose flour

½ teaspoon salt

¼ teaspoon baking soda

1 cup sour cream

1 cup chopped pecans

Preheat the oven to 350°F. Butter a 9-inch tube pan or two 9 x 5-inch loaf pans.

Using an electric mixer, cream the butter and sugar until light and fluffy. Add the vanilla and eggs, one at a time, beating thoroughly after each addition.

Sift the flour, salt, and baking soda together 3 times. Add the dry ingredients to the butter mixture alternately with the sour cream, beating well after each addition. Stir in the pecans and pour into the prepared pan(s). Bake for 60 to 70 minutes, or until a toothpick comes out clean. Cool for 5 minutes in the pan(s) before removing them to a wire rack to cool thoroughly.

Pound Cake

Barbara J. Warren

Makes 3 loaves

4½ cups cake flour, sifted

1½ teaspoon salt

½ teaspoon mace

1 pound (4 sticks) butter,
   at room temperature

2¼ cups granulated sugar

2 teaspoons vanilla

9 eggs, beaten

Preheat the oven to 325°F. Line the bottoms and sides of 3 (9 x 5 x 3-inch) loaf pans with waxed or parchment paper.

Sift together the flour, salt, and mace.

Cream the butter until smooth, then add the sugar, mixing well to incorporate. Add the vanilla, then the eggs in four portions, beating well after each addition. Add the flour mixture ½ cup at a time and mix until thoroughly incorporated.

Pour the batter into the prepared pans, spreading the dough higher at the edges than at the center. Bake on the lower rack of the oven for 20 minutes, then increase the temperature to 350°F. and bake for 40 minutes more, until a crack appears on the top of the loaves and they are lightly browned.

Cool the loaves in their pans on cake racks for 5 minutes, then remove them from the pans to finish cooling.

Marbled Pound Cake

Makes 12 servings

1½ cups all-purpose flour

¼ teaspoon salt

⅛ teaspoon baking soda

¼ pound (1 stick) unsalted
butter, at room temperature

1¼ cups granulated sugar

3 eggs, at room temperature

1 teaspoon vanilla

Few drops almond extract

½ cup sour cream

3 ounces semisweet
chocolate, melted

Preheat the oven to 350°F. Butter and lightly flour a 9 x 5 x 3-inch loaf pan.

In a medium mixing bowl, combine the flour, salt, and baking soda. Stir to mix well.

Using an electric mixer on medium speed, cream the butter until fluffy. Gradually add the sugar, beating until light and fluffy. Add the eggs, one at a time, beating for 1 minute after each addition. Scrape the sides of the bowl as needed. Add the vanilla and almond extract and beat well. Add the flour mixture alternately with the sour cream, beating after each addition just until combined.

Divide the batter in half. Stir the melted chocolate into one half of the batter.

Drop alternate spoonfuls of plain and chocolate batter in the pan and gently stir through the batters, creating a marbled effect. Bake for about 1 hour, or until a wooden toothpick inserted in the center comes out clean. Cool for 10 minutes in the pan before removing to a wire rack.

Mile-High Lemon-Buttermilk Cake
with Lemon Filling

Makes 12 servings

Cake

4 cups cake flour

1 teaspoon baking soda

½ teaspoon baking powder

½ pound (2 sticks)
  unsalted butter

3 cups granulated sugar

1 teaspoon lemon extract

2 cups buttermilk

6 egg whites

Lemon Filling

1 cup granulated sugar

¼ cup cornstarch

¼ teaspoon salt

1 cup water

3 egg yolks

1 tablespoon unsalted butter

4 teaspoons shredded
  lemon zest

½ cup lemon juice

Frosting

1 cup milk

3 tablespoons all-purpose flour

½ pound (2 sticks) unsalted butter

1 cup granulated sugar

Lemon slices, for garnish

Preheat the oven to 350°F. Line three 9 x 2-inch round baking pans with waxed paper.

Combine the flour, baking soda, and baking powder.

In a large mixing bowl and using an electric mixer, cream the butter on high speed for 30 seconds. Add the sugar and beat until fluffy. Beat in the lemon extract. Add the flour mixture and buttermilk alternately, beating after each addition. Add the egg whites and beat at medium speed for 2 minutes.

Divide the batter among the prepared pans and bake for about 30 minutes, or until a toothpick inserted in the center of each cake comes out clean. Cool in the pans for 10 minutes before removing to a wire rack to cool.

Meanwhile, make the filling. In a saucepan, combine the sugar, cornstarch, and

salt. Gradually stir in the water and cook, stirring, until thickened and bubbly, about 2 minutes more.

Gradually stir about half of the hot mixture into the egg yolks. Return the sugar mixture to the saucepan and cook, stirring, for 2 minutes. Remove from the heat and stir in the butter, lemon zest, and lemon juice. Set aside to cool to room temperature.

To make the frosting, combine the milk and flour in a small saucepan and cook, stirring, over medium heat until the mixture thickens, then cook for

1 minute more. Set aside to cool.

In small mixing bowl, beat the butter for 30 seconds, then add the sugar and beat until fluffy. Add the cooled milk mixture and beat until fluffy.

To assemble: Set aside ¼ cup of the Lemon Filling. Place one cake layer on a serving plate and spread with half of the remaining filling. Add the second cake layer and spread with the other half of the filling. Add the third cake layer and frost the cake and sides. Drizzle the cake with the reserved filling and garnish with lemon slices.

Lemon Yogurt Cake with Yogurt Cream Topping

Makes 8 to 10 servings

Lemon Yogurt Cake

2¼ cups all-purpose flour

1 teaspoon baking powder

½ teaspoon baking soda

¼ teaspoon cream of tartar

⅛ teaspoon salt

¼ pound (1 stick) unsalted
   butter, cut in chunks,
   at room temperature,
   plus more for pan

1¼ cup granulated sugar

2 whole eggs

4 egg whites

1 cup lemon yogurt
   (not nonfat)

Zest of 1 lemon

¼ cup lemon juice

2 teaspoons vanilla

Berry Topping

1 quart seasonal berries, such as raspberries,
   blackberries, strawberries, sliced peaches
   or a mixture

⅓ cup granulated sugar, or to taste

Lemon Yogurt Cream

½ cup heavy cream

4 teaspoons confectioners' sugar

2 cups smooth lemon yogurt

Preheat the oven to 325°F. Line a 9-inch round cake pan with parchment or waxed paper. Butter and flour the sides of the pan.

Mix the cake flour, baking powder, baking soda, cream of tartar, and salt in a medium bowl; set aside.

Using an electric mixer, cream the butter. Add the sugar, a little at a time, beating constantly. One by one, add the eggs and egg whites, beating after each addition. Add the yogurt and mix in; add the lemon zest, lemon juice, and vanilla. Beat until well combined.

Sift the flour mixture over the batter and gently fold it in. Distribute the batter evenly in the prepared pan. Bake in the lower third of oven for 50 to 60 minutes, or until the cake is golden and a toothpick inserted in the center comes out clean. Let the cake cool in the pan on a wire rack for 10 minutes. Turn the cake out onto the rack and cool completely.

Meanwhile, make the Berry Topping. Mix the fruit and sugar, stirring well. Let sit at least 30 minutes, or until the fruit is juicy.

To make the Lemon Yogurt Cream, beat the cream just until soft peaks form. Add the sugar and continue beating until stiff. Carefully fold in the yogurt and refrigerate up to one hour until serving time for best texture.

To serve, cut the cake in wedges and top each serving with fruit and a dollop of yogurt cream.

Carrot Cake

Makes 12 servings

1⅓ cups whole wheat flour

1 cup all-purpose flour

2 teaspoons baking soda

1½ teaspoons
  ground cinnamon

¼ teaspoon salt

¼ pound plus 4 tablespoons
  (1½ sticks) unsalted butter

1 cup honey

⅔ cup plain yogurt

2 eggs

1½ teaspoons vanilla

1 ⅓ cups shredded carrots

Cream Cheese Frosting

3 ounces cream cheese,
  at room temperature

4 tablespoons unsalted butter

1 teaspoon vanilla

2 cups confectioners' sugar

Preheat the oven to 350°F. Butter and flour a 13 x 9 x 2-inch baking dish.

Combine the flours, baking soda, cinnamon, and salt; set aside.

Using an electric mixer, cream the butter on high speed for 30 seconds. Gradually beat in the honey, yogurt, eggs, and vanilla. Stir in the carrots. Add the flour mixture and beat on medium speed for 2 minutes. Pour the batter into the prepared baking dish and bake for about 35 minutes, or until a wooden toothpick inserted in the center of the cake comes out clean. Cool on a wire rack.

To make the Cream Cheese Frosting, using an electric mixer, cream the cream cheese, butter, and vanilla on low speed until fluffy. Gradually beat in the confectioners' sugar.

Spread over the cool cake.

Chocolate Fudge Cake

Makes 1 (13 x 9 x 2-inch) cake

¼ pound (1 stick) unsalted
  butter, at room temperature

1 cup granulated sugar

2 large eggs,
  at room temperature

1 teaspoon vanilla

2 cups all-purpose flour

½ cup unsweetened
  cocoa powder

1 teaspoon baking powder

1 teaspoon baking soda

1 cup sour cream

1 cup chopped walnuts

¾ cup semisweet
  chocolate chips

Frosting

4 tablespoons unsalted butter,
  at room temperature

3 ounces unsweetened
  chocolate, melted

2 cups confectioners' sugar

½ cup sour cream

2 teaspoons vanilla

Preheat the oven to 350°F. Butter and flour a 13 x 9 x 2-inch metal baking pan.

Using an electric mixer, cream the butter for 1 minute. Add the sugar gradually, then the eggs and vanilla, beating until well combined, about 2 minutes. Scrape down the sides of the bowl as necessary; set aside.

Whisk together the flour, cocoa, baking powder, and baking soda. Add the flour mixture to the butter mixture, alternating with the sour cream, until well combined. Fold in the walnuts and chocolate chips.

Spread the batter evenly into the prepared pan and bake for 35 minutes, or until a toothpick inserted in the center comes out clean. Cool thoroughly before frosting.

To make the frosting, using an electric mixer, cream the frosting ingredients until smooth.

Dirt Cake

Makes 12 servings

1 (20-ounce) package
cream-filled chocolate
sandwich cookies

8 ounces cream cheese,
at room temperature

4 tablespoons unsalted butter,
at room temperature

1 cup confectioners' sugar

2 (¾-ounce) packages instant
vanilla pudding mix

3½ cups cold milk

1 cup heavy cream

2 tablespoons
granulated sugar

1 (8-inch) brand-new
terra-cotta flower pot,
washed and dried

Gummy worms

Silk or plastic flowers

Place the cookies in the bowl of a food processor and process until the cookies are finely crushed; set aside.

Using an electric mixer, combine the cream cheese, butter, and confectioners' sugar until smooth.

In a separate bowl, mix the pudding and milk until well blended.

Fold the pudding into the cream cheese mixture.

Whip the cream to soft peaks, then add the granulated sugar and beat to stiff peaks. Gently fold this mixture into the cream cheese mixture.

Cover the hole in the bottom of the terra cotta pot with a foil square, then place one cup of the crushed cookies in the bottom of the pot. Top with one-third of the pudding mixture, and continue layering until the pot is full, ending with crumbs on top. Chill for several hours or overnight. Prior to serving, decorate the top with gummy worms and silk or plastic flowers.

Black Forest Cake

Makes 12 to 16 servings

Cakes

8 eggs

1 cup granulated sugar

1 teaspoon vanilla

½ cup cocoa

½ cup all-purpose flour

¼ pound (1 stick)
  unsalted butter, melted,
  plus more as needed

Kirsch Syrup

½ cup water

3 tablespoons
  granulated sugar

3 tablespoons kirsch
  (cherry brandy)

Cherry Filling

17 ounces pitted dark sweet cherries

⅛ teaspoon ground cloves

3 tablespoons cornstarch

3 tablespoons cold water

Frosting

3 cups heavy cream

½ cup confectioners' sugar, sifted

¼ cup kirsch

½ teaspoons vanilla

Preheat the oven to 325°F. Butter and flour three 8-inch layer pans.

Using an electric mixer on high speed, combine the eggs, sugar, and vanilla until fluffy and thick, about 10 to 15 minutes.

In a separate bowl, sift together the cocoa and flour. Sprinkle a small amount of this cocoa mixture over the egg mixture and gently fold in. Repeat with the remaining cocoa mixture. Gently fold in the butter, one tablespoon at a time.

Pour the batter into the prepared pans and bake for 15 to 20 minutes or until a wooden pick inserted in the centers comes out clean.

Cool for 5 minutes before removing the cakes from the pans.

Meanwhile, make the Kirsch Syrup. Combine the water and sugar in a small saucepan set over high heat. Bring to a boil, stirring until the sugar is dissolved. Cool, then stir in the kirsch.

Place the cakes on baking sheets and gently prick each layer with a fork or toothpick. Brush each cake evenly with the syrup and let stand for at least 10 minutes.

To make the Cherry Filling, drain the cherries, reserving ¾ cup of the juice. In a small saucepan, combine the cherry juice, 1 cup of cherries, and cloves; bring to a boil.

In a small bowl, combine the cornstarch and water and add to the boiling cherry juice. Boil for 1 minute, stirring constantly, or until clear and thickened. Cool.

To make the frosting, beat the cream with an electric mixer on high speed until it thickens slightly. Gradually add the confectioners' sugar, beating until stiff peaks form. Add the kirsch and vanilla, beating only until well-combined.

To assemble, place one cake layer on a serving plate and spread with Cherry Filling. Place a second cake layer over top and spread with 2 cups of the Frosting. Top with the remaining cake layer and spread the top and sides with the remaining Frosting. Chill for several hours. Just before serving, garnish the top with the remaining cherries.

Chocolate Cherry Layered Cake

Makes 1 (8-inch) cake

4 ounces sweet
  baking chocolate

½ cup hot water

1 teaspoon vanilla

¼ pound (1 stick)
  unsalted butter

1½ cups granulated sugar

2 eggs

2 cups all-purpose flour

1 teaspoon baking soda

¼ teaspoon salt

1 cup sour cream

Cherry Filling

1 (16-ounce) can pitted sour cherries

2 tablespoons cornstarch

¼ cup granulated sugar

2 teaspoons brandy

Cocoa Whipped Cream Frosting

2 cups heavy cream

½ cup confectioners' sugar

1 teaspoon vanilla

2 tablespoons cocoa

Chocolate curls, for garnish

Preheat the oven to 350°F. Butter and flour 2 (8-inch) cake pans.

Break the chocolate into small pieces and place in a heavy saucepan set over low heat. Add the water and stir until the chocolate melts. Add the vanilla and remove from the heat to cool.

Using an electric mixer, cream the butter, sugar, and eggs until light and fluffy. Blend in the chocolate mixture.

Combine the flour, baking soda, and salt. Add, alternately with the sour cream, to the chocolate mixture beating until batter is smooth. Pour evenly into the prepared pans and bake for 30 to 35 minutes or until a wooden toothpick inserted in the center comes out clean. Cool on a wire rack for 15 minutes before removing the cakes from the pans to finish cooling.

Meanwhile, make the Cherry Filling. Drain the cherries, reserving ¾ cup of the syrup. Combine the cornstarch and sugar in a heavy saucepan and gradually add the reserved syrup. Cook over medium heat, stirring constantly, until the mixture is clear and thickened. Stir in the cherries and brandy. Cool.

To make the Cocoa Whipped Cream Frosting, beat the cream until it thickens slightly. Gradually add the sugar, vanilla, and cocoa. Beat until stiff peaks form.

To assemble, place one cake layer on a plate and spread with Cherry Filling. Top with the second cake layer and frost the cake. Garnish with shaved chocolate curls.

Perfect Spice Cake

Makes 8 servings

Cake

2¼ cups cake flour, sifted

1 teaspoon baking powder

1 teaspoon salt

1 teaspoon cinnamon

¾ teaspoon baking soda

¼ teaspoon ground cloves

1⁄16 teaspoon ground pepper

¼ pound plus 4 tablespoons
   (1½ stick) unsalted butter

1 cup granulated sugar

¾ cup brown sugar,
   firmly packed

1 teaspoon vanilla

3 eggs

1 cup buttermilk

Filling

1½ cups chopped dates

½ cup orange juice

1 teaspoon grated orange zest

¼ cup walnuts

Frosting

2 egg whites

¾ cup brown sugar, firmly packed

¾ cup granulated sugar

1½ teaspoons light corn syrup

¼ teaspoon cream of tartar

⅓ cup minus 2 tablespoons cold water

Dash salt

1 teaspoon vanilla

3 ounces cream cheese

Preheat the oven to 350°F. Butter and flour
two (9-inch) cake pans.

To make the cake, sift together the cake
flour, baking powder, salt, cinnamon, baking
soda, cloves, and pepper; set aside.

Using an electric mixer, cream the butter
and sugars until light and fluffy. Add the vanilla
and the eggs, one at a time, beating after each
addition. Add the dry ingredients alternately

with the buttermilk and beat well. Pour the dough into the prepared pans and bake for 30 minutes or until a toothpick inserted in the center comes out clean. Cool the cakes in the pans for 10 minutes before removing to a wire rack to cool completely.

Meanwhile, make the filling. In a saucepan set over medium heat, cook the dates and orange juice, stirring, until the dates are tender and the mixture is thick, about 2 to 3 minutes. Add the orange zest, remove from the heat, and allow to cool. Add the walnuts.

To make the frosting, set a medium-sized saucepan with about 2 inches of water over high heat and bring to a boil.

While the water is coming to a boil, in a metal bowl that can be set over the saucepan to act as a double boiler, combine the egg whites, sugars, corn syrup, cream of tartar, water, and salt a medium-sized bowl. Using an electric mixer, beat for 1 minute. Place the bowl over the saucepan with boiling water and beat constantly for 7 minutes. Remove the bowl from the heat and add the vanilla. Set the mixture aside to cool to lukewarm.

In a separate bowl, beat the cream cheese until smooth. Gently fold into the frosting.

To assemble the cake, spread the filling between the cake layers, then frost the cake.

Pineapple Upside Down Cake

Makes 6 servings

¼ pound (1 stick) unsalted butter, at room temperature

½ cup brown sugar

½ cup pineapple juice

3 to 4 canned pineapple rings, drained (do not use fresh pineapple)

¾ cup all-purpose flour

1 teaspoon baking powder

¼ teaspoon salt

¾ cup granulated sugar

2 large eggs

Heavy cream, whipped, for serving

Preheat the oven to 375°F. Line the bottom of a round 8 x 2-inch cake pan with parchment or wax paper.

Melt 4 tablespoons of butter, and combine with the brown sugar and ¼ cup of the pineapple juice. Pour into the prepared cake pan, and arrange the pineapple rings over top; set aside.

Combine the flour, baking powder, and salt.

In a large mixing bowl and using an electric mixer, cream the remaining 4 tablespoons of butter with the sugar. Add the eggs, one at a time, beating well after each addition. Add the flour mixture and beat on low speed until well-combined. Stir in the remaining ¼ cup pineapple juice.

Pour the batter over the pineapple slices and bake for 30 to 35 minutes. Cool for 10 minutes in the pan before carefully inverting the cake onto a serving platter. Remove the pan and paper. Serve warm with whipped cream.

Rhubarb Cake

Makes 1 (13 x 9-inch) cake

¼ pound (1 stick) unsalted
butter, at room temperature

1 cup brown sugar, packed

¾ cup granulated sugar

1 egg

1 teaspoon vanilla

2 cups all-purpose flour

1 teaspoon baking soda

½ teaspoon salt

1 cup buttermilk

1½ cups fresh rhubarb, cut fine

1 teaspoon cinnamon

Preheat the oven to 375°F.

Butter a 13 x 9-inch pan.

Using an electric mixer, cream the butter, brown sugar, and ½ cup of granulated sugar. Add the egg and vanilla and beat until well-blended.

Sift together the flour, baking soda, and salt, then add to the butter mixture alternately with the buttermilk. Stir in the rhubarb and pour into the prepared pan.

Combine the remaining ¼ cup granulated sugar with cinnamon, and sprinkle evenly over top of the cake. Bake for 30 to 35 minutes. Remove from the oven and place on a wire rack to cool before serving.

Yogurt Glazed Pecan Cake

Makes 1 (8-inch square) cake

Glaze

1 cup granulated sugar

½ cup water

¼ cup honey

1 teaspoon lemon juice

½ cup plain yogurt

Cake

¼ pound plus 4 tablespoons
   (1½ sticks) unsalted butter,
   at room temperature,
   plus more for pan

¾ cup granulated sugar

3 eggs

1 cup all-purpose flour

1½ teaspoons baking powder

½ teaspoon cinnamon

¼ teaspoon salt

¼ cup plain yogurt

1 cup chopped pecans

Preheat the oven to 350°F.

To make the glaze, combine the sugar, water, honey, and lemon juice in a small pan set over high heat. Bring to a boil, then lower the heat slightly and boil gently for 7 minutes. Remove from the heat.

Add 2 tablespoons of the sugar mixture to the yogurt, mixing well. Gradually pour the yogurt mixture into hot glaze, stirring constantly. Return to the heat and boil for 2 minutes. Set aside to cool.

Using an electric mixer, cream the butter. Gradually add the sugar, beating until light and fluffy. Add the eggs, one at a time, beating well after each addition.

In a separate bowl, sift together the flour, baking powder, cinnamon, and salt. Stir in to the butter mixture, alternately with the yogurt, until well-blended. Stir in the pecans, then pour into a buttered 8-inch square pan. Bake for 30 minutes. While the cake is hot, pour the cooled glaze over top. Cool for 1 hour before serving.

Lemon Kiwi Torte

Makes 8 to 12 servings

1 teaspoon unflavored gelatin

2 tablespoons water

1 cup granulated sugar

Zest and ⅓ cup juice of
  2 lemons

¼ pound (1 stick)
  unsalted butter

2 egg yolks, beaten

8 ounces (1 cup) mascarpone
  cheese, slightly softened

1 (10½-inch) prepared sponge
  or angel cake

2 kiwi, peeled and sliced

In a small bowl, combine the gelatin with the water; set aside.

In a 2-quart saucepan set over medium-low heat, combine the sugar, lemon zest and juice, and butter. Cook, stirring occasionally, until the mixture is almost boiling. Remove from the heat.

Stir in 1 cup the hot lemon mixture into the beaten egg yolks, stirring vigorously. Return the egg mixture to the pan with the rest of the lemon mixture. Over medium-low heat, cook until the mixture becomes very thick, about 15 minutes, whisking continuously—do not boil. Add the softened gelatin and stir until completely dissolved.

Pour the lemon mixture into a large bowl to cool to room temperature.

Whisk the mascarpone cheese into the lemon mixture, then pour over the sponge cake and spread evenly to the edge. Refrigerate for several hours. Just before serving, garnish with kiwi slices.

Fruitcake with
Mascarpone Chantilly

Makes 10 to 12 servings

2 cups extra fancy fruitcake
mix, or assorted candied
fruit, chopped

2 cups pecans, chopped

4 cups all-purpose flour

1 pound (4 sticks) butter

2 cups granulated sugar

6 large eggs

2 tablespoons orange zest

2 teaspoons vanilla

1 teaspoon baking powder

Mascarpone Chantilly

2 cups heavy cream

½ cup confectioners' sugar

½ teaspoon vanilla

½ cup mascarpone cheese,
at room temperature

¼ cup sour cream

TIP: For extra flavor, drizzle
sherry, Marsala, or port
wine over the cake before
refrigerating.

Preheat the oven to 300°F. Butter and floured a 10-inch tube pan.

In a medium bowl, combine the fruitcake mix, pecans, and 1 cup of flour. Toss to coat and set aside.

Using an electric mixer, cream the butter and sugar until light and fluffy. Add the eggs one at a time, beating well after each. Beat in the orange zest and vanilla.

Combine the remaining flour and the baking powder, then gradually add this mixture to the butter mixture. Fold in the reserved fruit mixture. Spread the dough into the prepared pan and bake for 1½ to 2 hours or until a toothpick inserted near the center comes out clean. Cool the cake for 10 minutes, then remove the cake from the pan and transfer to a wire rack. Refrigerate.

To make the Mascarpone Chantilly, beat the cream on low until thickened. Add the confectioners' sugar and vanilla. Beat to stiff peaks and set aside.

Combine the mascarpone and sour cream, then fold into the heavy cream.

To serve, cut the cake into slices and top each slice with a generous dollop of Mascarpone Chantilly.

Fruit Kringle

Makes 10 to 12 servings

Dough

2½ cups all-purpose flour

¼ teaspoon salt

¼ pound (1 stick) unsalted
butter, at room temperature

1 teaspoon active dry yeast

2 tablespoons warm water
(105°F. to 115°F.)

2 large eggs

2 tablespoons
granulated sugar

⅓ cup buttermilk

Filling

⅔ cup granulated sugar

½ cup brown sugar

1 teaspoon cinnamon

1 cup chopped dried fruit

¼ cup cinnamon chips

4 ounces cream cheese,
at room temperature

½ cup chopped nuts

1 cup confectioners' sugar

⅓ cup heavy cream

In a large bowl, combine the flour and salt. Using 2 knives or a pastry cutter, cut in the butter.

In a small bowl, dissolve the yeast in the warm water.

In another bowl, combine the eggs, sugar, and buttermilk. Stir in the yeast mixture, then the flour mixture. Stir to make dough. Cover with plastic wrap and refrigerate the dough overnight.

The next day, preheat the oven to 375°F.

To make the filling, combine the sugar, brown sugar, cinnamon, chopped fruit, cinnamon chips, cream cheese, and chopped nuts in a medium bowl. Set aside.

Divide the dough into 3 parts. Roll one piece into a 15 x 8-inch rectangle. Carefully spread one-third of the filling lengthwise across the bottom half of the dough rectangle. Fold the dough over in half and pinch to seal; fold all seams underneath. The finished rectangle should be approximately 14 x 4-inches. Transfer to a baking sheet and repeat with the remaining dough and filling.

Bake for 25 to 30 minutes or until golden brown. Cool to room temperature.

Combine the confectioners' sugar and cream and drizzle over the Kringle before serving.

Triple Nut Torte

Makes 12 to 16 servings

2½ cups granulated sugar

1 cup heavy cream

1 cup pecans,
coarsely chopped

¾ cup slivered almonds

¾ cup walnuts,
coarsely chopped

½ pound (2 sticks)
unsalted butter

1 egg

½ teaspoon vanilla

2¾ cups all-purpose flour

1 egg white

1 teaspoon water

Confectioners' sugar,
for dusting

Preheat the oven to 350°F.

In a heavy 2-quart saucepan set over medium heat, melt 2 cups of sugar, stirring constantly. Add the cream, stirring briskly until well-combined. Stir in the pecans, almonds, and walnuts and set aside to let cool.

Using an electric mixer, cream the butter and remaining ½ cup sugar until light and fluffy. Blend in the egg and vanilla. Add the flour and mix well.

Spread 2 cups of the dough onto the bottom and 1½ inches up the sides of a 10-inch springform pan. Spread the nut mixture evenly over the dough in the pan.

Roll the remaining dough, between wax paper, to a 10-inch circle. Place the dough circle over the nut mixture and pinch the edges to seal.

In a small bowl, combine the egg white with the water, and brush it over the dough. Bake for 1 hour. Let cool before dusting with confectioners' sugar.

Apple Brown Betty

Mary C. Taylor

Makes 5 servings

6 slices stale bread,
  torn into bite-sized pieces

6 tablespoons butter, melted

6 Granny Smith apples,
  trimmed and sliced

1 cup sugar

1 teaspoon ground cinnamon

¼ teaspoon salt

½ cup water or apple cider

Preheat the oven to 400°F. Butter a 12 x 9-inch baking pan and set aside.

Place the bread in a shallow pan and toast lightly, about 3 minutes. Place the toasted bread in a large bowl and drizzle with the remaining butter. Toss with a fork to coat the bread.

Pour one-third of the bread into the prepared pan and cover with half of the apples.

In a separate bowl, combine the sugar, cinnamon, and salt. Sprinkle half of the mixture over the apples. Add another layer of bread, the remaining apples, and the rest of the sugar mixture. Drizzle water over all, cover with foil, and bake for 30 minutes. Uncover and bake for 10 minutes longer or until the top is brown and crusty.

Cheddar Apple Crisp

Makes 6 to 8 servings

4 cups crisp and tart apples
   such as Braeburn or
   Granny Smith, peeled, cored,
   and sliced
1 tablespoon lemon juice
⅓ plus ½ cups brown sugar,
   firmly packed
½ cup rolled oats
¼ cup all-purpose flour
1 teaspoon ground cinnamon
¼ pound (1 stick)
   unsalted butter
4 ounces (1 cup) sharp
   Cheddar cheese, shredded
Ice cream or whipped cream,
   for serving
Additional shredded Cheddar
   cheese, for garnish

Preheat the oven to 350°F. Butter an 8- or 9-inch square pan.

Combine the apples, lemon juice, and ⅓ cup brown sugar, and arrange in the prepared pan.

Combine the oats, flour, and cinnamon and, using 2 knives or a pastry cutter, cut in the butter until the mixture is crumbly; gently mix in the cheese. Sprinkle evenly over the apple mixture, and bake for 25 to 30 minutes.

Serve with ice cream or whipped cream and garnish with cheese.

Strawberry-Rhubarb Cobbler

Makes 8 servings

Cobbler

¾ cup plus ⅓ cup
  granulated sugar

1 tablespoon cornstarch

2 teaspoons cinnamon

1 pound rhubarb,
  cut into 1-inch pieces

1 pint (2 cups) strawberries,
  halved or quartered

1 cup all-purpose flour

1 teaspoon baking soda

¼ teaspoon salt

4 tablespoons unsalted butter,
  at room temperature

1 large egg

¼ cup buttermilk or
  heavy cream

Cinnamon-Sugar Topping

1 tablespoon granulated sugar

½ teaspoon cinnamon

Ice cream or whipped cream,
  for serving

Preheat the oven to 375°F. Butter an 11 x 7-inch baking dish or 1½-quart shallow casserole dish.

In a large bowl, combine the ¾ cup of sugar, cornstarch, and cinnamon; mix well. Add the rhubarb and strawberries; toss well and transfer the mixture to the prepared baking dish.

In a small bowl, combine the flour, baking soda, and salt; set aside.

Using an electric mixer, cream the butter and the remaining ⅓ cup sugar until light and fluffy. Beat in the egg. On low speed, beat in half of the flour mixture. Beat in the buttermilk then the remaining flour mixture.

Drop the batter by heaping tablespoonfuls into 8 mounds over the fruit.

Combine the sugar and cinnamon, then sprinkle over the batter. Bake for 34 to 40 minutes or until the fruit is bubbly and the topping is golden brown. Transfer to a wire rack and let stand for at least 40 minutes before serving.

Serve warm or at room temperature with ice cream or whipped cream.

Season's Best Strawberry Shortcake

Makes 6 servings

Topping

⅓ cup honey

2 tablespoons lemon juice

3 pints strawberries,
   cored and sliced

Shortcake

2 cups all-purpose flour

2 tablespoons
   granulated sugar

3½ teaspoons baking powder

¼ pound (1 stick) unsalted
   butter, chilled

¼ cup sour cream

¼ to ½ cup milk

Cream

1 cup heavy cream

⅓ cup confectioners' sugar

1 teaspoon vanilla

½ cup sour cream

Preheat the oven to 425°F.

To make the topping, combine the honey and lemon juice in a medium bowl, then stir in the strawberries. Cover with plastic wrap and chill.

To make the shortcakes, combine the flour, sugar, and baking powder. Using 2 knives or a pastry cutter, cut in the butter until the mixture resembles fine crumbs. Add the sour cream and mix lightly with a fork. Stir in just enough milk to form a soft dough.

On a lightly floured surface, roll the dough out to ½ inch thickness. Cut with a 3-inch biscuit cutter and place on an ungreased baking sheet. Re-roll any leftover dough as necessary to make 6 shortcakes. Bake for 15 minutes or until the tops are golden brown. Remove to a wire rack to cool.

Meanwhile, beat the cream until soft peaks form. Add the confectioners' sugar and vanilla, and continue beating until stiff peaks form. Fold in the sour cream and chill.

To serve, split the shortcakes in half. Place the bottom halves on serving plates and top with strawberries and cream; repeat layers.

Buttery Caramels

Makes 5 dozen

½ cup pecans

2 cups granulated sugar

¼ pound (1 stick)
  unsalted butter

2 cups heavy cream

¾ cup light corn syrup

Preheat the oven to 350°F. Butter the inside of an 8-inch square glass baking dish.

Toast the pecans on a baking sheet for about 8 minutes or until fragrant. Let them cool, then chop finely. Sprinkle the pecans evenly over the bottom of the prepared dish; set aside.

In a heavy 3-quart saucepan set over medium heat, combine the sugar, butter, cream, and corn syrup. Bring to a boil, stirring constantly. Place a candy thermometer in the pan and cook, stirring frequently, until the temperature reaches 245°F., or when a tablespoon of the mixture dropped into very cold water forms a firm ball. (It is important to stir the mixture after it reaches a soft ball stage to prevent sticking.)

Pour the caramel over the pecans in the dish and let cool to room temperature, for about 1 hour. Run a knife around the dish edges and invert the dish to release the caramel. Using a wet, sharp knife and with a sawing motion, cut the caramel into small squares. Let the squares cool completely before wrapping each square in plastic wrap.

Creamy Caramels

Makes 2 pounds

2 cups granulated sugar

Pinch salt

2 cups light corn syrup

¼ pound (1 stick) butter

2 cups evaporated milk

2 teaspoons vanilla

Butter a 9-inch square baking pan.

Heat the sugar, salt, and corn syrup in heavy saucepan to boiling. Boil to 245°F (firm ball stage), stirring occasionally. Add the butter and milk slowly so the boiling doesn't stop. Continue to cook, stirring constantly until the mixture reaches 242°F. (medium ball stage). Remove from the heat and stir in the vanilla. Pour into the prepared pan and allow to cool completely before cutting.

Butterscotch Patties

Mary E. Taylor

Makes 40

1 cup granulated sugar

1 cup light corn syrup

1 teaspoon white vinegar

¼ pound (1 stick) butter

Heat the sugar and corn syrup in a heavy saucepan over medium heat until the sugar dissolves, about 10 minutes. Add the vinegar and bring to a boil until it reaches 260°F. (hard ball stage). Add the butter and continue cooking until the temperature reaches 270°F. (soft crack stage).

Remove from the heat and drop ½ teaspoonfuls of candy onto buttered pans. Cool completely before removing from pans.

Buttery English Toffee

Makes 4 dozen

1 pound (4 sticks)
  unsalted butter

2 cups granulated sugar

⅓ cup water

1 teaspoon vanilla

1 cup chopped pecans

12 ounces mini
  chocolate pieces

¼ cup ground pecans

In a 4-quart saucepan set over medium heat, combine the butter, sugar, water, and vanilla, stirring constantly, and heat to boiling. Cook until the temperature reaches 260°F. on a candy thermometer.

Add the pecans and continue cooking to 290°F., stirring constantly. Pour onto a buttered 15 x 10 x 1-inch jelly roll pan. Cool for 2 minutes, then sprinkle with chocolate pieces. Cover the pan with a baking sheet to soften the chocolate, then, using a knife, spread the chocolate over the toffee. Sprinkle with ground nuts and cool completely before breaking the toffee into pieces with a knife.

Old Almond Toffee

Katharine O'Boyle

Makes 1 pound

1 pound (4 sticks) butter

2 cups granulated sugar

½ cup coarsely
   chopped almonds

Combine all of the ingredients in a heavy saucepan set over medium low heat. Stirring constantly, heat to a gentle boil until the mixture reaches 305°F. (hard crack stage) or until it is a golden brown color. Pour out onto a large baking sheet and spread flat with an oiled spatula. Let stand for 5 minutes, then loosen the bottom with a spatula and mark into squares. When the toffee is completely cool, break into pieces.

Oatmeal Toffee

Makes 16 squares

6 tablespoons butter, melted

2 cups oatmeal

½ cup dark brown
   sugar, packed

¼ cup dark corn syrup

½ teaspoon salt

2 teaspoons vanilla

1 cup semi-sweet
   chocolate chips

¼ cup chopped walnuts

Preheat the oven to 450°F. Butter an 8-inch square pan.

In a large bowl, combine the butter, oatmeal, sugar, corn syrup, salt, and vanilla. Pour into the prepared pan and bake for 12 minutes until golden brown. Turn the oven off, remove the toffee from the oven, and sprinkle it with the chocolate chips. Return the toffee to the oven to let the chocolate chips melt. Once they've melted, spread the chocolate over the toffee and sprinkle with walnuts. Allow to cool before cutting into squares.

Peanut Butter Bon Bons

Makes 5 dozen

¼ pound (1 stick) unsalted
  butter, at room temperature
1½ cups creamy peanut butter
2 cups confectioners' sugar
1 teaspoon vanilla
12 ounces milk chocolate chips

Line a baking sheet with parchment or waxed paper. Set aside.

Place the butter, peanut butter, sugar, and vanilla in a medium mixing bowl. Using a heavy-duty mixer, mix the ingredients into a smooth dough.

Shape two teaspoons of dough into a ball, then repeat with the rest of the dough. Place the balls on the baking sheet and refrigerate.

Melt the chocolate chips in a small saucepan set over low heat.

Remove the peanut butter balls from the refrigerator, and stick a toothpick into a ball and carefully dip the ball into the chocolate, leaving the top one-fourth of the ball uncovered. Place the ball on the baking sheet, remove the toothpick, and continue until all of the balls are coated. Refrigerate until the chocolate is firm.

Eggnog Fudge

Makes 2 dozen

¼ pound (1 stick)
  unsalted butter

¾ cup eggnog

2 cups granulated sugar

10 ounces white chocolate,
  broken into pieces

½ teaspoon ground nutmeg

1 (7-ounce) jar
  marshmallow crème

1 cup chopped pecans

1 teaspoon rum or rum extract

In a heavy 2½- to 3-quart saucepan set over high heat, combine the butter, eggnog, and sugar; bring to a rolling boil while stirring constantly. Reduce the heat to medium and continue cooking and stirring for 8 to 10 minutes or until a candy thermometer reaches 234°F.

Remove from the heat and stir in the chocolate and nutmeg. Add the marshmallow crème, pecans, and rum and beat until well blended. Pour into a buttered 8- or 9-inch square pan and cool until room temperature; cut.

Cream Mints

Makes 2 dozen

2 tablespoons butter

2 tablespoons shortening

2 tablespoons warm water

2 tablespoons
  peppermint extract

Food coloring,
  your choice of color

2 cups confectioners'
  sugar, sifted

Cream the butter and shortening together and add the water. Beat until the mixture is creamy, then add the peppermint extract and food coloring. Add the confectioners' sugar gradually until it is completely mixed and smooth.

Shape into a roll and wrap in cling film or waxed paper. Chill.

Slice into serving sizes.

Chocolate Icing

Makes enough to ice 36 cookies

2 squares
  unsweetened chocolate

4 tablespoons butter, melted

2 cups confectioners' sugar

¼ cup heavy cream

1 teaspoon vanilla

2 tablespoon light corn syrup

Melt the chocolate in the microwave for 15 to 20 seconds; set aside.

Place the butter in a bowl and add the confectioners' sugar and cream in batches, mixing constantly with an electric mixer set on lowest speed. Beat in the vanilla, chocolate, and corn syrup until smooth and shiny, about 4 minutes.

French Buttercream Frosting

Mary C. Taylor

Makes enough for 3 (9-inch) cake layers

⅔ cup granulated sugar

¼ cup all-purpose flour

¼ teaspoon salt

¾ cup whole milk

½ pound (2 sticks)
  butter, chilled

2 teaspoons vanilla

1 teaspoon rum extract

Place the sugar, flour, and salt in a saucepan and mix completely then stir in the milk until smooth. Place the saucepan over medium heat and cook, stirring constantly, until the mixture is very thick. Remove from the heat and pour into a medium-sized mixing bowl. Cool to room temperature.

Remove one stick of butter at a time from the refrigerator and cut it into tablespoons. Beat the butter into the mixture, 2 tablespoons at a time, being sure that it is well incorporated after each addition. When all of the butter is incorporated, add the vanilla and rum extract and beat an additional minute. The frosting will be fluffy, but still a bit stiff.

Mocha Butter Frosting

Makes enough for 2 (8-inch) cake layers

4 tablespoons butter,
  at room temperature

2 cups confectioners' sugar

1 cup brewed coffee, cooled

¼ teaspoon salt

1 tablespoon light corn syrup

1 teaspoon vanilla

Cream the butter until smooth and shiny, then gradually blend in the sugar, alternating with 3 tablespoons of coffee each time. Beat well to incorporate after each addition. Beat in the salt, corn syrup, and vanilla until the mixture is smooth and shiny, about an additional 3 minutes.

Lemon-Butter Jelly

Makes 2½ cups filling

¼ pound (1 stick) butter

2 cups granulated sugar

2 tablespoons all-purpose flour

3 eggs, beaten

½ cup plus 1 tablespoon
  lemon juice

½ ounce Limoncello, optional

½ teaspoon lemon zest

Melt the butter in a saucepan and remove from the heat.

In a separate bowl, combine the sugar and flour. Add the eggs and beat well, then stir in the butter. Add the lemon juice and Limoncello, stirring well to incorporate.

Cook this mixture over a double boiler, stirring constantly for 10 to 12 minutes until the mixture is clear and thick. Remove from the heat and stir in the lemon zest. Pour into a covered bowl and refrigerate.

Spreads, Sauces, and Condiments

———— ∞∞∞ ————

Herb Butter

½ pound (2 sticks) salted
  butter, at room temperature
1 tablespoon fresh thyme
1 tablespoon fresh sage
2 tablespoons flat-leaf parsley
1 tablespoon fresh chives
1 teaspoon fresh
  rosemary, chopped

Place the butter and herbs in a medium mixing bowl and, using an electric mixer fitted with the paddle attachment, beat until light and fluffy. Use as a spread or a marinade for poultry, fish, or meat.

Herb and Cheddar Butter

¼ pound (1 stick) salted butter,
  at room temperature
2 tablespoons Cheddar
  cheese spread
¼ teaspoon dill weed

Place the butter, cheese spread, and dill in a medium mixing bowl and, using an electric mixer fitted with the paddle attachment, beat until light and fluffy.

Scrape the butter mixture into a small bowl, serving crock, or butter mold and cover tightly, or shape into a log and wrap in grease-proof paper (plastic, wax, or parchment) for storing and slicing as needed.

Lemon Parsley Butter

¼ pound (1 stick) salted butter, at room temperature

2 tablespoons chopped parsley

1 tablespoon lemon juice

1 tablespoon minced onion

2 teaspoons grated lemon zest

¼ teaspoon white pepper

TIP: This goes really well with poultry, veal, seafood, broccoli, spinach, and rice.

Place the butter, parsley, lemon juice, onion, lemon zest, and pepper in a medium mixing bowl and, using an electric mixer fitted with the paddle attachment, beat until light and fluffy.

Scrape the butter mixture into a small bowl, serving crock, or butter mold and cover tightly, or shape into a log and wrap in grease-proof paper (plastic, wax, or parchment) for storing and slicing as needed.

Italian Butter

¼ pound (1 stick) salted butter, at room temperature

2 tablespoons grated Parmesan cheese

½ teaspoon Italian seasoning

⅛ teaspoon garlic powder

TIP: Serve this with crusty breads, baked chicken, zucchini, and pasta.

Place the butter, Parmesan, seasoning, and garlic powder in a medium mixing bowl and, using an electric mixer fitted with the paddle attachment, beat until light and fluffy.

Scrape the butter mixture into a small bowl, serving crock, or butter mold and cover tightly, or shape into a log and wrap in grease-proof paper (plastic, wax, or parchment) for storing and slicing as needed.

French Bread Spread

¼ pound (1 stick) unsalted
   butter, at room temperature

1 ounce (¼ cup) grated
   Parmesan cheese

¼ cup chopped fresh parsley

4 garlic cloves, minced

¼ teaspoon salt

⅛ teaspoon pepper

2 teaspoons paprika, optional

Place the butter, Parmesan cheese, parsley, garlic, salt, pepper, and paprika in a medium mixing bowl and, using an electric mixer fitted with the paddle attachment, beat until light and fluffy.

Scrape the butter mixture into a small bowl, serving crock, or butter mold and cover tightly, or shape into a log and wrap in grease-proof paper (plastic, wax, or parchment) for storing and slicing as needed.

TIP: To serve this with French Bread, cut the bread in half lengthwise and lightly toast. Spread the butter on the bread halves and grill or broil until hot and bubbly.

½ pound (2 sticks) plus
  1 tablespoon salted butter,
  at room temperature
¼ cup finely diced shallots
Salt to taste
2 tablespoons dry vermouth,
  or dry white wine
2 tablespoons fresh sweet
  marjoram, finely chopped,
  or 2 teaspoons dried
⅛ teaspoon finely ground
  white pepper

Heat 1 tablespoon of butter in a small saucepan over medium heat. Add the shallots and season with a pinch of salt. Sauté until soft, but do not brown. Add the vermouth, and simmer until the pan is almost dry. Set aside to cool completely.

Place the butter in a medium mixing bowl and, using an electric mixer fitted with the paddle attachment, beat until light and fluffy. Add the marjoram and pepper, and beat to incorporate, scraping down the sides. Add the cooled shallot mixture and beat to combine. Taste for salt and pepper.

Scrape the butter mixture into a small bowl, serving crock, or butter mold and cover tightly, or shape into a log and wrap in grease-proof paper (plastic, wax, or parchment) for storing and slicing as needed.

TIP: Serve this herb-flecked butter on everything from mashed potatoes to dinner rolls. It's also wonderful for rubbing under the skin of turkey and chicken.

Creamy Truffle Butter

Recipe inspired by
The Del Bar, Lake Delton

½ cup heavy cream

¾ cup (2 ounces) Shiitake
mushrooms, finely chopped

¾ cup (2 ounces) Cremini
mushrooms, finely chopped

1 tablespoon finely
chopped shallots

2 tablespoons Marsala wine

1 teaspoon white truffle oil

¼ pound (1 stick) salted butter,
at room temperature

In large skillet, heat the cream to boiling, then add the mushrooms and shallots. Cook over high heat, stirring for 3 minutes or until all of the liquid is boiled away. Scrape the mushroom mixture to the side of the pan, then add the Marsala to loosen the browned bits on the bottom of the pan. Stir in the truffle oil and remove from the heat to cool.

In food processor, mix the cooled mushroom mixture with the butter until well blended.

Scrape the butter mixture into a small bowl, serving crock, or butter mold and cover tightly, or shape into a log and wrap in grease-proof paper (plastic, wax, or parchment) for storing and slicing as needed. Chill until firm.

TIP: This butter goes well with New York strip or tenderloin steaks.

Horseradish Butter

¼ pound (1 stick) salted butter, at room temperature

1 tablespoon prepared horseradish

1 teaspoon Dijon mustard

TIP: Add this butter to sandwiches, beef, or ham

Place the butter, horseradish, and mustard in a medium mixing bowl and, using an electric mixer fitted with the paddle attachment, beat until light and fluffy.

Scrape the butter mixture into a small bowl, serving crock, or butter mold and cover tightly, or shape into a log and wrap in grease-proof paper (plastic, wax, or parchment) for storing and slicing as needed.

Cheddar Butter Spread

¼ pound (1 stick) unsalted butter, at room temperature

4 ounces (1 cup) Cheddar cheese, shredded

1 garlic clove, minced or ⅛ teaspoon garlic powder

1 teaspoon lemon juice

½ teaspoon basil

¼ teaspoon thyme

⅛ teaspoon pepper

Place the butter, cheese, garlic, lemon juice, basil, thyme, and pepper in a medium mixing bowl and, using an electric mixer fitted with the paddle attachment, beat until light and fluffy.

Scrape the butter mixture into a small bowl, serving crock, or butter mold and cover tightly, or shape into a log and wrap in grease-proof paper (plastic, wax, or parchment) for storing and slicing as needed.

Dutch Cheese and Beer Spread

2 pound ball (8 cups)
  Edam cheese*

¼ pound plus 4 tablespoons
  (1½ sticks) butter, cubed and
  at room temperature

2 tablespoons chopped
  fresh chives

2 teaspoons Dijon mustard

½ cup amber or dark beer,
  at room temperature

Cocktail rye or pumpernickel
  bread slices

*Tip: Gouda can be substituted for Edam. If the cheese is not available in ball form, this spread may be served in your favorite serving bowl.

Cut the top off of the cheese to create a flat surface. With a butter curler or melon baller, remove the cheese from the center, leaving a ½-inch thick shell. Shred enough of the cheese removed from the ball and the top to measure 4 cups. Reserve the remaining cheese for another use.

In large bowl, place the shredded cheese, butter, chives, and mustard; mix with a spoon until blended. Stir in the beer until blended. Spoon the spread into the hollowed cheese ball; reserve any remaining spread to refill the ball. Chill until serving time. Serve as a spread with cocktail bread.

Butter-Cheddar Cheese Dip and Spread

4 tablespoons unsalted butter,
  at room temperature
3 ounces (¾ cup) Cheddar
  cheese, finely shredded
Worcestershire sauce,
  as desired
3 to 4 teaspoons sour cream
Dash cayenne pepper
¼ teaspoon prepared mustard
2 tablespoons chopped
  stuffed olives

Place the butter, cheese, Worcestershire sauce, sour cream, cayenne pepper, and mustard in a medium mixing bowl and, using an electric mixer fitted with the paddle attachment, beat until light and fluffy. Add the chopped olives and mix well.

Scrape the butter mixture into a small bowl, serving crock, or butter mold and cover tightly, or shape into a log and wrap in grease-proof paper (plastic, wax, or parchment) for storing and slicing as needed.

Bacon Cheese Log

4 tablespoons salted butter,
  at room temperature
8 ounces cream cheese,
  at room temperature
12 slices (about ½ pound)
  bacon, cooked crisp
2 green onions, thinly sliced
6 or 8 ounces Cheddar
  cheese spread
½ cup finely chopped pecans
Chopped parsley

Using an electric mixer, cream the butter and cream cheese until smooth. Add the bacon and green onions, mixing until thoroughly blended.

Shape into a log about 8 inches long, wrap in grease-proof paper (plastic, wax, or parchment) and refrigerate overnight.

Coat the log with cheese spread and roll in pecans and garnish with snipped parsley. Chill and serve with lightly salted crackers.

Maple Butter

¼ pound (1 stick) unsalted
  butter, at room temperature
1 tablespoon pure maple syrup

Place the butter and maple syrup in a medium mixing bowl and, using an electric mixer fitted with the paddle attachment, beat until light and fluffy.

Scrape the butter mixture into a small bowl, serving crock, or butter mold and cover tightly, or shape into a log and wrap in grease-proof paper (plastic, wax, or parchment) for storing and slicing as needed.

Honey Butter

4 tablespoons salted butter,
  at room temperature
2 tablespoons honey

Place the butter and honey in a medium mixing bowl and, using an electric mixer fitted with the paddle attachment, beat until light and fluffy.

Scrape the butter mixture into a small bowl, serving crock, or butter mold and cover tightly, or shape into a log and wrap in grease-proof paper (plastic, wax, or parchment) for storing and slicing as needed.

Honey and Spice Butter

¼ pound (1 stick) unsalted
  butter, at room temperature.
1 tablespoon honey
½ teaspoon pumpkin pie spice

Place the butter, honey, and spice in a medium mixing bowl and, using an electric mixer fitted with the paddle attachment, beat until light and fluffy.

Scrape the butter mixture into a small bowl, serving crock, or butter mold and cover tightly, or shape into a log and wrap in grease-proof paper (plastic, wax, or parchment) for storing and slicing as needed.

Walnut Parsley Butter

¼ pound (1 stick) salted butter,
  at room temperature
¼ cup chopped parsley
¼ cup ground walnuts
⅛ teaspoon garlic powder

TIP: Serve this butter with seafood, lamb, pork, veal, green beans, pasta, or chicken Kiev.

Place the butter, parsley, walnuts, and garlic powder in a medium mixing bowl and, using an electric mixer fitted with the paddle attachment, beat until light and fluffy.

Scrape the butter mixture into a small bowl, serving crock, or butter mold and cover tightly, or shape into a log and wrap in grease-proof paper (plastic, wax, or parchment) for storing and slicing as needed.

Honey Sesame Butter

½ pound (2 sticks) salted
butter, at room temperature

2 tablespoons honey

1 teaspoon toasted
sesame oil*

3 tablespoons lightly
toasted sesame seeds*,
or a mix of black and
white sesame seeds

Salt to taste

*To toast sesame seeds, place the seeds in a single layer in an ungreased shallow pan. Bake at 350°F. for 5 to 10 minutes or until golden brown. Remove from pan to cool.

Place the butter in a medium mixing bowl and, using an electric mixer fitted with the paddle attachment, beat until light and fluffy. Add the honey, sesame oil, and sesame seeds and beat to incorporate, scraping down the sides. Taste for salt.

Scrape the butter mixture into a small bowl, serving crock, or butter mold and cover tightly, or shape into a log and wrap in grease-proof paper (plastic, wax, or parchment) for storing and slicing as needed.

TIP: This versatile butter turns simple vegetables into stunning side dishes—add a pat or two to green beans, snap peas, asparagus, carrots, and parsnips. The sweetness from the honey also makes it perfect for spreading on dinner rolls, breakfast breads, or bagels, and for topping pancakes, French toast, and waffles.

Almond Butter

¼ pound (1 stick) unsalted
   butter, at room temperature
2 tablespoons ground almonds
½ teaspoon almond extract

Place the butter, almonds, and almond extract in a medium mixing bowl and, using an electric mixer fitted with the paddle attachment, beat until light and fluffy.

Scrape the butter mixture into a small bowl, serving crock, or butter mold and cover tightly, or shape into a log and wrap in grease-proof paper (plastic, wax, or parchment) for storing and slicing as needed.

Praline Butter

¼ pound (1 stick) unsalted
   butter, at room temperature
2 tablespoons ground pecans
1 tablespoon brown sugar

Place the butter, pecans, and brown sugar in a medium mixing bowl and, using an electric mixer fitted with the paddle attachment, beat until light and fluffy.

Scrape the butter mixture into a small bowl, serving crock, or butter mold and cover tightly, or shape into a log and wrap in grease-proof paper (plastic, wax, or parchment) for storing and slicing as needed.

Orange Butter

¼ pound (1 stick) unsalted
  butter, at room temperature
1 tablespoon orange
  juice concentrate
1 teaspoon grated orange zest

Place the butter, orange juice, and zest in a medium mixing bowl and, using an electric mixer fitted with the paddle attachment, beat until light and fluffy.

Scrape the butter mixture into a small bowl, serving crock, or butter mold and cover tightly, or shape into a log and wrap in grease-proof paper (plastic, wax, or parchment) for storing and slicing as needed.

Orange Honey Butter

¼ pound (1 stick) unsalted
  butter, at room temperature
3 tablespoons honey
1 teaspoon grated orange zest

Place the butter, honey, and zest in a medium mixing bowl and, using an electric mixer fitted with the paddle attachment, beat until light and fluffy.

Scrape the butter mixture into a small bowl, serving crock, or butter mold and cover tightly, or shape into a log and wrap in grease-proof paper (plastic, wax, or parchment) for storing and slicing as needed.

Bittersweet Chocolate Orange Butter

3 ounces bittersweet
chocolate (at least 70%
cocoa), chopped

½ pound (2 sticks) salted
butter, at room temperature

2 tablespoons unsweetened
cocoa powder

2 tablespoons finely grated
orange zest

2 tablespoons
confectioners' sugar

½ cup roasted and salted
pistachio nuts, chopped into
halves and quarters

TIP: This luscious butter makes
even the simplest bread or
roll special. Try it on toast, bis-
cuits, pancakes, French toast,
waffles, or bread pudding. It's
especially lovely with banana
bread and holiday breads,
such as Stollen.

Melt the chocolate in the microwave on low at
1 minute intervals, stirring until just melted
and smooth. Allow the melted chocolate to cool
enough to touch.

Place the butter in a medium mixing bowl
and, using an electric mixer fitted with the paddle attachment, beat until light and fluffy. Beat
in the cooled chocolate, cocoa, zest, and sugar.
Scrape the sides of the bowl as necessary to
incorporate all of the ingredients. Stir in the
pistachios.

Scrape the butter mixture into a small bowl,
serving crock, or butter mold and cover tightly,
or shape into a log and wrap in grease-proof
paper (plastic, wax, or parchment) for storing
and slicing as needed.

Bourbon Cherry Butter
with Orange

½ cup dried cherries

¼ cup bourbon

½ pound (2 sticks) salted
butter, at room temperature

2 tablespoons orange zest

2 tablespoons confectioners'
sugar, or to taste

1 tablespoon orange or
Angostura bitters, or
additional bourbon, optional

TIP: This butter combines all
the elements of the classic Old
Fashioned cocktail and conse-
quently finds a cozy place in
the holiday kitchen and on the
holiday table. Use it with pork,
ham, duck, and turkey or try it
baked inside an acorn squash
or tossed with carrots, beets,
and sweet potatoes. It's
also wonderful as a spread on
bread, rolls, or muffins.

In a small bowl, soak the cherries in bourbon, stirring occasionally, until the bourbon is almost completely absorbed. This will take from 2 to 12 hours. (To speed the process, lightly heat the cherries in bourbon, but cool completely before adding to butter.)

Place the butter in a medium mixing bowl and, using an electric mixer fitted with the paddle attachment, beat until light and fluffy. Add the cherries, zest, sugar, and bitters and beat to incorporate, scraping the sides of the bowl as needed.

Scrape the butter mixture into a small bowl, serving crock, or butter mold and cover tightly, or shape into a log and wrap in grease-proof paper (plastic, wax, or parchment) for storing and slicing as needed.

Pomegranate-Clementine Butter

½ pound (2 sticks) salted butter, at room temperature

¼ cup reduced pomegranate syrup, or pomegranate molasses (do not reduce), chilled*

2 tablespoons finely grated Clementine zest**

1 tablespoon confectioners' sugar, or more to taste

¼ cup toasted and chopped almonds, hazelnuts, or pecans, optional

*To make pomegranate syrup, boil 16 ounces of pomegranate juice in a heavy saucepan over medium-low heat until reduced to ¼ cup. You can also use pomegranate molasses, which is available from many specialty grocers or at ethnicgrocer.com.

**Any orange or mandarin variety may be substituted for Clementines.

Place the butter in a medium mixing bowl and, using an electric mixer fitted with the paddle attachment, beat until light and fluffy. Beat in the pomegranate syrup, zest, and sugar, scraping the sides of the bowl as needed. Stir in the nuts.

Scrape the butter mixture into a small bowl, serving crock, or butter mold and cover tightly, or shape into a log and wrap in grease-proof paper (plastic, wax, or parchment) for storing and slicing as needed.

Cranberry Orange Butter

½ pound (2 sticks)
  unsalted butter
⅓ cup whole berry
  cranberry sauce
2 tablespoons sweet
  orange marmalade

Place the butter in a medium mixing bowl and, using an electric mixer fitted with the paddle attachment, beat until light and fluffy. Slowly add the cranberry sauce and marmalade, and mix to combine.

Scrape the butter mixture into a small bowl, serving crock, or butter mold and cover tightly, or shape into a log and wrap in grease-proof paper (plastic, wax, or parchment) for storing and slicing as needed.

Cranberry Sage Brown Butter

½ pound (2 sticks) unsalted
  butter, at room temperature

½ cup onion, finely diced

1 garlic clove, minced

2 tablespoons chopped
  fresh sage

1 teaspoon sea salt

1 teaspoon freshly
  ground pepper

¼ cup dried cranberries,
  finely diced, optional

In a medium skillet, melt ¼ pound of butter over moderate heat. When the butter begins to foam, add the onion and garlic and continue cooking until the butter turns a nut brown color. Remove from the heat and stir in the sage, salt, and pepper; cool completely.

Place the remaining butter in a medium mixing bowl and, using an electric mixer fitted with the paddle attachment, beat until light and fluffy. Add the brown butter mixture and beat to incorporate, scraping down the sides. Stir in the cranberries.

Scrape the butter mixture into a small bowl, serving crock, or butter mold and cover tightly, or shape into a log and wrap in grease-proof paper (plastic, wax, or parchment) for storing and slicing as needed.

TIP: This flavorful butter is equally good with or without dried cranberries. Use it during the holidays on potatoes, vegetables, or meats. It is also delicious year round tossed with pasta or as the final touch on broiled or grilled fish.

½ pound (2 sticks) unsalted
butter, at room temperature

⅓ cup pumpkin purée, strained
to remove excess water

1 tablespoon finely grated
orange or lemon zest

1½ to 2 tablespoons
Chinese five-spice powder

Salt to taste

Confectioners' sugar or
honey powder for sweeter
applications

¼ cup chopped walnuts
or pecans

Place the butter in a medium mixing bowl and with an electric mixer fitted with a paddle attachment and beat until light and fluffy. Scrape down the sides. Add the pumpkin purée, zest, and five-spice powder, scraping down the sides of the bowl as necessary. Taste and add more five-spice powder and salt, as needed. Add confectioners' sugar and the walnuts; taste again for salt.

Scrape into a small bowl, serving crock, or butter molds and cover tightly; or shape into a long roll in grease-proof paper (plastic, wax, or parchment) for storing and slicing as needed.

TIP: This butter is a great accompaniment for breakfast pastries or dinner breads and muffins, or in the kitchen when preparing turkey, ham, or other pork dishes. This butter adds richness and flavor to sweet potatoes, carrots, parsnips, and beets.

Strawberry Butter

¼ pound (1 stick) unsalted butter, at room temperature

1 tablespoon strawberry preserves, or your favorite flavor

Place the butter and strawberry preserves in a medium mixing bowl and, using an electric mixer fitted with the paddle attachment, beat until light and fluffy.

Scrape the butter mixture into a small bowl, serving crock, or butter mold and cover tightly, or shape into a log and wrap in grease-proof paper (plastic, wax, or parchment) for storing and slicing as needed.

Caramel Sauce

¾ cup granulated sugar

6 tablespoons unsalted butter

⅓ cup corn syrup

1½ cups heavy cream

¼ teaspoon salt

Combine the sugar, butter, corn syrup, and ½ cup of the cream in a heavy medium-sized saucepan. Bring to a boil over medium-high heat, then reduce the heat to medium-low and continue to boil, uncovered, until the sauce is thickened and golden brown, 10 to 12 minutes, stirring frequently. Gradually stir in the remaining 1 cup of cream and the salt. Return to a boil, stirring constantly. Serve warm.

Hot Fudge Sauce

½ cup heavy cream

3 tablespoons unsalted butter,
  cut into small pieces

⅓ cup granulated sugar

⅓ cup brown sugar, packed

Dash of salt

½ cup unsweetened
  cocoa, sifted

In a heavy saucepan, heat cream and butter over medium heat until boiling. Stir in sugars until dissolved. Reduce heat; quickly stir in salt and cocoa. Remove from heat. Serve immediately.

Honey Butter Sundae Sauce

¼ pound (1 stick)
  unsalted butter

¾ cup honey

¼ teaspoon cinnamon

Dash of salt

½ cup heavy cream

1 teaspoon orange extract

In a saucepan, melt the butter, then add the honey, cinnamon, and salt. Stir in the cream until smooth; add the orange extract.

TIP: Use this delectable sauce for a Waffle Sundae. Toast frozen waffles and place 2 squares in a dessert dish. Scoop vanilla ice cream on waffles. Top with warm Honey Butter Sauce and garnish with fresh orange sections, chopped nuts and a maraschino cherry.

Béchamel and Velouté Sauces

Makes 1½ cups

2 tablespoons minced shallots

4 tablespoons butter

3 tablespoons all-purpose flour

½ teaspoon salt

2 cups whole milk

1 egg yolk, beaten

In a saucepan set over medium-low heat, sauté the shallots in 1 tablespoon of butter until soft, about 5 minutes. Add the remaining butter and allow it to melt. Whisk in the flour and salt, being sure to incorporate into the butter, leaving no lumps. While you are still whisking, slowly add the milk. Cook, stirring constantly, until the mixture thickens and boils, about 7 minutes. Reduce the heat.

In a separate bowl, add 2 tablespoons of the sauce to the yolk and then add that mixture to the rest of the sauce, cooking an additional minute and stirring constantly, taking care not to allow the mixture to boil.

VARIATION: To make this a velouté sauce, which is used with vegetables, fish, and other white meats, substitute a vegetable, fish, or other stock for the milk.

Hollandaise Sauce

4 egg yolks

1 tablespoon cold water

¾ cup clarified butter
 (from 1½ sticks)

½ teaspoon salt

Dash white pepper

1 teaspoon lemon juice

Bring 2 cups of water to a boil in the lower part of a double boiler. Lower the heat to a simmer and, in the top of the double boiler, add the egg yolks and water. Whisk rapidly until the mixture starts to thicken. Gradually add the butter, whisking constantly until it is completely incorporated. Add the salt, pepper, and lemon juice.

NOTE: If the sauce starts to thicken too quickly, remove the top of the double boiler from the heat and, while whisking, sit it into another pan of ice water to slow the cooking process. Then continue with recipe.

Béarnaise Sauce

1 small onion, chopped

1½ teaspoons dry tarragon

¼ teaspoon black pepper

½ cup white wine, like a Chablis

1 cup clarified butter
  (from ½ pound)

6 egg yolks

3 tablespoons tarragon vinegar

In small pan set over medium heat, bring the onion, tarragon, pepper, and wine to a simmer. Let the mixture simmer, uncovered, until the liquid reduces to a few tablespoons; about 6 to 8 minutes.

Meanwhile, in another small pan set over low heat, warm the butter.

Blend together the egg yolks and tarragon vinegar, until well mixed.

When the wine has reduced, turn on the blender and-very slowly-add the butter to the egg yolk mixture. Blend a few seconds to incorporate. Then, slowly add the wine reduction and let the blender run for a few seconds.

Blue Cheese Sauce

4 tablespoons unsalted butter

3 tablespoons all-purpose flour

½ teaspoon salt

1½ cups milk

1 ounce (¼ cup) crumbled
   blue cheese

In a saucepan, melt the butter, then stir in the flour and salt. Remove from the heat and gradually stir in the milk. Return to the heat and cook, stirring constantly, until thickened. Cook an additional 2 minutes, then gradually add the blue cheese, stirring until the cheese is melted.

Cheddar Cheese Sauce

4 tablespoons unsalted butter

¼ cup all-purpose flour

½ teaspoon salt

2 cups milk

2 cups medium white sauce

6 ounces (1½ cups) shredded
   sharp Cheddar cheese

1 teaspoon
   Worcestershire sauce

Dash cayenne pepper

Melt the butter in a saucepan, then stir in the flour and salt until smooth. Cook over medium heat for about 1 minute. Remove from the heat, then gradually add 1 cup of the milk, stirring until blended. Return to the heat and stir constantly until the mixture begins to thicken. Add the remaining 1 cup of milk and heat just to boiling. Cook for 1 to 2 minutes over reduced heat. Add the cheese, Worcestershire sauce, and cayenne pepper. Heat, stirring constantly until cheese melts.

Gouda Cheese Sauce

4 tablespoons unsalted butter

¼ cup all-purpose flour

½ teaspoon salt

2 cups milk

8 ounces (2 cups) shredded
  Gouda cheese

1 teaspoon
  Worcestershire sauce

¼ teaspoon garlic salt

Melt the butter in a saucepan, then stir in the flour and salt until smooth. Cook over medium heat for about 1 minute. Remove from the heat, then gradually add 1 cup of the milk, stirring until blended. Return to heat and stir constantly until the mixture begins to thicken. Add the remaining 1 cup of milk. Heat just to boiling and cook for 1 to 2 minutes.

Gradually add the cheese, Worcestershire, and garlic salt. Heat, stirring constantly, until the cheese melts.

Provolone Cheese Sauce

4 tablespoons unsalted butter

¼ cup all-purpose flour

½ teaspoon salt

2 cups milk

6 ounces (1½ cups) shredded
  provolone cheese

4 ounces mushrooms, drained
  and chopped

½ teaspoon grated onion

½ teaspoon
  Worcestershire sauce

¼ teaspoon paprika

Melt the butter in a saucepan, then stir in the flour and salt until smooth. Cook over medium heat for about 1 minute. Remove from the heat and gradually add 1 cup of the milk, stirring until blended. Return to the heat and stir constantly until the mixture begins to thicken. Add the remaining milk and heat just to boiling, then cook 1 to 2 minutes.

Gradually add the cheese, mushrooms, onion, Worcestershire, and paprika. Heat, stirring constantly, until the cheese melts.

Index

NOTE: *Italicized* page references indicate photographs.